STAR TREK

ALL GOOD THINGS:
A *NEXT GENERATION* COMPANION

TITAN

WWW.TITAN-COMICS.COM

THANK YOU

Titan would like to thank the casts and crews of *Star Trek: The Next Generation*, CBS Television, Paramount Pictures, and John Van Citters, Marian Cordry and Risa Kessler at CBS Consumer Products for their invaluable assistance in putting this volume together.

Star Trek
All Good Things: A Next Generation Companion
ISBN: 9781785855948
Published by Titan
A division of Titan Publishing
Group Ltd.,
144 Southwark Street,
London
SE1 0UP

Collecting the best articles and interviews from *Star Trek* Magazine.

First Edition May 2017
10 9 8 7 6 5 4 3 2 1

Printed in China.

Editor Christopher Cooper
Senior Editor Martin Eden
Art Director Oz Browne
Publishing Manager Darryl Tothill
Publishing Director Chris Teather
Operations Director Leigh Baulch
Executive Director Vivian Cheung
Publisher Nick Landau

Contributors:
David Bassom, Tara Bennett, Paula M. Block, Bryan Cairns, Keith R.A.Decandido, Rod Edgar, Terry J. Erdmann, Allyn Gibson, Robert Greenberger, K. Stoddard Hayes, Simon Hugo, Pat Jankiewicz, Justin Keay, Kevin Lauderdale, William Leisner, Rich Matthews, David A Mcintee, Joe Nazzaro, Scott Pearson, Jill Sherwin, Paul Simpson, Ian Spelling, and Calum Waddell.

Please note:
The interviews collected in this volume were originally printed in *Star Trek Magazine*, some of which date back almost 20 years. In order to maintain the originality of the material, we have not modified the interviews unless absolutely necessary.

STAR TREK

ALL GOOD THINGS:
A NEXT GENERATION COMPANION

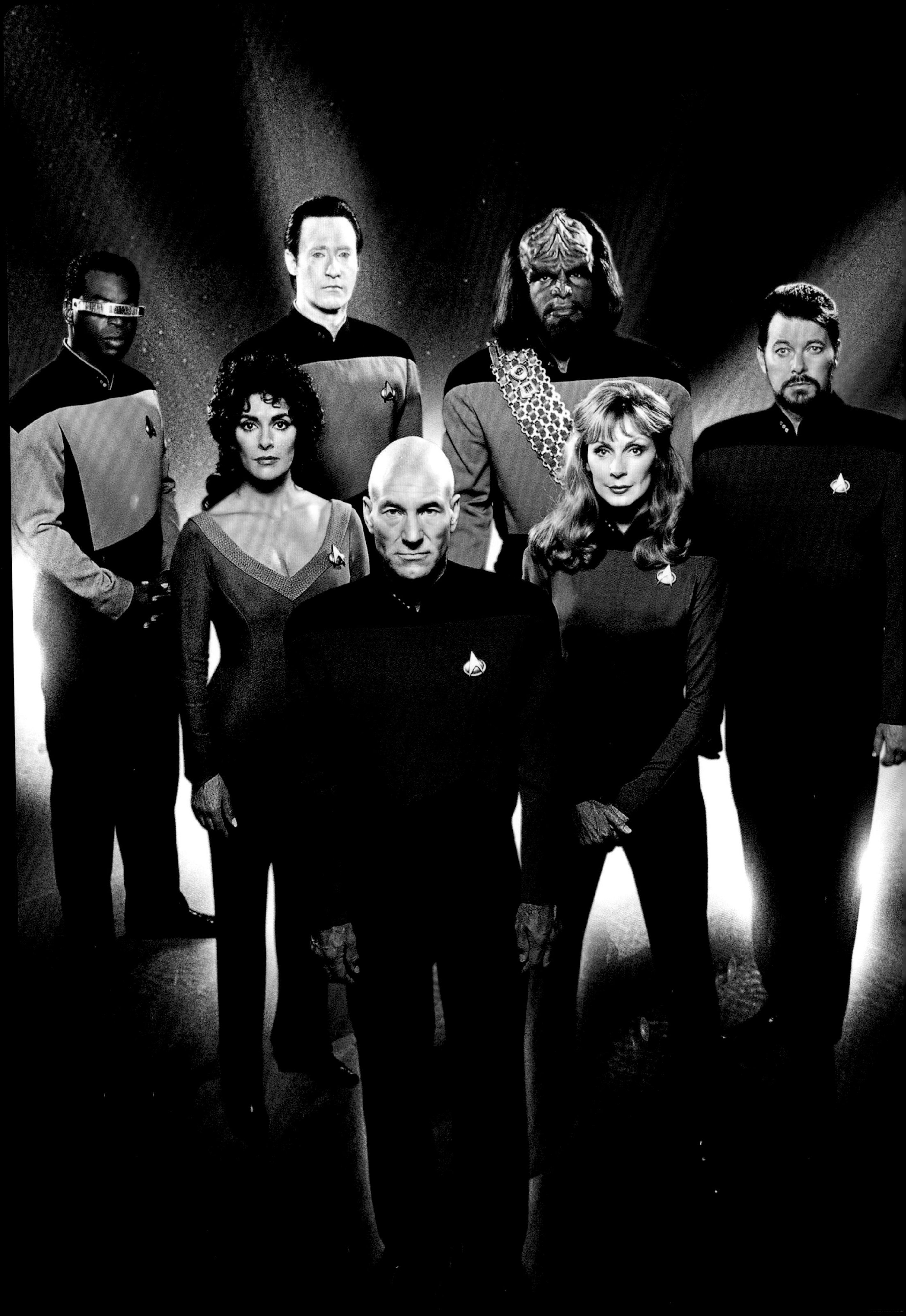

CONTENTS

MAKE IT SO...

Classic cast interviews and behind-the-scenes features from the pages of *Star Trek Magazine*, celebrating the 30th anniversary of *Star Trek: The Next Generation*.

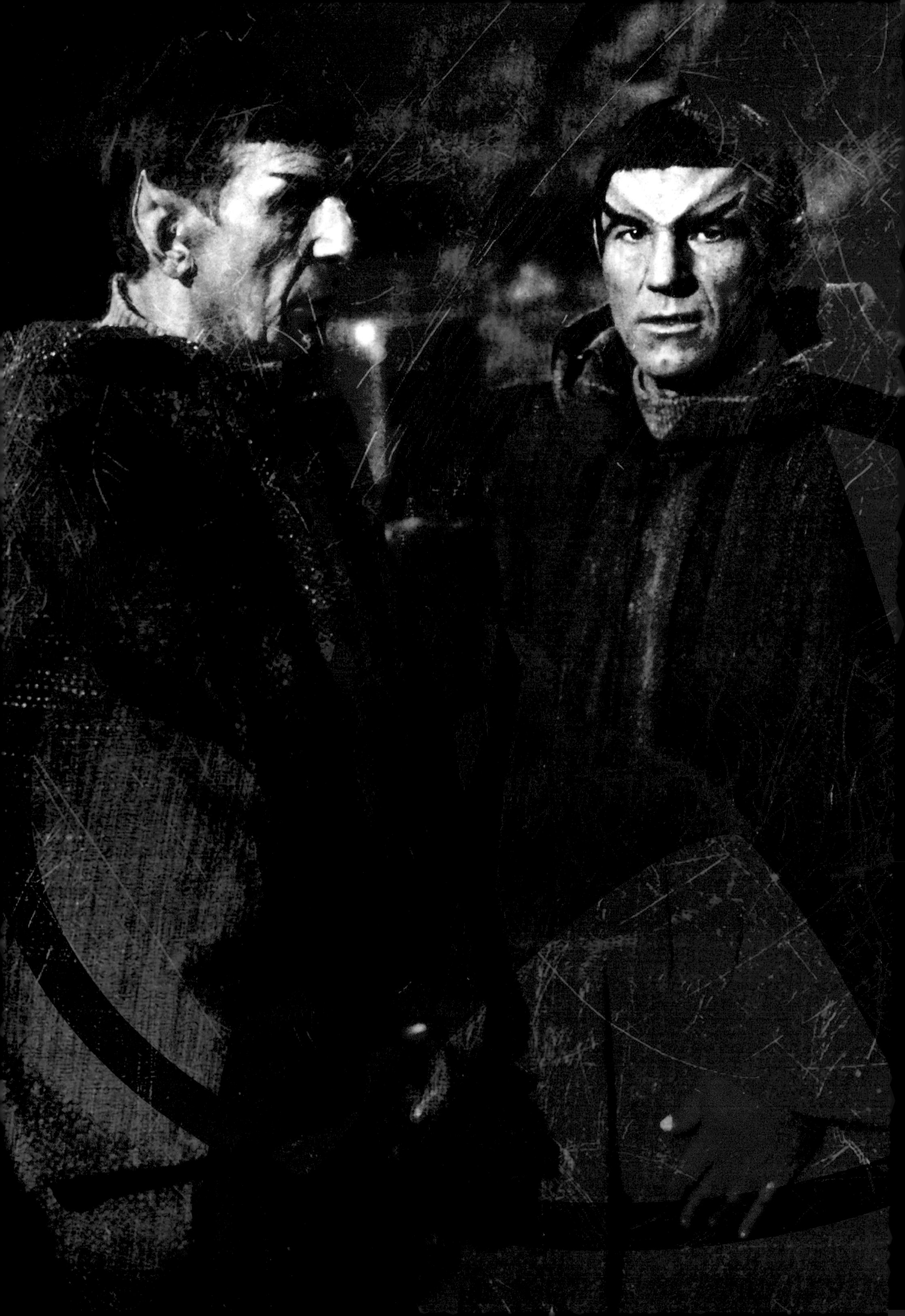

The Next Generation Season 1 cast
(Left to right: Wil Wheaton, Denise Crosby, LeVar Burton, Jonathan Frakes, Patrick Stewart,
Gates McFadden, Michael Dorn, Marina Sirtis, and Brent Spiner)

A NEW BEGINNING

2017 marks the 30th anniversary of *Star Trek*'s live action return to television
screens. John Ainsworth and Lee Mansfield examine how *The Next Generation*
redefined *Star Trek* and changed the science fiction TV landscape forever...

n 2017, it's hard to imagine a *Star Trek*
universe that consisted of just one TV series,
with one captain, one crew, and one starship.
But from 1966 until 1987, that's exactly what
it was. For those who watched, loved, and lived
it, the unique appeal of *Star Trek* wasn't so
much the often-quoted 'Wagon Train to the
Stars' adventures of the starship *Enterprise* in
the far future, but the characters aboard that
ship and their relationship with each other. In
short, as far as most *Trek* viewers were

concerned, Kirk, Spock, McCoy and their
extended 'family' of semi-regular characters
were *Star Trek*. But in 1987, that definition was
challenged with the arrival of *Star Trek: The
Next Generation* – and nothing would ever be
the same again...

With the cancellation of the original *Star Trek*
in 1969, fans had to wait 18 years before a new
live-action *Star Trek* series was back on their TV
screens. It seems strange then to recall that *The
Next Generation* didn't receive a universally warm

TWENTY YEARS AFTER ITS
FIRST BROADCAST, THE
ORIGINAL SERIES WAS
STILL THE SINGLE MOST
WATCHED DRAMA SERIES
IN SYNDICATION

welcome from long-time *Trek* fans. Many were at least suspicious of the new series and some were even hostile towards it. The reason was of course that these would not be the new adventures of Kirk, Spock, and McCoy but an entirely new crew on a new starship – even a new *Enterprise*!

These days, 'Iconic' has a tendency to be a rather devalued compliment, attributed far too readily, yet there can be few people who would disagree that James T. Kirk, Mr. Spock, and Dr 'Bones' McCoy are pop culture icons of the 20th Century. So it's perhaps not too difficult to see that the concept of *Star Trek* without them was, at least, a little controversial. Many *Star Trek* fans felt that they had 'kept the faith' in the years since the original TV series had ended, and had firm ideas about what was and wasn't *Trek*. Far from being 'wilderness years', as they might be viewed from today's perspective, 1969 to 1979 was a period in which the fans themselves

took ownership of the series, promoting and celebrating the adventures of their heroes in a variety of creative endeavors, including fanzines, fiction-writing, costume-making and even composing songs. Through regular conventions, the *Star Trek* fan community prospered, despite (or perhaps even because of) the absence of new TV episodes. Making appearances at these fan-organized conventions were the *Star Trek* actors who had played the show's memorable characters, and they became known and loved by their fans.

Professionally published novels, comic books, and a short-lived animated TV series (featuring the voices of the original cast), plus of course regular re-runs of the 79 live-action episodes, helped keep *Star Trek* alive in the 1970s. The news of a new *Star Trek* series – *Star Trek Phase II* – was announced in 1977, but there was disappointment when it became clear that Leonard Nimoy would not be returning to the role of Spock. Instead, a new Vulcan science officer would be taking his place along with other new regular characters. However, this all became academic when plans for the new TV series were dropped, to be replaced by a theatrically-released big screen adventure.

THE LONG WAIT

Released in 1979, *Star Trek: The Motion Picture* may not have received universal praise, but it did at least feature the entire original cast of the TV series – including Spock, with Leonard Nimoy having reconsidered his position when the project moved from TV series to movie. *Star Trek* was back at last, and with the highly successful release of *Star Trek II: The Wrath of Khan* in 1982, its future

as an ongoing movie series seemed assured. But, as good as the movies were, three years seemed a long time to wait for each new adventure. What fans really wanted was a weekly TV show.

By 1986, Paramount, who owned the *Star Trek* property, decided that they also wanted a new *Star Trek* TV series. Twenty years after its first broadcast, the original TV series was still the single most watched drama series in syndication and the movies were box office sensations. *Star Trek* was big business, and Paramount reasoned that they could capitalize on its popularity by producing a new TV show. The only stumbling block, however, was the regular *Star Trek* cast. With *Star Trek IV: The Voyage Home* about to hit movie theaters, the actors were by now used to receiving movie star salaries. A TV series couldn't hope to match those salaries and remain profitable. There was also a fear that a TV show with the same cast might harm demand for future films. The simple but brave decision that Paramount made to address these concerns was to have an entirely new cast. Recasting the roles of Kirk, Spock, McCoy and the rest was inconceivable – at least in 1986 – so the new cast would play a completely new starship crew.

After initially declining to be involved, original series creator Gene Roddenberry joined the production team of the new show as

Star Trek creator Gene Roddenberry on the set of the *Enterprise*-D

Data (Brent Spiner) is reunited with his cat, Spot, in *Star Trek: Generations*

The new transporter room set included parts from the original series

executive producer. Much loved by *Star Trek* fans, Roddenberry's appointment went some way to reassure fans that the new show would still be genuine *Star Trek*.

With the passage of time since the demise of the original show, Roddenberry had had time to ponder and refine his vision of the *Star Trek* universe and the future of humanity as he saw it. Although not a 're-boot', as we have seen with the recent *Battlestar Galactica* series, *Star Trek: The Next Generation* would definitely be an evolution of the concept whilst retaining the essence of optimism and self-betterment. By cleverly setting the new show in a time period some 80 years after the original series and

movies, Roddenberry gave himself room to make a variety of changes to the *Trek* universe without contradicting what had gone before.

Prior to 1986, the *Star Trek* universe felt very open – limitless and pioneering. It was essentially the story of three archetypes – the Warrior (Kirk), the Priest (Spock), and the Healer (McCoy) exploring "strange new worlds" on a dangerous frontier together, encountering "new life and new civilizations" and having to improvise a kind of 'gunboat diplomacy' against the hostile or dangerously alien. Although this was still an element of *The Next Generation*, many episodes would focus on the internal problems of the United Federation of Planets and Starfleet with stories revolving around new technologies, politics, and diplomacy, and set on worlds already within the Federation's boundaries. This was a much more developed and stable Federation, one that had expanded its borders and was now buffeting against the territories of the other 'known' powers. Captain Kirk would often have to make his own decisions, with Starfleet Command several days away by subspace radio. On the *U.S.S. Enterprise* of *Star Trek: The Next Generation* though, Captain Picard would frequently be obliged to consult with his superiors who were only the touch of a button away.

PASS THE SHAKE

The depiction of personal relationships had also evolved, based on Gene Roddenberry's beliefs

that, in the future, interaction between humans and other intelligent civilized peoples would be far more harmonious, and individuals would not be motivated by baser desires.

Perhaps one of the most significant developments in *Star Trek: The Next Generation* over the original series was the sense that this was much more of an ongoing story. Although each episode was a self-contained adventure, there was also an additional level of appreciation to be found by watching the series episode by episode. Empires rise and fall, relationships begin and end, familiar characters make recurring appearances. 'Soap opera' series such as *Dallas* and *Dynasty* had broken the mould of prime time U.S. TV drama in the 1980s by daring to tell an ongoing story that required the viewer to watch each week. Although *Star Trek: The Next Generation* couldn't be described as a soap opera, it certainly took a step in that direction. The success of the series proved that the format could work in a science fiction drama series and the idea would be employed by other genre shows in the future. Today, 25 years later, it is the norm for genre shows to have quite complex, ongoing story 'arcs' and *The Next Generation* is, at least in part, responsible for this.

That *Star Trek: The Next Generation* was a huge success – both for Paramount and, ultimately, in the eyes of the fans – is now a matter of record. Although there were a few

SQUARE PEGS

So much of *Star Trek*, in all of its various incarnations, has been about exploring the human condition. How better to do that than by allowing the audience to examine humanity – and thereby themselves – through the eyes of characters that are not human but are forced to co-exist with humans. The aloof and logical Vulcan Spock was the only alien aboard the original *Enterprise* and was the first to fill this role. Although we learn that he himself was half-human, he had clearly adopted the Vulcan approach to life and was frequently puzzled by illogical, emotional human behavior.

In *Star Trek: The Next Generation*, the android Data, who was devoid of emotions, became determined to understand what it was to be human. Running throughout the entire seven seasons of the series and on into the following movies, this thread eventually reached something of a conclusion when, thanks to a tiny computer chip, Data was actually able to experience emotions first-hand.

fans who did part company with *Trek*, unable to take to the new crew and the new look of the series, for the most part even those that had doubts came to embrace the new show and the three spin-off series that were born from its success. *Star Trek: The Next Generation* proved to be a whole new beginning for the *Star Trek* franchise, attracting many new fans too young to have seen and enjoyed the original series on its first broadcast. What is perhaps less well recognized though, is that *The Next Generation* proved to be a turning point in the history of U.S. TV broadcasting as well as in *Star Trek* history.

Having decided to produce their new *Star Trek* series, Paramount attempted to sell it to the 'Big Three' television networks – NBC, ABC, and CBS. However, despite *Star Trek*'s continued success as a syndicated TV show, none of the networks were willing to commission an entire series – NBC and ABC wanted to see a pilot first, and CBS requested a mini-series. Fox was just about to launch its own network and were keen to have the series on their new channel, but were only able to commission 13 episodes. With a firm belief in the strength of *Star Trek*, Paramount was unwilling to compromise and wanted to retain total control over its new show. So it took the unusual decision to broadcast *Star Trek: The Next Generation* in first-run syndication on independent stations and affiliate stations of the Big Three networks that could choose to opt out of network programming. The show was given to these local stations for free, but in exchange, Paramount would receive a share of the advertising revenue generated from its screening. As an added incentive, re-runs of the still popular original series would only be made available to channels that took the new

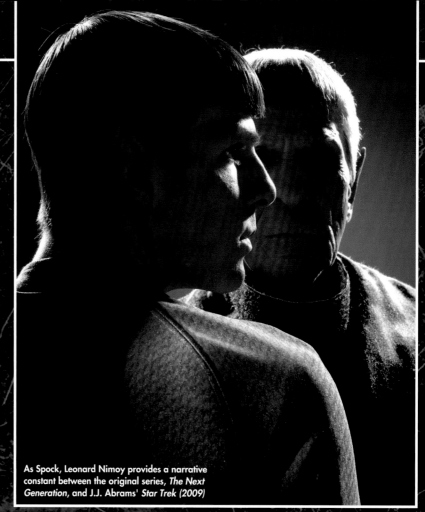

As Spock, Leonard Nimoy provides a narrative constant between the original series, *The Next Generation*, and J.J. Abrams' *Star Trek (2009)*

WITH A FIRM BELIEF IN THE STRENGTH OF STAR TREK, PARAMOUNT WAS UNWILLING TO COMPROMISE.

show. In 1986, this was a virtually unheard of way of selling a new drama series, but it was a strategy that worked with the revenue from advertising actually proving greater than the typical fee that the networks would have paid for the series. *Star Trek: The Next Generation* attracted an average audience of 20 million viewers, regularly beating the ratings of other top syndicated and networked shows.

A NEW WORLD

Such was the success of Paramount's pioneering approach to the sale and broadcast of *Star Trek: The Next Generation* that other shows soon followed, adopting the same model with similar success, and by 1994 there were more than 20 hour-long shows in first-run syndication. Many of these were genre shows including *Friday the 13th: The Series*, *Freddy's Nightmares*, and *War of the Worlds* – all of which were based (however loosely) on existing movie properties.

Star Trek: The Next Generation had spectacularly demonstrated that not only was there life in *Star Trek* but in the science fiction genre as well. A wealth of new sci-fi shows, both in first-run syndication and on the networks would premier over the next few years. Some would not last but others became huge hits, including *The X-Files*, *Buffy the Vampire Slayer*,

Patrick Stewart as Captain Jean-Luc Picard

Like *The Next Generation*, *Star Trek (2009)* energized a new generation of *Star Trek* fans

Hercules: the Legendary Journeys and its spin-off show, *Xena: Warrior Princess, Babylon 5,* and *Forever Knight. Star Trek: The Next Generation* had set a ball rolling and it's still rolling today, with a crop of new sci-fi and fantasy shows debuting every new season.

Of course, *The Next Generation* would give rise to its own spin-off series that would further explore the ever more diverse *Star Trek* universe with new characters in new situations. However, although *Deep Space Nine, Voyager,* and *Enterprise* enjoyed varying degrees of success, none ever quite reached the heights attained by their ground-breaking progenitor.

With no new *Star Trek* show having aired since 2005, we have once again entered another comparatively quiet period. However, much as *The Next Generation* did in 1986, J.J. Abrams' 2009 *Star Trek* movie has both reinvented and reinvigorated the franchise whilst maintaining a direct connection with its illustrious past. And this time it has come full circle, returning to the iconic characters of the original series, Kirk, Spock, and McCoy – now played by a new young cast. The long and complex fictional history established in the preceding series and movies has been deftly set aside, while being neither contradicted or ignored. Everything is new again, and the adventure continues…

PASSING ON THE TORCH

To help underline the connection of *Star Trek: The Next Generation* to the original series, the very first episode – "Encounter at Farpoint" included a one-scene cameo appearance by Doctor 'Bones' McCoy. With the help of make-up and prosthetics, actor DeForest Kelley played the now very elderly Leonard McCoy and was seen to give his blessing to the new *Enterprise* and her crew. Further crowd-pleasing appearances by the show's original stars were to follow with engineer Montgomery Scott – or 'Scotty' – appearing in the episode "Relics", while Spock featured in the two part "Unification" story.

History was to repeat itself with the cast of *Star Trek: The Next Generation* making occasional appearances in the spin-off *Trek* shows that followed it. The *Enterprise*'s head of security, Worf, became a regular character in the latter seasons of *Deep Space Nine*; Deanna Troi and fellow *Enterprise* crewman Reginald Barclay made semi-regular appearances in *Voyager*; and both Troi and William Riker were seen in new flashback sequences in the final episode of *Enterprise*. As well as being popular with the fans, each of these crossovers served to emphasise that *Star Trek* was now one big, interconnected universe.

The most recent such handover was in the 2009 *Star Trek* movie, where the Spock of 'our' universe is seen to travel into his own past at a point where the timeline diverges in an alternate direction. The presence of both Spock and the actor who plays him, Leonard Nimoy, united the origins of *Star Trek* with its exciting new future, making them one.

The real McCoy. DeForest Kelly makes a cameo appearance in the *TNG* pilot episode, "Encounter at Farpoint"

STARFLEET'S NEXT GENERATION

With the launch of *Star Trek: The Next Generation* on September 28th, 1987, Gene Roddenberry's already 20-year-old science fiction creation broke new ground. *The Next Generation* not only built upon the dramatic foundations laid by the original series but, over seven seasons, it took the popularity of *Star Trek* to ever greater heights.

At its core was a group of actors and characters, led by Patrick Stewart's Captain Jean-Luc Picard, who would become every bit as iconic as Kirk's crew...

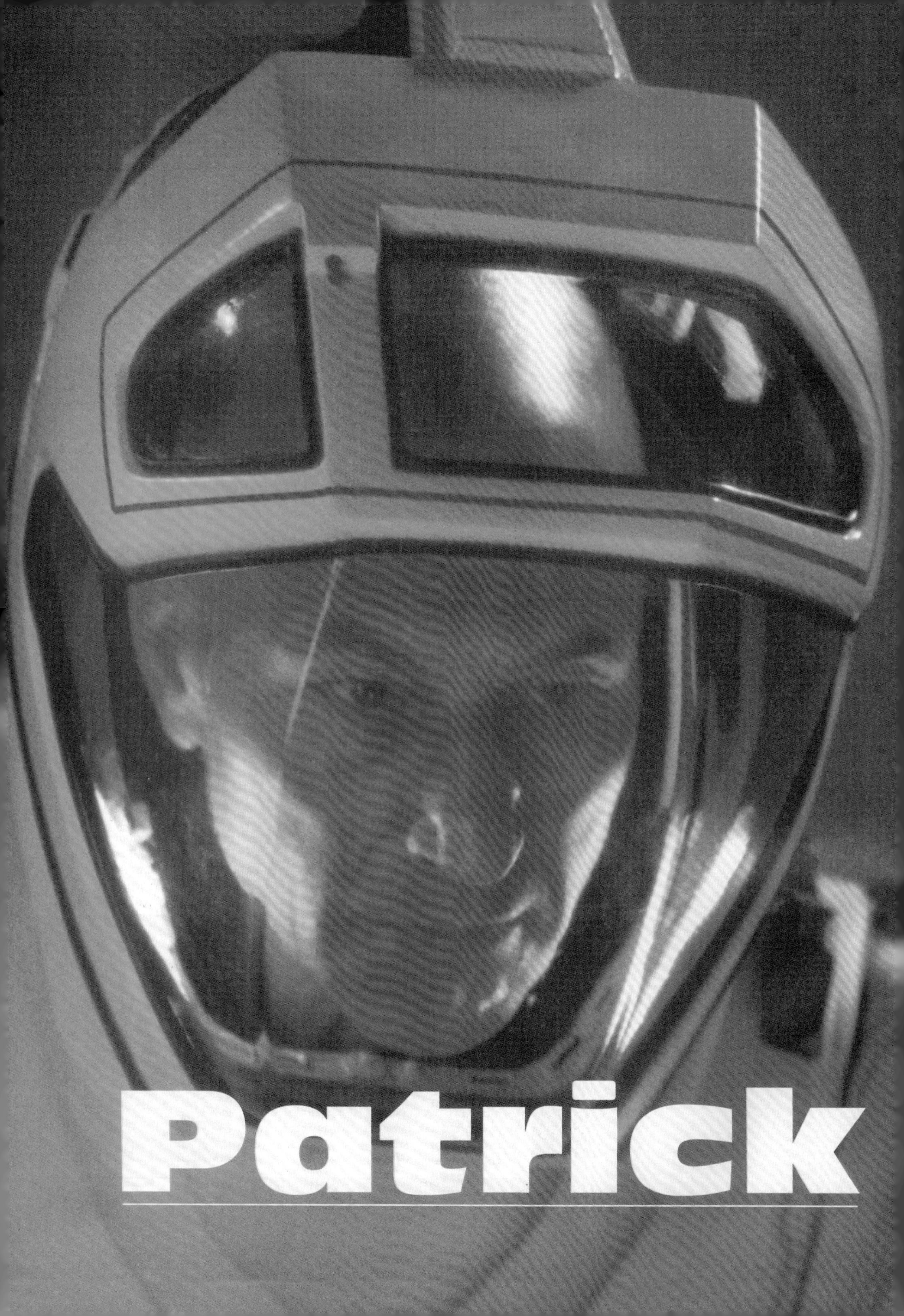

Patrick

"This is proving to be as good an experience as I hoped it would be..."

A Captain's Revenge

In interview with Ian Spelling, Patrick Stewart reveals how his role as *Captain Picard* is more the Captain Ahab of space...

Patrick Stewart disappears swiftly into the New York City skyline.

It's a bizarre sight. Trekkers are used to seeing Stewart's *Star Trek: The Next Generation* alterego, Captain Jean-Luc Picard, whisking about in the *U.S.S. Enterprise* or beaming from one place to another via the transporter. But on this day, even though Stewart sports full Starfleet regalia, he is pedalling into the distance on a rather ordinary 20th Century bicycle, and that Manhattan skyline is nothing but a giant set, the streets of the Big Apple as seen on the *Paramount Pictures* backlot in Hollywood. And Stewart, after an interview in his trailer, is returning to the set of *Star Trek: First Contact*.

Such a great, ironically appropriate coda to the Stewart interview is his exit by bike that it makes perfect sense to start an article about Stewart with the anecdote. In moments, Stewart will be back before the camera, taking his cues from Director Jonathan Frakes, just as he was about an hour earlier. It was then that Stewart shared the set with Michael Dorn, Marina Sirtis, Frakes, Brent Spiner and Gates McFadden on one of the rare *Star Trek: First Contact* production days in which almost the entire cast was working at the same time. It was moments after Frakes called "Cut" on a scene in which Worf arrives on the *U.S.S. Enterprise* from an embattled *U.S.S. Defiant* that Stewart strode over to his trailer to talk. "This is proving to be as good an experience as I hoped it would be and an even better one in one particular instance, and that is the work we are all doing here with Jonathan as our director," Stewart says earnestly as he juggles lunch, an inter-

view and some paternal concern about his cat, Bela, who is a bit under the weather. "It's been very nice so far to be back here with everyone, to be playing Picard once again, but I am most pleased that Jonathan earned the job and that he has so heartily embraced the task.

"He is bringing everything he learned while he was acting in and directing episodes of *Star Trek: The Next Generation* to *Star Trek: First Contact*, and it is paying off, for us and for Jonathan. One can see that, given the scale of this movie, a director – and a first-time director at that – might have been overwhelmed by it all. On the contrary, Jonathan stands so tall while he's directing, literally and figuratively. I had a visitor on the set the other day and they said, 'This is amazing. I have never seen the director of a movie this complicated appear to be as relaxed and at ease as Jonathan is.' He's really doing a wonderful job of it. It's thrilling to be here – as we were when Jonathan directed his first episode of the television series – for what I think is going to be a very grand directing career for Jonathan."

Stewart is equally enthusiastic about *Star Trek: First Contact* as a whole. While he ultimately liked *Star Trek Generations* and felt the David Carson-directed film did a reasonably good job of passing the torch from the original *Star Trek* crew to that of *Star Trek: The Next Generation*, he feels it was a dark film, one in which too much time was spent focusing on a Picard who was noticeably distracted and brooding. The captain was that way, understandably so, because he was surrounded by death. After all, we learnt that his brother and nephew had died senselessly in the opening reels. *Captain Kirk*

Opposite: *Captain Picard prepares to take on the Borg in* Star Trek: First Contact
Left: *Picard bids farewell to* Star Trek: The Next Generation *in* All Good Things

Stewart

Right: *Suffering at the hands of the Cardassians sans replicator in* Chain of Command
Far right: *A Captain's Holiday... and a little romance with* Vash *(Jennifer Hetrick)*
Below left: *To the captain and his trusty Number One, defence is* A Matter of Honor
Below right: Captain *Jellico (Ronny Cox) briefs Picard on his secret mission in* Chain of Command

(William Shatner) perished while fighting *Soran* (Malcolm McDowell) with him. And the *U.S.S. Enterprise* went down in a blazing ball of flames.

Although battling the dreaded *Borg*, as Picard and his compatriots do in *Star Trek: First Contact*, can't exactly be called the foundation of a celebratory *Star Trek* outing, Stewart promises that the film's tone and his character's demeanour are very different from those on view in *Star Trek Generations*. "We have a wonderful story, a different kind of story from the first film. It's a great adventure. It uses most of the principal characters effectively," Stewart notes. "The film's actually quite dark at times, and that is necessarily so, it being a story featuring the Borg. I feel especially pleased with it in terms of what we do with Picard this time. Here, despite the Borg connection, we see him being very much the Captain. We see him on the *U.S.S. Enterprise*, on the Bridge and in command, which is where he should be and what he should be doing."

Much of Picard's lighter side will be reflected in his rela-

"The film's actually quite dark at times... it being a story featuring the Borg."

tionship with *Lily Sloane*, the scientist played in *Star Trek: First Contact* by Alfre Woodard. Sloane is the associate of *Zefram Cochrane* (James Cromwell), and it is she who winds up on the *U.S.S. Enterprise* like Alice in Wonderland. Stewart won't go so far as to describe their relationship as a romance, but he reveals that there is a "definite attraction and appeal that grows out of the experiences they share together." It was Stewart who initially suggested to the film's producers that a black actress be cast as Sloane, determined to counter present day racism with some 24th Century-style acceptance. "Racism is a reality, I suppose. But it is not a part of my universe," he insists. "This was one of my reasons, from the beginning, for suggesting a black actress for Lily: It's absolutely at the heart of what *Star Trek* is all about, because I don't see it as an issue. I see

"I see in Lily a tremendously attractive, intelligent woman being played by a tremendously attractive, intelligent woman and a brilliant actress."

Patrick Stewart PROFILE

BIRTHDAY: 13 July
BIRTHPLACE: Great Britain

Selected Credits:
THEATRE
A Christmas Carol (Winner of a Drama Desk Award for Best Solo Performer and an Olivier Award nomination for Best Actor)
The Tempest – Prospero

TELEVISION
I, Claudius (1976) – Sejanus
Tinker, Tailor, Soldier, Spy (1980) – Karla
Smiley's People (1982, mini-series) – Karla
Playing Shakespeare (1984, mini-series) – Himself
Star Trek: The Next Generation (1987-1994) – Captain Jean-Luc Picard
500 Nations (1995, voice)

FILM
Hedda (1975) – Ejlert Loevborg
Little Lord Fauntleroy (1980, TV) – Wilkins
Hamlet, Prince of Denmark (1980, TV) – Claudius
Excalibur (1981) – Leondegrance
The Plague Dogs (1982, voice) – Major
Dune (1984) – Gurney Halleck
Wild Geese II (1985) – Russian General
Lifeforce (1985) – Doctor Armstrong
The Doctor and the Devils (1985)
Code Name: Emerald (1985) – Colonel Peters

Lady Jane (1986) – Henry Gray, Duke of Suffolk
L.A. Story (1991) – Maitre d'
Robin Hood: Men in Tights (1993) – King Richard
Alistair MacLean's Death Train (1993, TV) – Malcolm Philpott
Star Trek Generations (1994) – Capt. Jean-Luc Picard
The Pagemaster (1994, voice)
Liberation (1994, narrator)
In Search of Dr. Seuss (1994, TV) – Sgt. Mulvaney
Gunmen (1994) – Loomis
Let It Be Me (1995)
Jeffrey (1995) – Sterling
The Canterville Ghost (1996, TV) - Sir Simon de Canterville (also co-producer)
Star Trek: First Contact (1996) – Captain Jean-Luc Picard
Safe House (1996)
Smart Alec (1997)
Prince of Egypt (1998)

Sources: The International Movie Database, Paramount Pictures

in Lily a tremendously attractive, intelligent woman being played by a tremendously attractive, intelligent woman and a brilliant actress."

Ultimately, Stewart sounds happy that he has returned to the character that has given him financial security, made him a star and allowed him to pursue any number of other exciting projects outside the *Star Trek* galaxy. Since *Star Trek Generations*, Stewart has hardly slowed down to catch his breath. He sashayed through a wonderful part as a gay man in the Paul Rudnick comedy, *Jeffrey*, gave *Party of Five* star Neve Campbell the creeps in *The Canterville Ghost*, and played a dance instructor in a film entitled *Let*

It Be Me, with Jennifer Beals, Leslie Caron and Campbell Scott. He has hosted a well-received evening of the famous US comedy show *Saturday Night Live* (in which, yes, he skewered *ST:TNG* to a nice crisp), lent his unmistakable voice to a wide variety of television commercials and educational CD-ROM games, and even turned up on the children's programme, *Sesame Street*, to promote the virtues of the letter 'B'.

The actor also took to the stage in the summer of 1995 as a fierce Prospero in a production of *The Tempest*. Initially a free, outdoor show in New York's famed Central Park (as part of its annual Shakespeare Festival), *The Tempest* proved so popular that it was transferred to Broadway for a sold-out run of several months. Clearly, Stewart is as proud of *The Tempest* as he could possibly be. "The experience was as good as any I've ever had," he enthuses. "It was simply an exhilarating experience. It was the first show to transfer from the Park to Broadway in, I think, 18 years. The show before it was *The Pirates of Penzance*. I don't know how long it had been since a

Above left: *Even during working hours, Stewart finds time to go back to his roots...*
Left: *Undercover operation... Picard poses as a renegade archaeologist in* **Gambit**

17

Stewart on Stewart

Speaking at the Pasadena Grand Slam Convention earlier this year, Patrick Stewart talked on many topics to a packed audience

On his commitment to *Star Trek*...

"I have heard stories that Patrick doesn't want to do Star Trek any more and this is nonsense. I want to be the first actor in the history of the world who can continue in a successful movie franchise like Star Trek, making every movie better and better and better than the one before it, and at the same time fill my working life in between with other movies, with theatre work, with whatever I want to do. And so it's very, very important to me that our movies are the best movies that we can make and that we go on making them. And that, I guess, is that!"

On how he gained the role of Captain Jean-Luc Picard...

"After having met me, Gene [Roddenberry], God rest his soul, had said, 'Absolutely, definitively, no question about it, this is not the actor.' And others who were kind of part of my campaign team were told to shut up and never mention the name Patrick Stewart again. It just wasn't going to wash. Well, many, many, many months later it came up again and they agreed to see me one more time. And so I guess it worked out. I can remember when I used to answer this question and it was still fresh in my mind. I can remember when the feelings of that time were still very fresh. I cannot think of anything that I have done that I could be prouder of that would go on for longer than this. I want to see Star Trek: The Next Generation continuing as long as we can put one foot in front of the other.

"Why did I say yes? Because it was irresistible. Because it was too damned exciting. If I'd said 'no' and gone back to London, and sat in my house and waited for the phone to ring for the next whatever I would do, I could never have been comfortable with myself for the rest of my life, that I had passed on an opportunity like this."

On his favourite episode...

"The episode is The Offspring. It's a favourite because I think it represents so perfectly the best of what Star Trek is, and it is yet another awesome performance by Brent Spiner, who gave so many in the seven years of the series. There's also an amazing guest star performance from Hallie Todd who played the offspring. You should be able to let go of that kind of thing, but it still gets me that performances like this got totally overlooked by certain organisations, when the time came to pat people on the back and say well done, you know. It still irritates me. But I'm trying to let go of those things. But also it happened to be Jonathan Frakes' first episode that he directed, so that's very meaningful too, because the work that Jonathan did on that paved the way for me, LeVar and Gates to do our work subsequently."

On his favourite film...

"There was a movie that changed my perception of movies and what acting could be and the kinds of stories that acting could tell, and that was On the Waterfront, which I saw when I was 13, and I saw it three times in one week. It entirely changed my notions of what movies were, what acting was, and even though I didn't live on the New Jersey waterfront (far from it!), in a sense that film was about things that I understood. They were also part of my life too. And I'd never seen a movie like that before. It's reality.

"Until then, my movie world had largely been that of Hollywood musicals, Debbie Reynolds movies, and so forth. This was quite different. It connected with my life more directly than other things which I've enjoyed."

... and on his cat, Bela!

"... was brought to me by Jackie, my assistant, just two years ago. She was an earthquake victim. She had been found living in a collapsed parking structure somewhere near Northbridge after the January quake.

"I really didn't have any plans of owning a cat and Jackie said, 'well, just have a look at her and if you don't want her, I'll take her away', knowing full well that the moment I looked into those blue eyes I would fall. And fall I did... she's just fine. She's a travelling cat. Because of circumstances I cannot go into here, she does not live with me in Los Angeles, but whenever I go somewhere she goes with me. She has had three extended visits to New York and she went to Vancouver, and is just fantastic. She's getting very cool about travel these days!"

Left: *Picard and* Data *(Brent Spiner) lead a team in an attack against the Borg in* Star Trek: First Contact
Below: *As the Borg take over the ship, Picard and Lily Sloane (Alfre Woodard) make for the Holodeck in an attempt to escape*
Bottom: *Captain on the bridge... and ready to fight*

Shakespeare production had transferred. Certainly, it was a number of years before a US production of Shakespeare had played on Broadway. I've actually been harassing (*Tempest* director) George C. Wolfe about another project. It's not *Richard III*, which, if you look closely at *Star Trek: First Contact*, is in Picard's ready room (in a glass case). It would be one of the tragedies."

As if all that weren't enough, Stewart has a full slate of upcoming films on the way, including a thriller, *Safe House*, and a comedy, *Smart Alec*. "I play an ex-DIA agent in *Safe House*," Stewart reveals, "DIA being the Defense Intelligence Agency, who has barricaded himself inside his Hollywood Hills home using the latest security technology that can be found. He believes that his life has been threatened by a man who was once his boss, an admiral who is now running for President of the United States. The admiral is killing off all of the people who used to work for him and who may have dirt on him.

"And I have a lot of dirt on him for things he did while he was with the DIA. My character is the last guy alive, but no one believes him because he is in the early stages of Alzheimer's Disease. Everyone thinks his paranoia is part of the disease. So, as the actual danger to his life gets closer, his ability to deal with the threat, with anything around him, gets worse and worse. We don't have a distributor for the film yet, but I think that it may come out very, very well."

Stewart has also completed principal photography on *Smart Alec*, a comedy that was shot on location in Canada immediately after *Star Trek: First Contact* wrapped up. "It's an action-comedy and I get to play a luminously unpleasant character," Stewart says, smiling broadly. "The major conflict of the story is the competition between this super-criminal that I play and a teenager [played by Vincent Kartheiser], who was in the movie *Alaska*." The film was released in the United States in August. "He's a wonderful young talent," Stewart continues. "The best way I can describe the film is to say that it will be a little like *Home Alone* in spirit and in its comedy."

These days, Stewart seems to be doing rather well for

This page: *Picard as captain of the U.S.S. Enterprise NCC-1701-E in Star Trek: First Contact*

"I have always said I would not mind coming back to Star Trek and to Picard as long as I had the opportunity to do other things."

"I still feel that way."

And with that, Stewart takes one last bite of his salad, pets his beloved Bela good-bye for now, and hops on that bicycle which will shuttle him back to the *U.S.S. Enterprise* bridge.

It really is quite a sight. ∎

himself. He lives in Los Angeles most of the time, but maintains a residence in London, and is romantically involved with *Star Trek: Voyager* producer Wendy Neuss. He recently sang at the Hollywood Bowl and will be taking to the stage come December in a limited-run Los Angeles production of his popular one-man show, Charles Dickens' *A Christmas Carol*. He hopes to direct a small film in the future, perhaps even a film version of *The Merchant of Venice* in the style of Sir Ian McKellen's *Richard III*.

So positive have Stewart's experiences away from *Star Trek: The Next Generation* been that he is actually looking forward to reprising his role as Jean-Luc Picard every few years in future films. Indeed, *Star Trek: The Next Generation* and Picard have not, as Stewart once feared like some fear the plague, stood in the way of his pursuing other opportunities, other roles that allow him to fully express himself as an actor.

"I was absolutely determined to be in a state of preparedness in my career as an actor to move on after *Star Trek: The Next Generation* went off the air, and I think I was successful in doing that," Patrick Stewart says as the conversation comes to a close. "I have always said I would not mind coming back to *Star Trek* and to Picard as long as I had the opportunity to do other things.

Patrick Stewart as Jean-Luc Picard,
Captain of the *U.S.S. Enterprise*-D

John de Lancie as Q, the omnipotent thorn in *The Next Generation*'s side

JOIN THE Q

Whether you think of him as Picard's arch-nemesis or humanity's enigmatic shepherd, John de Lancie's colorful Q is one of the most loved bad guys in *Star Trek* history. Bryan Cairns spoke to the actor about *Trek*, computer games... and *My Little Pony*?!

Q (de Lancie) visits Quark's Bar in the *DS9* episode "Q-Less"

"IT OCCURRED TO ME THAT Q WAS OMNIPOTENT, BUT TOO STUPID TO KNOW IT."

When John de Lancie descended on Hollywood, clearly he had a message in mind: Resistance is futile! With a body of work that has now spanned 35-plus years, the busy actor conquered the film world with credits that include *The Hand that Rocks the Cradle*, *The Fisher King*, *Crank 2*, and *Reign Over Me*. De Lancie didn't slow down in TV-land either, racking up appearances in shows ranging from *Breaking Bad* and *The West Wing*, to *The Six Million Dollar Man*, *Legend*, *Stargate SG-1*, and recent stints on *Torchwood: Miracle Day* and *The Secret Circle*. He's voiced video games such as *Assassin's Creed III* and *Interstate '76*, as well as animated projects including *My Little Pony: Friendship is Magic*, *Duck Dodgers*, and *The Real Adventures of Jonny Quest*. Then there's his stage work, the operas he's directed and, well, the list goes on and on and on.

Regardless of his impressive resumé, it's the almighty Q that remains his most recognizable, and beloved role. Looking back to those early *Trek* days, de Lancie obviously brought a certain energy and intensity to the Q audition that impressed the casting directors.

"At the time, I was playing Roald Amundsen, who was the Arctic explorer," says de Lancie. "I had a sense of that in my body. I had also played Lord Byron, who was from *Mad, Bad and Dangerous to Know*. It was sort of a combination of these two characters."

Back in 1987, all eyes were on *Star Trek: The Next Generation*'s premiere, "Encounter at Farpoint." Viewers were introduced to Captain Jean-Luc Picard commanding the *U.S.S. Enterprise* and a crew of fresh dedicated faces eager to complete their first mission. That almost didn't happen since en route to speak with the Bandi, the ship came across an enigmatic super being named Q, who decided to put humanity on trial.

"Patrick [Stewart] and I had rehearsed a little before I left to go to Japan," recalls de Lancie about shooting the pilot. "I was gone a month before coming back to be on *Next Generation*. I arrived Sunday night from Japan and was on the set at 6am for *Star Trek*. I was mostly jetlagged. I remember there was a lot of attention to detail. It was an unusual situation because most people do not have the opportunity to get a second chance, as it were. Gene [Roddenberry], some of the producers and the original costumer were there. Everybody was really excited to be back, so there was all of that going on. It was an exciting time is what I remember."

GOOD Q/BAD Q

The closest thing to an intergalactic prankster, Q originated from the Q Continuum and often demonstrated a crazy amount of power. Mysterious and mischievous, Q's motives for interacting with the *Enterprise* have never clearly been defined.

"I don't know if I spent a great deal of time asking that," offers de Lancie. "I do know that there's a technical issue when you play certain characters – not least the kings, wizards, and the all-powerful – and that is that after you've sort of strutted around the room a couple of times, being very kingly, there isn't much else to do. That goes with being omnipotent. In this case, it occurred to me that Q was omnipotent, but too stupid to know it. Or that he was all-powerful, but with clay feet, and he was needy. He was really needy, which is something I think makes someone more interesting, rather than just being kingly."

Q puts humanity on trial in "Encounter at Farpoint"

An instant fan favorite, Q was to have sporadically plagued Picard and friends throughout the first season. That was the game plan, but was not how things worked out.

"After the first week, Gene came up to me and said, 'We're going to bring you back six or seven times per year,'" reports de Lancie. "Then he

came up to me on the lot and said, 'We can't do that because the audience is going to wait for The Trickster.' There's nothing else for me to say. It's like somebody else's dinner party. You're either invited or you're not."

De Lancie subsequently appeared in season two's "Hide and Q", where Q grants Commander

A romantic Q (John de Lancie) plays the love card, in *TNG* Season 4 episode "Qpid"

William T. Riker immense powers to tempt him to join the Q Continuum. Next up was "Q Who," where an irate Q transports the *Enterprise* light years across the galaxy, before vanishing himself. It was in this uncharted territory that the ship runs into the lethal Borg and barely manages to escape unscathed. For many Trekkies, Q's actions branded him a villain, a notion de Lancie does not share.

"Well, what I get is, 'When I first saw you, I really hated you. Then I really loved you. Then I saw you were really on their side,'" he laughs. "There's a whole arc there. You have to understand it was an arc that only lasted eight episodes in *Next Generation*. Of course, the material is important. I tried in each one of those episodes to bring out some sort of new facet. The best episodes invariably are the ones of a more philosophical nature."

"Deja Q" found Q stripped of his powers and stuck on the *Enterprise* during a crisis of gravitational proportions. Learning a lesson for a change, surely playing a humanized Q was a welcome shift in pace.

"It was sort of a comedic turn," says de Lancie. "The episodes that incorporated everything were 'All Good Things' and 'Tapestry.' You actually see him try and work with these people. In 'Tapestry,' in his own asshole-y way, he's trying to be a nice guy. In 'All Good Things,' you see in a way, he has really shepherded and protected these people and wishes them well."

Speaking of "All Good Things," de Lancie seemed thrilled to bookend the series and watch it come full circle.

"Yeah, very much so," he confirms. "It was something I appreciated and took seriously."

Recurring over seven seasons also put de Lancie in the unique position of being able to observe the show grow and evolve.

Q (de Lancie) was a pivotal character in both the pilot and final episodes of *The Next Generation*

"Jonathan Frakes [Riker] used to sit me down and say, 'Tell me everything you see,'" explains de Lancie. "I don't remember what I said anymore. I'm sure in my own way I was blunt and hopefully accurate."

Q & A-TYPE

Even after *The Next Generation* wrapped in 1994, de Lancie was recruited for one episode of *Star Trek: Deep Space Nine* and three more of *Star Trek: Voyager*. "The Q and the Grey" was an awkward episode where Q approached Janeway [Kate Mulgrew] to be the father of his child. She declined, but ultimately became the godmother of his son instead. Evidently, Q had a different relationship with Janeway than with Picard, so did de Lancie favor one captain over the other?

"WE WERE JUST TWO MEN WHO WERE VYING FOR WHO WAS ON TOP. IT WAS ALL VERY A-TYPE PERSONALITY."

"They were written for different dynamics" he counters, "The relationship between Picard and I was uncluttered by the potential for romance. We were just two men vying over who was on top. It was all very A-type personality. The Janeway situation had the potential for some romance. But they were so concerned she not play it that she was in any way tempted, infatuated, or in no way affected in a relationship/sexual level, I think they missed a big opportunity. That was the 800-pound gorilla in the room. We should have gone down that road and then have the rug pulled out, mostly from under me. It gave us so many possibilities, but we had to turn a blind eye to it. That dialogue, that experience, was just not as fulfilling."

In "Q2," Q arrives on the *U.S.S. Voyager* to introduce Janeway to her godson, Q Junior. Unfortunately, power corrupts, and the youngster was a bit of a hellion and wreaked havoc by instigating wars and pitting the *Voyager* against Borg vessels. If Q Junior bears an uncanny resemblance to his dear old TV Dad, there's a pretty good reason. Junior was played by de Lancie's real life son, Keegan.

"My agents called me and said, 'By the way, I don't know if you know this, but they are casting

Gerrit Graham joins John de Lancie as another member of the Q continuum, in *Voyager* episode "Death Wish"

Captain Q (de Lancie) makes his arrival felt on the *Enterprise* bridge ("Encounter at Farpoint")

Leonard Nimoy back in 1996. The endeavor involved various *Star Trek* actors performing great science fiction literature for audio. Recently released as digital downloads, people can finally hear that series again.

"I was delighted," de Lancie says of the development. "I worked hard to get them back up there on a website at a reasonable price. They can hear them all."

Q IS FOR QUADWRANGLE

De Lancie is also returning to the realm of video games with the *Quantum Conundrum*, where he tackles the wacky character, Professor Quadwrangle.

"I have not played the game yet," states de Lancie. "When I asked other people about it, the guy who did it, and my sons knew this as well, is a very famous game designer. He created a thing called *Portal*. I had asked my kids about it, who are now 24 and 27, and they were like 'Oh yeah, yeah! He did *Portal*, Dad! That's a big deal!' Same thing with *Assassin's Creed*, which I just did. That one I had seen. *Quantum* is a puzzle game and it's very clever. In the game, my rambunctious nephew comes to this extraordinary crazy mansion that I own. I am the scientist and have created all of these strange things and we, the audience, are making our way through the house. It's fun.

"Once I did a game about 15 years ago," he continues. "I go into the studio and was knocking off the lines. After about 20 minutes or so, I go, 'What's this game? I feel like it is drive-by shootings.' And the guy goes, 'Yeah, it is.' I went 'What?' Of course, I knew I was stuck. I couldn't say I wasn't going to do it. From then on, I've always asked about that type of stuff. 'We're not shooting people or killing people?' 'Oh, no, no, no. This is a fun puzzle game.'"

for the character of your son. Do you want me to submit Keegan?'" explains de Lancie. "'I don't know. Let me ask him.' I said 'Keegan, would you like to be in *Star Trek*? Obviously, you have to audition for it.' So he went in, auditioned and got past station number one. He had to audition two or three times and I believe they hired him because he did a really great job. I had nothing to do with it."

For de Lancie, the episode wasn't exactly a fitting final goodbye for Q, but it still must have been a pinch-me moment to have your son co-starring next to you in a *Trek* episode.

"Yeah, it was both great and… a lot of actors will understand this, but while part of acting involves being very attentive to the other people and what's going on, you have to keep some of your power for yourself, to do your job and maintain your presence," explains de Lancie. "In the case of my son, the majority of my attention was, 'How's Keegan doing?' If I go on a regular job, where someone might have a cold or an actor doesn't feel well or there's just an upset in their family, I am very sympathetic. But when we were acting, it's real tennis."

For some reason, there was never any discussion about beaming Q over to the

Enterprise series and the *TNG* feature films. That's okay, though. De Lancie's career still hit warp speed and upon inspection, is chock-full of fascinating genre roles.

"It was the thing that started me out as a kid," says de Lancie. "The best movie was a sci-fi movie. The second best was a war movie and the third was a western. After that, I just didn't go. All of a sudden, I was doing sci-fi. The first book I ever read was a sci-fi book. I just liked it. I have to say, this was at a time when sci-fi films were few and far between. If you liked that stuff, it was considered edgy or avant-garde. Now, it's become the canvas, whereas westerns used to be the canvas. I am delighted."

One of the projects de Lancie is most proud of is *Alien Voices*, which he formed along with

Q demonstrates humanity's drug-induced military past, in "Encounter at Farpoint"

Father and son cause trouble for Janeway, in "Q2"

To this day, the *Star Trek* fandom demonstrates unparalleled dedication to that mythology and the intergalactic exploits of the *Trek* characters. There are many *Star Trek* conventions, comic books, novels, this very magazine, and the next movie installment is scheduled for 2013. However, given his extensive and diverse resume, that doesn't mean de Lancie hasn't experienced other properties with devoted aficionados.

"Do you know anything about Bronies?" he asks. "I dare say they have as much presence at these conventions of late. I don't do that many conventions, but I did some *Torchwood* episodes, and they asked me to go to a convention in Los Angeles. I was up there with the whole cast and the first question out of somebody's mouth was about *My Little Pony*. It's like somebody asked an inappropriate question at dinner. I was on the stage with people going 'What's *My Little Pony*? I thought this was for *Torchwood*!'"

On April 28, 2012, the nine principal *TNG* cast members, including Stewart, Frakes, Brent Spiner, and Marina Sirtis, assembled at Calgary's *TNG* Exposed event, a full-blown reunion that had attendees in a frenzy. As an added surprise, an unscheduled de Lancie rushed on to the stage to help his friends and former co-stars celebrate the show's astounding 25th anniversary. Naturally, such a rare reunion made it easier to reflect and reminisce about some treasured memories.

"There are so many," says de Lancie. "I remember the opening sequence once I got back from Japan and started filming. I remember the specialness of the last show. I remember a scene I did with Jonathan, Kate [Mulgrew], somebody else and I, and we laughed and laughed and laughed."

"I've also had some very intense experiences with fans, where a father brought me his son, who was going to have a very serious operation the next day. You have to go, 'Wow! This is a lot of responsibility.' I enjoy meeting them. I made a whole group of them laugh the other night. I felt people would ask me about these shows and it was like asking about a dinner party I had hosted and cooked the dinner for and everyone still wanted to know about what the menu was. Now we're so far beyond that. It's been so many years that you know all the guests, you know the wine we drank and the food we ate. Now you are asking me to go back to when I went to the grocery store and started picking out the potatoes. And you know it so well that when I say, 'Well, okay, I got the potatoes,' people go, 'No, no, no! It's not that you got the potatoes. Remember! You picked that first potato up, you looked at it and it was perfect.'"

"DO YOU KNOW ANYTHING ABOUT BRONIES?"

Q (de Lancie) changes uniforms for his appearance in *Voyager* ("Q2")

A DATE WITH
DATA

BRENT SPINER, ALTER EGO OF *STAR TREK: THE NEXT GENERATION'S* LIEUTENANT
COMMANDER DATA, CELEBRATES 40 YEARS OF *STAR TREK* AND REMINISCES ON
HIS FORMER LIFE AS AN ANDROID WITH NICK JOY...

Pictures clockwise: *Masks; The Defector; Elementary Dear Data; All Good Things...; Encounter at Farpoint; Data; Sarek*

"MUCH AS I HATED WEARING THEM, THERE WAS SOMETHING ABOUT THE YELLOW CONTACT LENSES THAT FLIPPED ME INTO THE GEAR OF PLAYING THAT CHARACTER."

"Your challenge is to come up with something that I haven't already been asked over the last few days," Brent Spiner playfully poses. He's in London at the plush Dorchester Hotel, promoting the franchise's big four zero, and inevitably some reporters have been asking the same old questions. But for someone who has been in the public eye as Data for nearly 20 years, it's hardly surprising that he has heard them all before.

"I don't tire of talking about Data though," he quickly reassures. "I mean, what would be the point? There's nothing I can do about it. This character is going to be with me for the rest of my life, one way or another. I don't feel pigeonholed by the role, and a lot of other things have

happened as a result of playing it. Certainly going back to Broadway and doing the lead in a Broadway musical [John Adams in the revival of Founding Fathers musical *1776*] was as a result of the box office value that Data brought."

Spiner is enthusiastic about *Star Trek*'s birthday, but questions the year count. "Is it really 40 years? It feels like 90. Maybe I'm younger than I think! I recall it premiering like any other new show on NBC," the accomplished actor continues, "so September 8, 1966 in itself was no big deal for me. I guess that I really only got into it in the 1970s when I was at college and watched it in the afternoon during daily re-runs. All the guys I knew would come up from school to watch it."

While fans are celebrating the series' anniversary, many people are just as keen to play down the achievement, Spiner reveals. "I find it interesting that the people who don't watch *Star Trek* are always interested in telling you that they don't!" he observes.

"I don't understand that. They say 'I hear you've been on *Star Trek*. I have to say that I *never* watched it.' And I say to them, '*Why* are you telling me this? I don't care what you do or don't watch, but why do you feel the need to tell me?'

"It's all about respecting people's choices, and it's a good thing that the anniversary is high profile. It's a way of showing the fans that you respect their choice to watch and support the programs. We're recognizing that their choices are valid and that it's OK to embrace this whole phenomenon."

Star Trek was a little over 20 years old when Spiner landed the role of Data, and he recalls the significance of the appointment. "Was it a big deal because I'd got a role on *Star Trek*? In all honesty, I was more excited because it was going to be regular work and a good job," he confesses. "I was just happy to be employed at that time, and because the show had been pre-sold for a

DATA FILE

P layed by Brent Spiner in *Star Trek: The Next Generation* and the subsequent films, the android Data's desire to be more human gained ground during his years aboard the *U.S.S. Enterprise* NCC-1701-D, culminating in the fitting of an "emotion chip" built by his creator, Dr. Noonien Soong, by the time of *Star Trek Generations*.

The android served aboard the *U.S.S. Enterprise* as lieutenant and then later operations officer and second officer. In addition to his well-documented service under Captain Picard's command – including duels with android brother Lore – he also captained the *U.S.S. Sutherland* during the Klingon Civil War.

Transferring to the Sovereign-class *U.S.S. Enterprise* NCC-1701-E in 2372, Data helped Picard defeat the Borg and preserve the timeline. He met his end in 2379, sacrificing himself aboard Reman ship *Scimitar* in order to destroy the Thalaron beam generator and save the crew of *U.S.S. Enterprise*. Before his destruction, Data did however download his entire memory database into android prototype B-4, so perhaps Data lives on in it...

whole season, I knew that I was going to be working solidly for a year. I'd previously only worked in the theatre, where my longest run at that point had been three months. So, steady employment, and getting paid better than anything I'd ever had before, were important considerations to me."

The fact that Spiner took to Data immediately was also a great advantage. "I liked him as soon I'd read the pilot [*Encounter at Farpoint*]," he beams. "My agent sent me the script and said, 'Read it and see if there's a character that appeals to you.' Data appealed to me, so that's what I went after."

While the character had his attractions, there were times that Spiner considered how much easier his life would have been if he'd ended up playing Picard, Riker or La Forge. "Patrick [Stewart] could turn up a quarter of an hour before rehearsals started, but because of the extensive make-up that Data required, I'd have to be there at 4:45 every Monday morning," he recalls. "That start time got later as the week went on because they had to allow us a 12-hour turnaround between finishing the night before and starting again the next day, but Monday was always 4:45. On the positive side, it was very quiet in the make-up trailer with Michael Westmore, who was a great guy to be around at that time of the morning."

Patrick Stewart has boasted that when playing Captain Picard, he could be changed out of his 'spacesuit' and into street clothes in less than 10 minutes. "That's true," Spiner agrees. "The worst part of the make-up for me was the point at the end of a 16-hour day where everybody just changed out of their clothes, washed their faces and left, while I was just trying to get enough of the stuff off my skin so that I could go home and then *really* take it off." Regardless of how much purging he undertook, the make-up seemed to be permanent. "You know, I'm still finding gold make-up even now in places that I really shouldn't,"

he chuckles. "In the early days I used a product that was kerosene-based because it was the only thing that would cut through the make-up (and presumably a layer of skin). Nowadays I understand that they use something a little... kinder."

In addition to playing Data and twin brother Lore in the season four episode *Brothers*, Spiner also wore extensive prosthetics to play the aged Dr Noonien Soong. "That was a three hour make-up job," he confirms. "Wearing the make-up really helped me to find the voice and mannerisms of the character." In the same manner, Data's make-up design helped Spiner to keep focused on the android. "Much as I hated wearing them, there was something about the yellow contact lenses that flipped me into the gear of playing that character. It was something about not being able to see very well that made it easier to play an android. It wasn't so much that the lenses in themselves limited my peripheral vision, it was how the make-up reacted with them. First of all they applied a regular make-up base, which they powdered over with a thick layer of gold powder. Because powder moves, it would come off my face and go directly into my eyes, smearing the lenses. An hour into the day and I really couldn't see," he winces.

While Spiner came to terms with the demands of the make-up, he freely admits he was less successful in combating the effects of ageing. As time went by, it became increasingly apparent that the actor was getting older, while his character was not meant to age.

"Frankly, the age issue was never a problem when we started. No one could have predicted that we'd go seven years and four movies. I didn't think that the show would go beyond a year," he reveals. "I thought

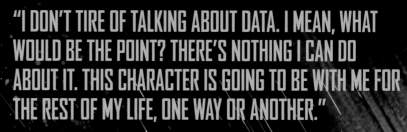

Pictures clockwise: *Nemesis*; *Data's Day*; *A Fistful of Datas*; *Brothers*; Data; *Descent* part II; *Datalore*

"I DO FIND IT INTERESTING THAT THE PEOPLE WHO DON'T WATCH *STAR TREK* ARE ALWAYS INTERESTED IN TELLING YOU THAT THEY DON'T!"

that we were attempting the impossible – trying to capture lightning in a bottle for a second time; but somehow it worked."

Time did inevitably catch up with Spiner, and the writers tried to deal with the issue in the show. "They talked about the problem and decided to write it into one of the episodes [*Birthright, Part 1*]. There was a scene with LeVar [Burton] and [Alexander] Siddig – who was guesting on our show from *DS9* – where they discussed a special ageing chip. I guess they thought it through and just dropped the idea," he suggests.

The audience was forgiving, even if time wasn't, and Spiner believes that it wouldn't have been a problem if he'd landed the job while younger. "It would all have been fine if I'd got that job ten years earlier. I was 38 when we first started doing *The Next Generation*, so when I finished the series I was 45. In the last film [*Nemesis*] I was in my early 50s. One really shouldn't be playing a child-like android at that point in your life! If I'd started at 28 I could have played it for 20 years without any noticeable change."

Spiner decided to halt the ageing process when developing the storyline for *Nemesis* with John Logan by taking the ultimate action – and killing Data off. "I'd like to clarify something here," Spiner interjects. "It was my decision, but I didn't *have* to kill Data. We were all pretty much aware that this was going to be our last film and as such thought we'd go for broke.

"We worked on the story with the intention of making it for the fans," Spiner recalls of his approach to what was the final *ST:TNG* movie. "With every *Star Trek* movie prior to that we tried to find a way to bridge the gap between the fans and the general public. Even reading the latest quotes from J.J. Abrams about the next movie, it makes sense for the movie to be as inclusive as

FAST FACTS

possible. With *Nemesis* we said 'Forget that! Let's make a movie for the fans, because that's the people who actually go to see the films.' And what happened? They didn't go! Usually the films opened big, even if they had a lot of competition, but *Nemesis* didn't even do that. This was a message from the fans that they were done with us," he feels, pausing. "It was unexpected."

Debates rage as to whether *Nemesis*' box office was down to poor scheduling, *Star Trek* fatigue, or the fact that it wasn't a great movie. Spiner avoids pointing the finger of blame. "You always make compromises with movies, but I think the final film was pretty close to what I originally imagined. You always overwrite your initial drafts, knowing that they will have to be cut down for pace. *Nemesis* was directed by an editor [Stuart Baird] where pace was his number one concern. A lot of stuff that was cut out of the movie was pretty good, while some of it wasn't. Could a better movie have been made from the material that was shot? Maybe. Maybe not."

If *Nemesis* had been the box office success that Paramount wanted, it seemed likely that a further installment would follow. While Data was killed when Shinzon's ship exploded, his memory had already been transferred to his brother B-4, thus giving Spiner the chance to return to the fold, albeit in a slightly different guise. "We probably would have come back and done another one," Spiner opines. "There was enough of Data within B-4 for Data's spirit to live again through him. Data's memory was now in B-4 and, ultimately, that positronic brain was going to kick in."

To date, there's hasn't been a new *ST:TNG* film. Spiner and John Logan did present a possible treatment for a follow-up, though this was not developed. "John and I had a great story that would bring together all the captains, crews and villains together at the same time. It was the 'Justice League' of *Star Trek*, but Paramount decided it was too expensive a move to make."

Not only was a further *ST:TNG* film put on ice, but *Star Trek: Enterprise* was cancelled after four seasons,

thus presenting fans with the prospect of no new *Star Trek* product in active development. Fortunately, a new movie is now being planned. "Neither the cancellation of *Enterprise* nor the announcement of the new film were a surprise to me," Spiner admits. "I think they're right to start a new movie franchise that will hopefully spawn a new series that in turn will spawn new movies. I think it was disappointing that they cancelled *Enterprise*, because I don't think that they [the viewers] ever quite 'got' it. *Enterprise* wasn't doing great numbers and they decided it wasn't cost-effective to keep it on. I disagree with their decision because I think that it was coming into its own in the fourth season. Like the other series that preceded it, it took a while to find its feet. I think they were getting good when they cancelled it. My experience on the show [as Arik Soong in three-part story *Borderland/Cold Station 12/The Augments*] was a really positive one."

Unfortunately, early cancellation was a fate that also befell Spiner's most recent TV show, the Brannon Braga-produced *Threshold*. Aside from that show, Spiner has kept a lower profile than his fans would like. "I'm just looking for my next project," he says. "I might do another CD." In 1991 he recorded *Ol' Yellow Eyes is Back*, a collection of classic songs, supported on some tracks by his *ST:TNG* co-stars. "I'm part-owner of a recording studio in Los Angeles, and one of my partners is a great engineer and producer. I suggested that we do another CD and he said 'Why not. At least we can get studio time cheap!'"

Spiner's most recent role is in teen 'chick flick' *Material Girls*, playing opposite Hilary and Haylie Duff. An opportunity arises to ask Spiner something completely new: who were scarier to act against – the Klingon Duras sisters or the Duff sisters? "Scary?" he chuckles. "I don't think that any of them were scary. The Duffs were really lovely girls and arguably they were only similar to the Duras sisters insofar as none of them had much experience with Planet Earth!" ◢

- Data was the fifth and next-to-last model created by Noonien Soong and his then-wife Juliana on the Omicron Theta science colony
- Doctor Soong was killed by Lore on Terlina III
- Data was activated on February 2, 2338 after he was found by members of a *U.S.S. Tripoli* away team after the Crystalline Entity had drained the life force from the 411-member colony on Omicron Theta.
- Data's interests include Sir Arthur Conan Doyle's detective Sherlock Holmes; art, theater and playing musical instruments, including the violin, guitar, oboe and flute. He can also dance and play poker and other card games
- Data weighs 100 kg and carries a concealed master on/off switch centered just below his right shoulder blade.
- Data's body was temporarily hijacked by Dr. Ira Graves, Soong's mentor, who was seeking to cheat death
- Data's rights as an intelligent being rather than Starfleet property were challenged and determined in his favor in 2365
- In addition to close friendships with Captain Picard, Tasha Yar and Geordj La Forge, Data had a pet cat called Spot that survived the destruction of the *U.S.S. Enterprise NCC-1701-D*

Pictures clockwise: *Generations;* Data playing poker; Spot; Juliana Soong; Dr Noonien Soong

Forbes Ahead

Michelle Forbes will always be remembered as the woman who properly introduced the *Bajorans* into *Star Trek*. Ian Spelling remembers the renowned actress and her feelings on and reasons for leaving the *Star Trek* universe...

Talented actress Michelle Forbes, with her jet black hair, even darker eyes and intense, formidable screen presence, scored big with *Star Trek* fans who loved her performance as the recurring character of *Ensign Ro* in *Star Trek: The Next Generation*. Ro introduced a number of vital, long-lasting elements into the *Star Trek* mythos. She was a Bajoran, somewhat unlikeable, and a Maquis renegade.

"Everyone kept referring to her strength and her outspokenness," Forbes said of her character in a recent interview in a US science fiction magazine, "but it disturbs me that Ro is con-

"[Ro]'s outspoken and she is who she is. I never thought of her as being strong."

stantly referred to as strong. "She's outspoken and she is who she is. I never thought of her as being strong. What is strong? People do tend to relate to her opinions or struggles and her outspokenness. If that makes her strong, fine, but she's also weak in trying to find her own way. Perhaps people just identify with her for that."

Forbes ultimately turned up on *ST:TNG* more than half a dozen times, in the episodes *Ensign Ro, Disaster, Conundrum, Power Play, Cause and Effect, The Next Phase, Rascals* (essentially a cameo) and the very last single episode show, *Preemptive Strike*. She considers *Ensign Ro, Conundrum* and *Preemptive Strike* her favourites as Ro. Of course, the actress also has a major soft spot for *Half a Life*, the 1991 episode that first

introduced her to the *Star Trek* universe, and to *ST:TNG*'s producers, writers and fans. Forbes played *Dara*, the daughter of *Dr Timicin* (played by David Ogden Stiers), a *Kaelon* who'd reached the age at which he was supposed to commit ritual suicide (60). *Lwaxana Troi* begged him to seek asylum, while Dara asked that he stick to Kaelon tradition. "I loved the story so much," Forbes says of the episode. "To me, it was about what we do with our elders and how we treat people at a certain age. It was also about dealing with intolerance and ignorance of other cultures. It struck a chord in me. I was pleased to be a part of [that episode]."

While Forbes graduated from Dara to Ro, she chose not to graduate from *Star Trek: The Next*

Below: *Ro,* Keiko *and* Guinan *are turned into the equivalent of 12-year-old children in* Rascals
Bottom (left and right): *After being taken on by Starfleet as an ensign in* Ensign Ro *and later promoted to a Lieutenant, Ro leaves Starfleet to return to her roots in* Preemptive Strike

2340 Ro Laren born on Bajor. She spends most of her childhood in Bajoran prison camps

2349 Witnesses her father's torture and murder

2358 (Date is conjecture) Escapes into the Federation from Bajor

2360 Enters Starfleet Academy

2364 Graduates from Starfleet Academy. Assigned to *U.S.S. Wellington*

2366 (Date is conjecture) Disobeys orders on Away Team mission to Garon II, leading to the death of eight crew members. She refuses to defend herself at her court-martial and is sent to prison on Jaros II

2368 Ro is released from prison. She is invited to remain on the *U.S.S. Enterprise* (Ensign Ro)
U.S.S. Enterprise suffers major systems damage. Ro is trapped on the Bridge with Counsellor Troi (Disaster)
U.S.S Enterprise crew lose their memory. Ro has a brief relationship with Will Riker (Conundrum)
Ro and Geordi La Forge are rendered invisible and presumed dead by the *U.S.S. Enterprise* crew (The Next Phase)

2369 Together with Guinan and Captain Picard, Ro is turned into a young child. Joins Starfleet's Advanced Tactical Training program (Rascals)

2370 Is promoted to full lieutenant. Completes Tactical Training program and is reassigned to *U.S.S. Enterprise*. After covert mission to infiltrate the Maquis, Ro leaves Starfleet and joins the Maquis in a fight against Cardassia (Preemptive Strike)

> "My being comfortable over the years had a lot to do with the cast and crew of Star Trek: The Next Generation and the show being such a good place to be."

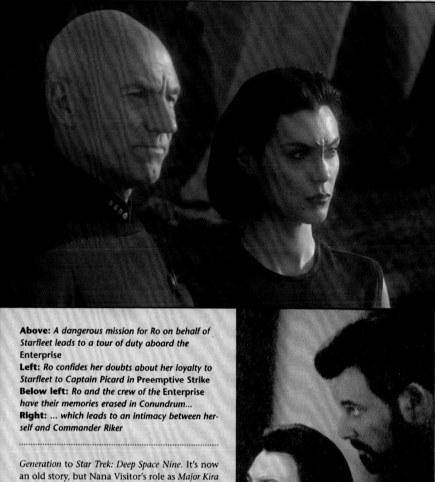

Above: A dangerous mission for Ro on behalf of Starfleet leads to a tour of duty aboard the Enterprise
Left: Ro confides her doubts about her loyalty to Starfleet to Captain Picard in Preemptive Strike
Below left: Ro and the crew of the Enterprise have their memories erased in Conundrum...
Right: ... which leads to an intimacy between herself and Commander Riker

Generation to Star Trek: Deep Space Nine. It's now an old story, but Nana Visitor's role as Major Kira on ST:DS9 was developed only after Forbes elected to pass on the offer of joining the series as a regular in order to pursue other film and television opportunities. Among those opportunities were the films Kalifornia, with Brad Pitt and X-Files star David Duchovny, and Swimming with Sharks, a scathingly funny black comedy about Hollywood and the motion picture industry. "I made the right choice for me," she explains. "Many people took it the wrong way. It's very hard for me to make a seven year commitment to anything, work-wise or otherwise. I want variety in my life and I want to play as many things as possible. I simply made a decision to hold out for variety and I hope people understand that."

Most recently, audiences have seen the Texan-born, New York City-based actress in such projects as John Carpenter's 1996 Escape from New York sequel Escape from LA, the television series The Prosecutors and, most notably, the long-running television drama Homicide: Life on the Streets, which screens on Channel 4 in the UK, in which she plays the show's Chief Medical Examiner, Julianna Cox. Her other credits include the soap opera The Guiding Light, the television drama Shannon's Deal, the little-seen vampire flick Love Bites (starring Adam Ant) and the stage play Call it Clover.

Looking back on her days with Star Trek, Forbes is obviously satisfied, seeing it as a good experience; a growing period, in a career that continues to evolve. "My being comfortable over the years had a lot to do with the cast and crew of Star Trek: The Next Generation and the show being such a good place to be," the actress enthuses. "The atmosphere on the set was so rare. Star Trek was like a family. Of course, there were little arguments and political things here and there, but nothing like it is on other shows and films. There was always just a real sense of community and family, and they were all welcoming to me when I came on. That's not always the case when you go on a show as a guest star."

There's little chance that Ro will return in an episode of either of the current Star Trek shows, a future series or film, but even if Forbes never does re-enter the 24th Century, there's no doubt that she made her mark on Star Trek, and that she will always be remembered for this. ■

> "It's very hard for me to make a seven-year commitment to anything, work-wise or otherwise."

Marina Sirtis

> "The favourite moments I have are always about something that made us laugh. Twice, I remember actually writhing on the floor with laughter, falling on the floor and laughing, and having to be pulled up to my feet. It was an incredible time."
>
> ### On *Star Trek: The Next Generation*

A CUT ABO

As well as running away with the vote for 'best hair' in our 'Ultimate *Star Trek*' survey, **Marina Sirtis** has been busy elsewhere in the *Star Trek* universe recently. Along with Dwight Schultz as *Reg Barclay*, Sirtis makes another appearance on *Star Trek: Voyager* as *Counselor Deanna Troi*, this time in the seventh season episode *Inside Man*. She's also been busy on this side of the Atlantic, guest starring in an episode of *Casualty*. **Abbie Bernstein** takes her pulse and asks about her favourite *Star Trek* stuff.

I t's no longer completely unheard of for actors to create roles on television and then play the same characters in feature films. However, Marina Sirtis is nearly unique in originating a role as a regular on one series – Deanna Troi in *Star Trek: The Next Generation* – playing the character in three films, then reprising the part as a guest in a different series, namely *Star Trek: Voyager*. After appearing in the sixth season instalments *Pathfinder* and *Life Line*, Troi makes another return in the seventh season episode *Inside Man*, once more deploying her empathic skills in the service of the Federation.

Speaking from her Los Angeles area home, Sirtis expounds on the changes in Troi. "It seems that the writers in the [*Star Trek*] films portray me slightly differently than the writers in the TV series do," she muses. "So when I'm doing *Voyager* now, it's the

Troi of *Next Gen*, the counselor, kind of sympathetic, the one who is called on when people are having problems – that Troi. And it seems that in the last two movies, I've become the wacky, zany Troi. You see another side of her personality. So it's not so much what I'm doing [as a performer] – it seems to be what the writers are doing and the context that they put me into."

Describing *Inside Man*, Sirtis says, "It's kind of a

VE

This page and opposite page, left to right: Marina and her co-stars through the years, from the early days of *ST:TNG* to *Star Trek: Insurrection* and *Star Trek: First Contact*

continuation of the Pathfinder project that Barclay set up. I can't say too much about the storyline, except I would hazard a guess that this Pathfinder thing has something to do with *Voyager* coming back to Earth, although it doesn't happen in my episode. I will be clear about that. Again, it's me and Barclay. I was talking to Michael Dorn [*Worf*] yesterday and I said, 'It's so funny, because I always seem to end up in a team of two.' First it was Troi and *Riker*, and then it was Troi and Worf, and then back to Troi and Riker in the movies, and now it's Troi and Barclay. It's great for the conventions, because they can double me up with three different people and get three different experiences."

After over a decade on the *Star Trek* convention trail, Sirtis still enjoys the experience. "They're a lot of fun," she says. For one thing, according to Sirtis, speaking at a convention is somewhat similar to acting in a stage comedy: "Over the years,

> **"After [*Star Trek: The Next Generation*] finished, instead of using the momentum of the show to get more work, which is what other people did, I was in denial about the show being over."**

obviously, I have been asked the same questions over and over again, and they have developed into this semi-stand-up comedy routine. I know what my answers are and you know where you're going to get the laughs. Like you know when you're going to get a laugh in a comedy, I know where I'm going to get a laugh on a certain reply, so there's a timing element to it which is the same. You come offstage from a play and you come offstage from a convention, and you're on

an adrenaline high in both cases. I really enjoy that aspect of it."

There are other rewards to doing conventions too. "I watched Denise [Crosby – *Tasha Yar*]'s movie *Trekkies* [a documentary about *Star Trek* fandom] for the first time this weekend – it was on cable. And something Majel [Barrett-Roddenberry] and Jimmy Doohan [*Scotty*] said about when you're onstage, the love that you get coming across from people is actually indescribable. The fans pay their hard-earned

"There's a part of me that is dreading the next movie, because it *will* be the last for us, but there's also a part of me that is looking forward to it being the last, because I can finally let go."

Brent Spiner (Data) with LeVar Burton (*Geordi La Forge*) and Marina Sirtis. Sirtis describes Spiner as "a very ironic person."

cash to come and see you many, many times, over and over again – it just blows my mind."

Once in a while, Sirtis acknowledges with amusement, it also blows her mind to realise how long she's been doing this. "I had a bit of a scare at a convention recently where a young lady had a gift for me and she came onstage. She showed me a photograph of a mother with a toddler and a baby, and she said, 'That's me.' I said, 'Where?' She said, 'I'm the baby in the photograph, taken at a convention 12, 13 years ago.' She was taller than me. I just said, 'OK, never do this to me again,'" relates the actress with a laugh. "I went into a decline immediately."

Although *Star Trek* fandom is international, Sirtis sees differences in the reception she gets from country to country. "When we go to Germany, it's like we're the Beatles," she laughs warmly. "It's unbelievable. They scream from the moment you walk onstage for about 10 minutes, until you can actually quiet them down so you can start to talk. In the US, I think they kind of feel that we're theirs. On a certain level, we are – it was an American show and they were the ones really that made us successful, so we do owe some kind of debt of gratitude to the American fans. In the UK, they totally get my sense of humour a hundred per cent. It's almost like a give-and-take thing in the UK. There's a real connection and a real to-ing and fro-ing of responses and… it is different. It's actually very special."

Sirtis recently returned to Britain to make her first appearance on a UK series in over a decade on an episode of the medical drama *Casualty*. "I'm a patient briefly, but I play a Labour MP. I'm a 'Blair babe', I think they call them. It was a real learning experience of what it's like to work in England, actually. In LA, it's a big concern that everyone look good, and in England, it's more about the acting. It was a kind of readjustment for me, having worked so long in Los Angeles, and being concerned about having a hair out of place, whereas in England, they couldn't care less – it was all about the performances."

Returning to work in her homeland was something the actress very much wanted to do. "I realised I hadn't worked [in England] for years," she reveals. "*Gadgetman* was about four or five years ago, and the time before that was *One Last Chance*, which I think was eight years ago. I thought that it was time for me to kind of poke my nose around the corner, because I sit and watch *Masterpiece Theatre* [the US public television showcase for BBC dramas] and I get really jealous, because they're doing such great work over there [in England]. Not that

Early publicity shot from *Star Trek: The Next Generation*

they don't do it [in the US], but they tend to do a different type of show in England, the classics and things like that, so I tend to get anxious that I'm not being thought of for those parts.

"I think because I've been in America for so long," she adds, "people just assumed that I didn't want to work in England, and that really wasn't the case. I think my career will basically be in those two countries, England and America."

English casting directors still remember Sirtis from her pre-*ST:TNG* days. Back then, the actress recalls, she was seen in a very non-Troi way.

"Before I got *Star Trek*, I was nine times out of 10 cast as the tough cookie, or sometimes the tart with a heart of gold. Then I got Troi, who was the total opposite and that was kind of weird for me, because I've never played anyone that *nice* before. I had to kind of stop and make sure that I wasn't letting the toughness that I usually played seep into the character. It was an ongoing challenge for the whole seven years and three movies, to be true to the character and maintain the sympathetic nature that she had,

and not to inject a lot of my kind of humour into her. I'm told I'm a funny person, but when I tried to do that, it wouldn't work. Jonathan [Frakes – Riker] would say to me, 'No, no, Marina, don't do that, it's not funny.' I really kind of had to battle sometimes to stay true to Troi."

It was also sometimes a battle for the *ST:TNG* cast to avoid being misunderstood by some overly literal-minded journalists. "They don't get irony in America most of the time," Sirtis observes. "We discovered that early on when we were doing interviews and Brent [Spiner – Data] – who's a very ironic person," she notes with a laugh – "read one of the interviews he'd done, and he said, 'You know what? Don't do irony. They don't get it.' They would write what he said down totally seriously and he'd come out looking bad."

One aspect of Troi that evolved over time was her accent. "I've always had to do accents," Sirtis explains, "because I look ethnic, especially in England, where I was not an English rose. I've done Greek, I've done French, Italian, Indian, Polish." Sirtis says she based Troi's accent originally on an Israeli friend. "She spoke English with an American accent. So Troi wasn't a complete copy of her accent, but it was based on that accent and then gradually, of course, she became less foreign-sounding because my mom was American and then my dad was American, so I tried to Americanise the accent much more. I think in the movies, I feel that she's almost American now."

A guest-starring stint as scientist Svetlana Markov on the recently-aired *Stargate SG-1* episode *Watergate* gave Sirtis the opportunity and motive to study a new accent: Russian. "On *Stargate*, I was actually amazed I got the part," she says, "because I was auditioning with a lot of real Russians, and actresses who were American but of Russian descent. I went in and called my manager and said, 'There's no way I'm going to get this part.' I think one of the reasons that I got it was because, in the audition speech, there was a lot of techno-babble. And of course, coming from where I come from, I was used to that, and it was easy for me to talk that way, and I learned it and it just flowed. So maybe that was where I had an edge.

"I have a dialect coach, and I went to see him after I'd got the part, because I wanted it to be right, but when I went in to audition, I just kind of made it up. I like the Eastern European accents, the Russian and the Polish – I don't know why, but they're fun."

Travelling through the galaxy via stargate rather than starship for a change was a blast, Sirtis reports. "It was a lot of fun to do. It's a very easy going set. They work a little faster than we worked on *Next*

Rock stars: Sirtis and Schultz as Deanna Troi and Reg Barclay in *Inside Man*. Like the nose, Reg

Gen. [*Stargate* lead and co-executive producer] Richard Dean Anderson is a joy to work with, and the rest of the cast are, also."

Even though she's surely been asked times beyond number by now, Sirtis enthusiastically responds when queried about her favourite *ST:TNG* experiences. "I remember before we ever started shooting, we'd come in to do make-up and hair tests. I was sitting in the hair chair, and Jonathan, who I hadn't met before, came bounding into the trailer and was so adorable and friendly and just Jonathan, that I knew this was going to be a fun show.

"On the first day of shooting *Encounter at Farpoint*," she continues, "we were on the planet, I think. Immediately, [the regular cast] were joking around and we got on and we were all laughing together, despite the fact that we were all, I presume, really nervous. There was this instant camaraderie that we had and it really impressed me as to how brilliantly the producers had cast these roles. The more we knew each other, the more comfortable we were with each other. The favourite moments I have are always about something that made us laugh. Twice, I remember actually writhing on the floor with laughter, falling on the floor and laughing, and having to be pulled up to my feet. It was an incredible time."

As for favourite episodes, Sirtis says, "There are a few, for different reasons. I like *Face of the Enemy*, because it was kind of the first time they expanded Troi, inasmuch as she kicked butt, but she wasn't possessed by an alien at the time – it was just Troi being strong and asserting herself. And I really enjoyed shooting *A Fistful of Datas*, because we all got to dress up as cowboys. There are so many episodes – I'm just picking two now to answer your question."

Sirtis is more hesitant in citing a favourite moment in terms of her own performance. "It was funny, because I would watch the episodes, and I would come in the next day to work and Brent's trailer was just down a bit from mine. I would go into Brent's trailer and say, 'Oh, Brent, I could've done so much more.' And he would always say, 'No, Marina, you did quite enough,'" she laughs. "I always felt that I could've been better. The only time I think I didn't feel that way was the drunk scene in *First Contact*, where I thought that I nailed it – I thought that was as good as it could be."

The *ST:TNG* regulars, including Sirtis, had three days off between wrap on the series finale and the start of filming on the first *ST:TNG* feature film, *Star Trek Generations*. After that, Sirtis says, "I don't think *Star Trek* affected my career. I think *I* affected my career. After the show finished, instead of using the momentum of the show to get more work, which is what other people did, I was in denial about the show being over. Which was stupid, but my world had kind of ground to a halt. I basically shot myself in the foot for about a year and turned down roles, wouldn't go in to read for certain things. I think I really missed an opportunity when the show finished."

These days, Sirtis is busy not only in front of the camera – besides *Stargate SG-1* and *Casualty*, she's also completed an episode of *Earth: Final Conflict* – but also on stage in the US in recent productions of *Neil Simon's Hotel Suite* and Joe Orton's black comedy classic *Loot*. What's next is an open question – although Sirtis will, of course, be in the next *Star Trek* feature film. She can't say much about the content at this point in time. "I know they've hired a writer and I know they have a story. Everything is kind of up in

Life's a beach: taking a stroll through the surf in *Inside Man*

the air right now because of the [Screen Actors Guild] strike that may happen next year. If there wasn't [the danger of] a strike, I would say we're going to be shooting it in the spring and it'll come out Thanksgiving as usual. However, I have heard rumours that we may not shoot it until the year after."

Sirtis says she looks ahead to the next movie with very mixed feelings. "As I've said before, I think many times – it was the best time of my life. I suppose officially, it's not over yet until we do the next movie.

"I always wanted to be an actor. Part of it is an escape. Part of it is just wanting to be in someone else's skin, which is what I've always wanted to do. I regard myself as a character actor."

There's a part of me that is dreading the next movie, because it *will* be the last for us, but there's also a part of me that is looking forward to it being the last, because I can finally let go. It's been very hard for me to let go and I think I need the closure of saying, 'OK, we've done the last movie and now it's over.'"

Fans needn't worry that they've seen the last of the actress, however. Sirtis reports that the reasons she took up performing are still as valid for her today as when she embarked on her career. "I always wanted to be an actor. Part of it is an escape. Part of it is just wanting to be in someone else's skin, which is what I've always wanted to do. I regard myself as a character actor. In America, they don't quite get it when an attractive person is a character actor, but I've always wanted to be someone totally different when I'm acting, and that's still the case. I'm not really interested in being myself in role after role and just wearing different clothes.

"I never even thought of doing anything else," she states finally, "and I still have that. In the quiet times, when I'm not busy, I don't think, 'Oh, maybe I could do something else.' That's never crossed my mind." ∎

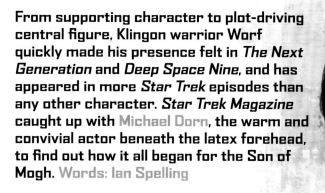

From supporting character to plot-driving central figure, Klingon warrior Worf quickly made his presence felt in *The Next Generation* and *Deep Space Nine*, and has appeared in more *Star Trek* episodes than any other character. *Star Trek Magazine* caught up with Michael Dorn, the warm and convivial actor beneath the latex forehead, to find out how it all began for the Son of Mogh. Words: Ian Spelling

Michael Dorn's mantra, for many years, has been this: Thanks to his decade-plus playing Worf in *Star Trek* series *The Next Generation* and *Deep Space Nine*, he doesn't need to work, but he likes to work. More than that, he loves it, especially when the role offers an acting challenge and the project doesn't require months and months of 16-hour days. So, he'll make a cameo for a friend or play a recurring role, and he'll do voiceovers for animated series or lend his support to a proposed Web series, which explains how such recent projects as *Ted 2, Con Man, Teenage Mutant Ninja Turtles*, and *Internity* (a pilot with Marina Sirtis) wound up on his IMDB filmography.

"You know, it's funny, but when I did *Castle*, those six episodes, that to me was a good time," Dorn says, referring to his recurring part as Dr. Carter Burke, Beckett's therapist on the romantic drama, which ended its run in Spring 2016. "I loved it. The part was great. It wasn't a huge part, but it was recurring, and the guy was a psychiatrist. I liked that. And also, it's become apparent that the business has changed. I have no idea what's coming up next for me. But I like roles like that."

Before CBS announced their new take on TV *Star Trek*, Dorn had been developing a proposal for a series based around his gruff but much-loved Klingon.

WORF

"There'd been a push for a Worf series, and that would've been great," Dorn says, "but since CBS decided to do their own show, the Worf spin-off seems to be in the outgoing file, so I took the basic story, did a page-one rewrite, and I wrote a science fiction show with that Gene Roddenberry feel of space travel, of going out there and discovering stuff. But there'd be no *Star Trek*, and not a lot of aliens. I'd want to star in that. That'd be more work than I'm doing now, but that's fine. Hopefully it'll be on cable, meaning there'd be more artistic freedom. Since they do fewer shows per year, you put more into each show, and I like that, too."

HIGH FLYING KLINGON

In fact, Dorn's imagination seems to be firing on all cylinders, and he's enthusiastic about the prospects for another new writing project he's devised. "The latest thing is a script I wrote a few years ago," Dorn explains, the excitement in his voice building. "It's an aviation story, which is my passion. It's about this Air Force base I visited, and I flew with these guys in Texas. It's called *High Flight*. It's kind of timeless. I'm just doing some script polishing, and I'm talking to the Air Force and another guy who does air-to-air photography. Hopefully, I'll be pitching it soon. I believe, on an ethereal level, there's something out there for me. Something really good's coming along. You never know, but I feel good about that."

Dorn, with characteristic cheeriness, still feels good about his time in the *Star Trek* universe, and his connection with the show now dates back a remarkable – and almost impossible-to-fathom – 30 years. In fact, Dorn played his character more often than any other actor has performed a character in *Star Trek*'s 50 years. He portrayed

Worf (Dorn) provides the muscle for yet another Away Team

Worf for the entire seven-year run of *The Next Generation*, appearing in nearly all 178 episodes, and he spent four seasons on *Deep Space Nine*, logging time in more than 100 episodes. Dorn also brought the Klingon back to life in the four *TNG* feature films, several video-games, an array of *Trek* audiobooks and videogames, and most recently for *Star Trek Online*. He even co-starred as Colonel Worf, a distant relation, in *Star Trek VI: The Undiscovered Country*. Having also directed three episodes of *Deep Space Nine* and one installment of *Star Trek: Enterprise*, Worf has proven to be an acting job that keeps on giving.

> ## "I DO FEEL VERY FORTUNATE, NOT ONLY BEING PART OF IT, BUT HAVING CREATED A CHARACTER THAT REALLY LIVES ON."

WORFISMS
THE QUOTABLE KLINGON
"KLINGONS DO NOT ALLOW THEMSELVES TO BE... PROBED."

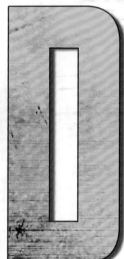

SPEED

"Offspring"

PLAYING FAVORITES

All these years after the fact, Dorn still has his favorite episodes of *The Next Generation* and *Deep Space Nine*.

His *Next Generation* episodes of choice – "The Offspring" and "The Drumhead" – are equally well regarded by most of his *TNG* co-stars. Of his 100-plus *DS9* hours, perhaps unsurprisingly, a pair of Klingon-centric episodes written by Ronald D. Moore – "Soldiers of the Empire" and "Once More Unto the Breach" – are the ones he rates best.

"In terms of showing Klingons in a different light than we'd ever seen before, I thought they were great," Dorn praises. "And there was some really, really good acting going on in those shows. 'Once More Unto the Breach' had John Colicos in his final performance. He died right after that. 'Soldiers of the Empire' had David Graf, who's [also] passed away, who was great, and Rick Worthy, who's in *The Magicians* now. It was directed by Levar [Burton], who turned into a wonderful, wonderful director. It had Terry and J.G. Hertzler, who was brilliant. In fact, that's what got me thinking about writing a Worf spin-off, those two episodes.

"The Offspring"

TNG Season 3, Episode 16
Data creates an android daughter.

"The Drumhead"

TNG Season 4, Episode 21
Picard is put on trial for treason.

"Soldiers of the Empire"

DS9 Season 5, Episode 21
Worf is assigned to General Martok's Bird-of-Prey.

"Once More Unto the Breach"

DS9 Season 7, Episode 7
Klingon warrior Kor seeks Worf's help.

"At first, when I got the job, I was just happy because I loved the original guys," Dorn marvels, "I was like, 'Oh, man, this is great.' I didn't think *The Next Generation* was going to go very long. I thought it was going to go a couple years, and we were going to make some money. I thought we'd be lucky if it went three years. When it was all over and done with, and we'd done *Nemesis*, the last movie, that's when it hit me how important our contribution is to the franchise, and how it just is never going to go away."

As *Star Trek* passes its half-century milestone, Dorn appreciates that it's always going to be a part of his life, and he has no qualms about that.

"It's the original cast's 50th anniversary this year, and our 30th is next year," Dorn reflects, "so, here we go again, because we had a big celebration for our 25th. It's pretty wild. And with the conventions, that's a job, too. That's another way of still being out there, and still talking to the fans. It's mind-boggling. But I do

Left: Michael Dorn

"I WROTE A SCIENCE FICTION SHOW WITH THAT GENE RODDENBERRY FEEL OF SPACE TRAVEL, OF GOING OUT THERE AND DISCOVERING STUFF."

feel very fortunate, not only being part of it, but having created a character that really lives on. I'm very proud of that."

NO TOKEN KLINGON

Early on in *The Next Generation*'s run, some fans voiced the sentiment that Worf served as the token alien on the bridge and, worse, that Captain Picard shot him down almost as often as he did Wesley. Dorn never agreed with that assessment, and for the most part still doesn't today.

"Not at all," he insists. "Even when I first started, I never thought of it as being shot down. At the time, you couldn't look at it over five years. You couldn't, in your head, piece together this video where you're getting shot down 50 times. People have gone and made that video of

clips, and when you look at it like that, then, yeah, he was shot down a lot. But it's one of those things. When I got the job, they really didn't know who Worf was, and they gave me no indication. I went to Gene [Roddenberry] after a couple of days and said, 'Look, what do you want from this guy? Who is he?' He told me to make the character my own. That gave me the license to create this gruff, surly, not-a-nice-guy character. He wasn't Mr. Friendly and ha-ha-ha, and laughing with everybody."

Dorn considered this was the way to go, which made sense because, in Dorn's words, initially Worf was "all over the place" – not in terms of personality, but in his varied job specification. When other characters left their stations at the conn, he took over; Worf navigated the *Enterprise*; he beamed down to planets on Away Missions "because he was a big, tough guy,"

WORFISMS
THE QUOTABLE KLINGON
"KLINGONS DO NOT FAINT."

Riker (Jonathan Frakes) and Worf (Dorn) talk tactics aboard the *Enterprise*

Michael Dorn as Worf, in *Star Trek: First Contact*

WORFISMS
THE QUOTABLE KLINGON

"CONGRATULATIONS. YOU ARE NOW FULLY DILATED."

and provided the muscle. Fans will remember that in the *Next Generation* pilot ("Encounter at Farpoint"), he was the captain of the saucer section. Dorn therefore assumed Worf would become, "the jack of all trades." Soon enough, though, and in the wake of Tasha Yar's demise (after Denise Crosby's departure from *TNG* towards the end of season one), Worf started to evolve, and he also climbed the ladder in terms of rank and responsibility aboard the *Enterprise*, ultimately emerging as Security Chief.

"I wasn't surprised I got more to do," Dorn observes, "I think they chose the actors, and I like to think that they chose me because I was a good actor. So it wasn't a shock to them, like, 'Oh, wow, he's good.'"

KLINGON JUSTICE

Dorn recalls the moment he knew that Worf was going places. "There was a show, the one where we go down on this planet and Wesley gets us in trouble, and they're all in these skimpy outfits with blonde hair," he laughs, remembering first season episode "Justice." "This really cute girl comes up to me and gives me a hug, because 'I hug everybody that comes down on this planet.' She gives me a hug and, while she's hugging me, I look at the rest of them and say, 'Nice

planet.' For some reason, the producers went crazy over that line. They just went crazy. They thought it was the funniest thing they've ever heard.

"And *that* was when it started, with the, 'Well, let's give him some more,'" Dorn adds, "So they started to write more Worf lines, where Worf would just basically say... something. They'd be talking, and they'd say, 'Well, Worf, what do you think?' And he'd give some terse four-word answer."

Ah, the Worfisms.

"Exactly," Dorn confirms. "So that's where it started. Then, after having me everywhere, they put me in charge of Security after Tasha died. Interestingly enough, they didn't want Denise to leave. They just did not want that to happen, because Tasha was becoming a popular character, extremely popular. So, I think they were going, 'Oh my God. What are we gonna do? Are we going to hire another woman for Security?' I think somebody said, 'Wait a minute... Worf! Security. Security. Worf!' They just went, 'Oh my God, it's perfect.'"

Worf earned his share of dramatic moments, but he stole a lot of laughs, too. Dorn, for one, believes that comedy comes out of drama, and he asserts that, "I wasn't playing comedy." The writers, he notes, didn't necessarily create jokes for Worf. They may have thought they were writing "fairly cute" lines, "but I played it for real, not for comedy, and that brought out the hilariousness of it all."

WORFISMS
THE QUOTABLE KLINGON

"I DO NOT LIKE SWIMMING. IT IS TOO MUCH LIKE... BATHING."

Lt. (Jr. Grade) Worf ("Encounter at Farpoint")

Colonel Worf (*The Undiscovered Country*)

Governor Worf ("All Good Things...")

KLINGON HONOR

Dorn always remained vigilant in order to ensure that Worf's comedy value never undermined the character, or his Klingon honor. If the writers handed him a cute line, Dorn delivered that line "the way that I wanted to say it." And he got the result he desired. Other characters – and viewers – would look at Worf, Dorn explains, and think, "Oh, jeez, Worf, lighten up," which generated laughs while retaining the Son of Mogh's no-nonsense demeanor.

"I've got to say, on *DS9*, they made an effort to try to be funny, to make Worf funny, and when I protested I got a lot of resistance, which was very interesting," Dorn notes. "Really, that's when I got very protective. But I got some resistance. I have no reason why they wanted him to do that. I think they thought, 'OK, it's too heavy. Let's do something funny,' but whenever you do something funny, it takes the substance out of the character."

Speaking of *Deep Space Nine*, Dorn shocked many people when he agreed to join the *Trek* spin-off in its fourth season. After all, Dorn made it clear after shooting the final season of *Next Generation* and then *Generations* back to back, he only would endure intensive make-up sessions for the occasional *TNG* feature. Years ago, when addressing what changed his mind, Dorn joked about the dollar signs executive producer Rick Berman dangled in front of him. Now, however, Dorn spins a different story, though Berman still figures into it.

"Actually, the real story is that I was in Baltimore, doing a video game for a few days," Dorn explains, referring to *Mission Critical*. "I'm in my hotel room and Rick calls. He goes, 'Hey, Michael, how you doing?' I said, 'Hey, Rick. What's going on?' Then he says, 'Look, I want to ask you a question. What do you think about coming back on *Deep Space Nine*?' I went, 'Oh, sounds interesting.' He says, 'OK. Well, I'll get back to you.' That was the conversation. So, it wasn't difficult, and I can't tell you why it wasn't difficult, because right after the show and movie were over, I did say, 'I'm never going to put that make-up on again. Forget it. It's over. Thank God.' But, for some reason, when Rick asked, 'Do you want to do it?' I said, 'Yeah, sounds interesting.' And that was it."

WORF FACTOR 10

The addition of Worf and Dorn to the *Deep Space Nine* tapestry provided a story spark, gave the show's publicists a fresh hook with which to generate features in the media, and helped spike the series' ratings. The writers, as Dorn puts it, "wrote some wonderful stuff for me, opening up the character and giving him more dimensions than he had on *The Next Generation*."

Worf's Klingon heritage always received plenty of attention, especially on *Deep Space Nine*, where the writers paired him with Jadzia Dax, played by Terry Farrell, with whom Dorn shared a tremendous chemistry.

"I didn't realize how many scenes, how many shows, focused on Terry and I until I watched a whole bunch of videos this guy put together [on YouTube] of our relationship on *DS9*," Dorn admits, "And it was a very, very great and deep relationship. Since we knew each other very well, the relationship you saw on the screen was even more scintillating, and more comfortable, because we were so comfortable with each other."

Dorn voiced Worf for *Star Trek Online* last year, and sort of reprised the character in Seth McFarlane's *Ted 2*. It makes one wonder how he might react if Bryan Fuller called him up and invited him to return as the character yet again in the new *Star Trek* series.

"You never say never," Dorn says. "But it really would depend – and it's not just *Star Trek*, it's anything I do now. My first question is, 'Can I read the script?' I'd base my decision on the script, on what it is they want me to do, and 'What is he going to be?' and 'How is he going to be treated in these episodes?' I'd base my decision on that. I've guarded the character for 14 years now (since *Nemesis*). So I'm not going to throw it all away just because they say, 'Oh, would you like to come on the show?' I'd say, 'Well, yeah. But what are you going to do?'" ▲

"I PLAYED IT FOR REAL, NOT FOR COMEDY, AND THAT BROUGHT OUT THE HILARIOUSNESS OF IT ALL."

STORM SELA

AS TASHA YAR, DENISE CROSBY FELT UNDERUSED, BUT HER ASSOCIATION WITH *STAR TREK: THE NEXT GENERATION* DIDN'T END THERE. PAT JANKIEWICZ TAKES THE ACTRESS BACK THROUGH SOME OF HER HIGHLIGHTS...

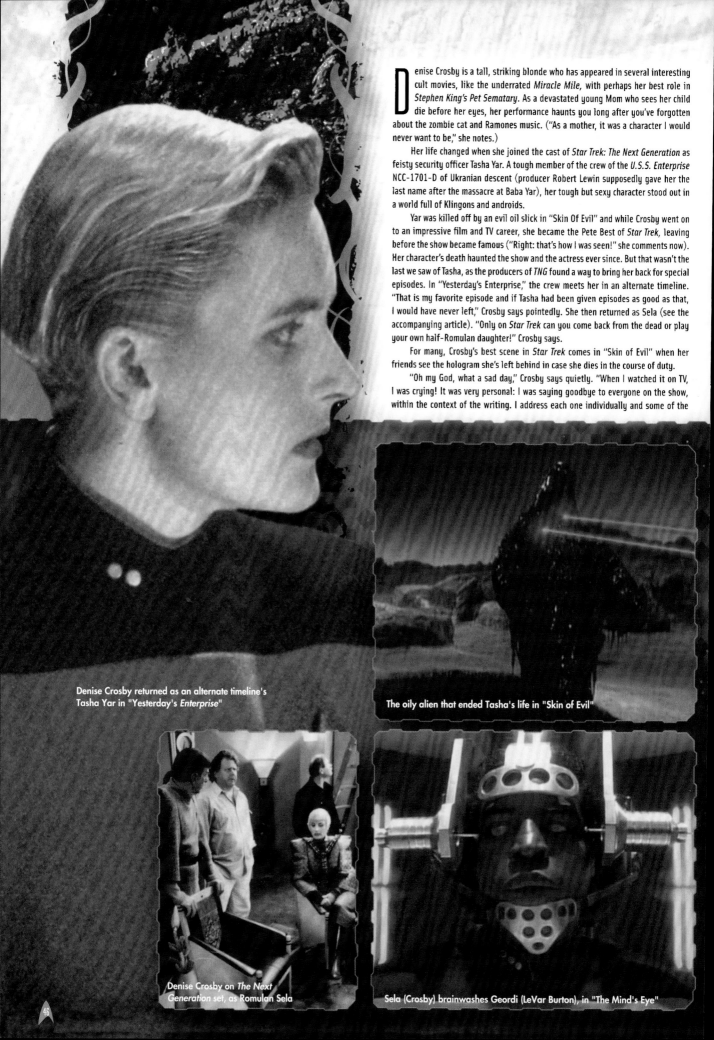

Denise Crosby is a tall, striking blonde who has appeared in several interesting cult movies, like the underrated *Miracle Mile,* with perhaps her best role in *Stephen King's Pet Sematary*. As a devastated young Mom who sees her child die before her eyes, her performance haunts you long after you've forgotten about the zombie cat and Ramones music. ("As a mother, it was a character I would never want to be," she notes.)

Her life changed when she joined the cast of *Star Trek: The Next Generation* as feisty security officer Tasha Yar. A tough member of the crew of the *U.S.S. Enterprise* NCC-1701-D of Ukranian descent (producer Robert Lewin supposedly gave her the last name after the massacre at Baba Yar), her tough but sexy character stood out in a world full of Klingons and androids.

Yar was killed off by an evil oil slick in "Skin Of Evil" and while Crosby went on to an impressive film and TV career, she became the Pete Best of *Star Trek,* leaving before the show became famous ("Right: that's how I was seen!" she comments now). Her character's death haunted the show and the actress ever since. But that wasn't the last we saw of Tasha, as the producers of *TNG* found a way to bring her back for special episodes. In "Yesterday's Enterprise," the crew meets her in an alternate timeline. "That is my favorite episode and if Tasha had been given episodes as good as that, I would have never left," Crosby says pointedly. She then returned as Sela (see the accompanying article). "Only on *Star Trek* can you come back from the dead or play your own half-Romulan daughter!" Crosby says.

For many, Crosby's best scene in *Star Trek* comes in "Skin of Evil" when her friends see the hologram she's left behind in case she dies in the course of duty.

"Oh my God, what a sad day," Crosby says quietly. "When I watched it on TV, I was crying! It was very personal: I was saying goodbye to everyone on the show, within the context of the writing. I address each one individually and some of the

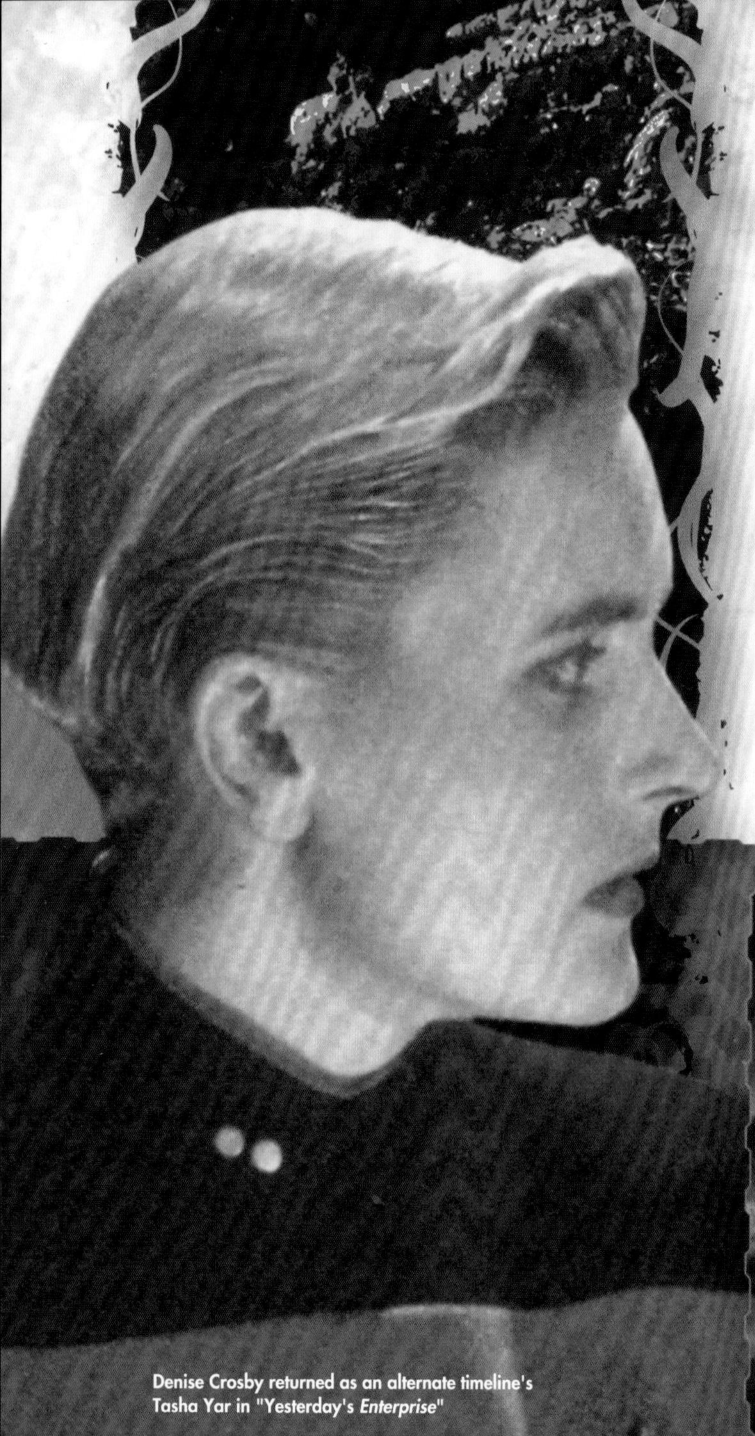

Denise Crosby returned as an alternate timeline's Tasha Yar in "Yesterday's *Enterprise*"

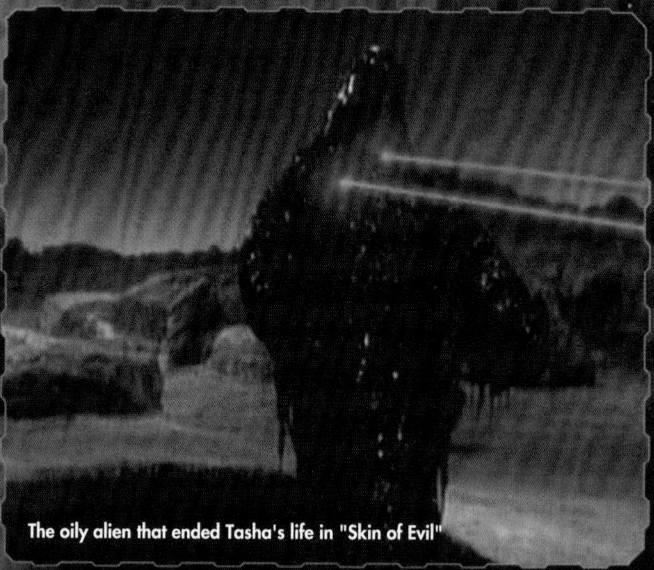

The oily alien that ended Tasha's life in "Skin of Evil"

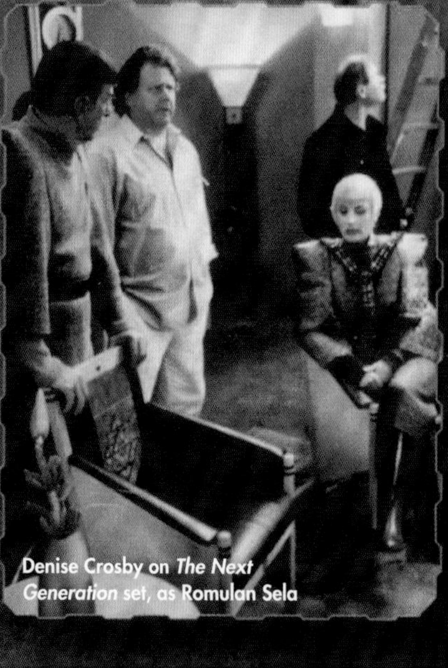

Denise Crosby on *The Next Generation* set, as Romulan Sela

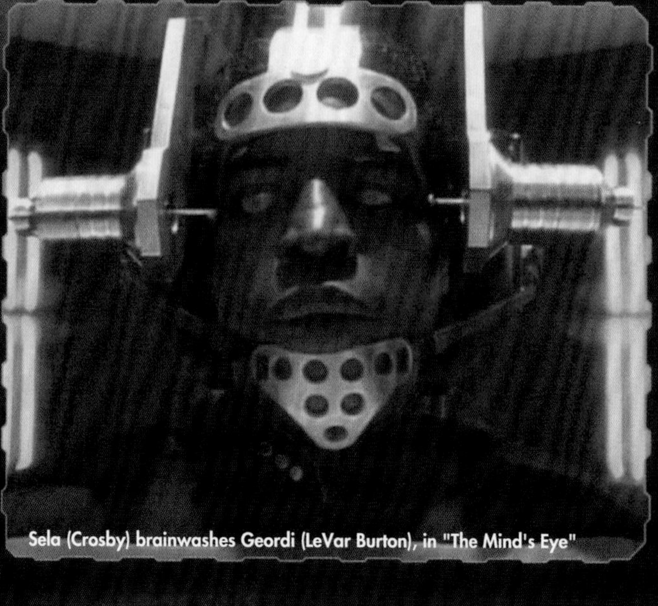

Sela (Crosby) brainwashes Geordi (LeVar Burton), in "The Mind's Eye"

things I was saying to them was very personal. What I said reflected a lot of my personal feelings. I touched on that, which made it very, very sweet and very touching."

She did have some good times on the show. One came when Crosby had a ringside seat for Southern California's devastating Whittier Narrows Earthquake. "Oh, that was a bad one," she shudders. "It was early in the morning and only Jonathan [Frakes] and I were working that day. Michael Westmore was doing my make-up and Jonathan had this habit of wearing a woman's hot pink Chanile bathrobe, because his uniform was too small.

"He had a faceful of shaving cream, because he shaved in those days, and the whole building started shaking, as people screamed 'Earthquake!' We all ran out into the Paramount lot, and as soon as we got out there, it stopped. But we all noticed Jonathan in his shaving cream and pink bathrobe, and *Entertainment Tonight* was suddenly there to talk to us! I pointed at Jonathan and said, 'Why don't you talk to him?'"

As for leaving the show, "I feel you've got to stay true to yourself," she declares. "It was painful, for me to leave the show towards the end of that season, but so many shows were going by while I just stood there. I felt this was not what I went to acting

NOW YOU SELA, NOW YOU DON'T

Robert Greenberger analyzes the role of Tasha Yar's daughter in the 24th Century *Star Trek* universe...

The Klingons benefitted from having great leaders, played by wonderful actors, and were indelibly cooler opponents for the Federation than the Romulans. After Mark Lenard's unnamed Romulan commander perished in "Balance of Terror," the Romulans were a faceless enemy until the also unnamed Romulan commander in "The Enterprise Incident." The same thing occurred on *Star Trek: The Next Generation* until Commander Tomalak and then... nothing until Sela.

As a result, writers have often turned to the blonde half-Romulan/half-human as a foil in comics, novels and even games. After all, there are so few Romulans to pick from and she's so dramatically rich.

Sela was cold, shrewd and calculating, the very embodiment of the Romulan race. Fans took to her, which prompted the producers to use her again and again. When casting for an opponent to actually emerge victorious over Picard in my novel *The Romulan Stratagem*, Sela was the only choice. Writing her was a delight given her driven desire to best Picard and through him, all of mankind.

Had Denise Crosby been happier during the first season of *TNG*, Sela never would have existed. The actress felt she wasn't being given enough to do on the ensemble's maiden voyage. As a result, she asked to leave the show and was rewarded by having Tasha Yar killed in "Skin of Evil."

By the beginning of the third season, Crosby had come to regret her decision, seeing how well things had gelled since her departure. Approaching the producers, she asked if there was any way for Yar to come back. This resulted in "Yesterday's Enterprise," one of the strongest offerings across the show's run. In short, a temporal rift opened and the U.S.S. *Enterprise-C* had drifted 22 years into the future. By being there, and not where they needed to be, things changed. When Tasha Yar learned from Guinan she should be dead, the security chief chose to leave the *Enterprise-D* to help the ship's predecessor fulfill its destiny.

The time anomaly also allowed the production staff to conceive of a new way for Crosby to recur on the series.

"The Mind's Eye" introduced audiences to Sela, who at the time was seen only in shadow and was coincidentally played by a different actress. When we finally met her in the two-part episode "Redemption," Sela had more than a passing resemblance to Yar and had quite the story to tell, revealing to Captain Jean-Luc Picard that her mother agreed to became the consort to General Volskiar, sparing the lives of others, which resulted in the birth of Sela in 2345.

Tasha's holographic memorial ("Skin of Evil")

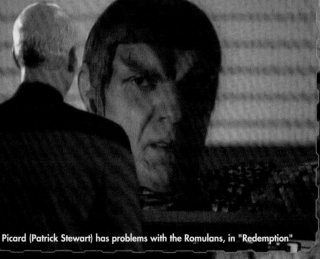

Picard (Patrick Stewart) has problems with the Romulans, in "Redemption"

An undesirable half-breed, she was raised and educated on Volskiar's private compound. Yar, though, still wanted to return home and attempted to escape with her four-year old daughter. Sela, though, didn't want to leave the only home she knew and called out to the guards. Her life was inextricably changed as she witnessed her mother being executed for treason. Burying the emotions she felt, Sela grew up fully embracing the Romulan way. And yet, she wore her anger plainly for all to see.

Despite her mixed heritage, her father's connections and her own skills earned Sela a place in the Romulan Star Empire's military. Her instructor, Saket, became her mentor and she excelled, rising through the ranks. At the young age of 22, Sela was a commander in the armed forces, already with influence in the Senate. As a result, Sela was given the tricky assignment of almost single-handedly destroying the Klingon Empire. Her complicated plan, as seen in "The Mind's Eye," involved assassinating a Klingon governor but using a brainwashed Geordi La Forge to do the actual deed. The entire plot was foiled by Data's intervention.

Sela finally appeared on camera in time to take advantage of K'mpec's death and foment a civil war within the Klingon Empire. Working alongside the delightful duo of Lursa and B'Etor, she backed Duras' illegitimate son Toral, offering materiel to the Romulan collaborators. Her revelatory meeting with Picard was memorable as she confirmed that she was the daughter of Tasha Yar. The captain managed to end the civil war, thwart Sela and the Klingon sisters, and install Gowron as Chancellor. Not quite Sela's anticipated outcome.

Despite two crushing defeats, Sela continued to think big and her next scheme involved invading Vulcan. She did this without realizing that Spock was on Romulus working with the underground reunification movement. Things got murkier for her when Picard arrived on the Romulan homeworld, seeking Spock but being on hand to stop the invasion. In the highly-rated two-parter "Unification" we saw her strut and preen, so proud of her schemes and her skills as a writer – but her grandiose schemes were always too contingent on everything working perfectly. She constantly underestimated the humans she professed to loathe, and the slightest kink in the plan meant everything tended to crumble.

After constant high profile defeats, it's little wonder she was reduced to commanding the rusting IRW N'ventnar. Feeling at the nadir of her young career, Sela was angrier than usual, blaming not herself but Picard for her woes. In The Romulan Stratagem, she and Picard found themselves representing their respective governments to woo the Eloshians. She relished the opportunity to beat Picard on a level playing field. When the race elected to ally with the Romulan Empire, Sela used the successful outcome to embarrass the Tal Shiar and regain fresh political capital.

She subsequently upgraded ships and wound up commanding a task force into Cardassian space. As seen in Peter David's Triangle: Imzadi II, she sought out her mentor Saket, who possessed a sample of a virus intended to decimate the Klingons. Not only did Sela find Saket at Lazon II's labor camp, but she encountered Thomas Riker, the improbable doppelganger of Enterprise First Officer William Riker. Although Saket died, he passed on the sample; Sela seduced Riker and used him to release the agent. To ensure he did as she demanded, and having clearly learned from her previous mistakes, Sela had Deanna Troi and Alexander Rozhenko kidnapped. The entire plan was foiled thanks to the involvement of Odo and the Excalibur's Commander Elizabeth Shelby.

What's interesting by this point is her utter determination to close off her human side without understanding the consequences. Instead, she took on repeated assignments that involved trying to ruin or destroy the Klingon Empire without pausing to ask why she was being given the same job again and again. Could the Romulans have so much disdain for the Klingons that they felt a hybrid could do the job? Or were they so smug that they used her as a symbol that even a half-breed could rub their faces in the ashes of defeat? The Sela vs. the Klingons theme was constant but rarely explored.

Her string of defeats continued to haunt her, as seen in the WildStorm miniseries The Killing Shadows by Scott Ciencin and Andrew Currie. There, she was an outcast from the military, roaming through space until her one-man craft is shot down. Lo and behold, so was Picard and the two had to form an uneasy alliance to survive the planet and their ninja-like captors.

The still-angry Sela's next chronological appearance was in the TNG chapter of the Double Helix novel crossover, Double or Nothing. She's once more in charge of a squadron of warbirds and they attacked the USS Independence and were happily picking off the escape pods until driven off by the Excalibur.

Most likely using her political connections, Sela wound up being rewarded for her actions by being promoted to Admiral a year later in 2376. As seen in the video game Star Trek: Armada, Sela was tasked with obtaining an Omega molecule which had come into the possession of the Ferengi and Cardassians. Her command tactics saw it to that Klingon patrol ships and Borg Cubes were crushed, before slipping through a wormhole and tricking the Borg into doing her dirty work: crushing a new Klingon civil war and killing Toral once and for all. She then destroyed her Borg allies although the collective ultimately wound up with the molecule.

Sela wound up being part of the Romulan delegation forming the alliance against the Dominion although her exploits during the War remain as yet unchronicled.

Her most recent appearance in the fiction was in the post- Star Trek Nemesis novel, Death in Winter by Michael Jan Friedman. Praetor Tal'Aura uses Sela as an agent, sending her to Kevratas, a Romulan holding, to manipulate public opinion away from both secession and the Federation. Her plan once again involved using a member of the Enterprise crew as her pawn, this time Beverly Crusher. Her seeming death was being blamed on the Kevratans which prompted Picard to come seeking the truth. The entire plan backfired and the Kevratans declared independence. Tal'Aura assigned Sela the task of remaining on the planet, away from Romulus, to monitor the situation.

For someone as ambitious and driven as Sela, no doubt still haunted by the images indelibly seared on a four year old's psyche, that posting is not likely to last long. When she will next turn up in the Star Trek universe remains unannounced but a character as rich as Sela is too good to stay out of the way for long. ▲

school for, and Tasha Yar was so much more than that: it was just too confining and not fulfilling. It was better to leave."

TNG was famous on the Paramount backlot for having a brutal shooting schedule, with 18 hour days being quite normal. "The 18 hour days you can handle, if you're doing scenes... But not if you're just standing there going, 'Aye Aye, Captain'. I used to ask them, 'Why can't you make fake legs?' I don't say anything, so just stick my fake legs up there and keep the camera below,' but they wouldn't do it!"

Because she left the show quietly, by her own choice, internet rumors spread that she was fired for all sorts of ridiculous reasons, like shooting a Playboy centerfold spread on set. "That's so funny... This has more rumors than anything!"

When she was immortalized in plastic as Tasha Yar, "That was the coolest! Come on, an action figure of me and getting on a Star Trek lunch pail? I am just pleased as punch: how many Oscar winners can say they had an action figure and their face on a lunch pail? That's a big thing for me, especially when Quentin Tarantino bought my action figure and one of John Travolta from Saturday Night Fever and put them together! I thought I really made it after that! I loved working with him on Jackie Brown."

Crosby made a couple of returns to TNG as Sela.

"Playing Sela was a challenge," she comments, "because she was half-human and half-Romulan. Because she was Tasha's daughter, I could show some elements of Tasha, but because she was half-Romulan, I also had to exhibit traits Tasha would not be familiar with."

Ironically, years before she walked through the Paramount backlot as an actress, she prowled it as a child. "I loved running around it as a kid," she shrugs. "My mom worked as a bookkeeper for Paramount, so I was on the set of *The Mod Squad* as a kid: it was after the original *Star Trek* series. One of the stars let me sit in his directors chair! I was excited, man, he was really sweet."

How does she feel about *TNG* now being 20 years old? "It's a constant surprise: I have been continuously surprised by *Star Trek* in my life. I thought it was a goofy thing to do at first, but it obviously resonated with so many people. I mean, I just did *Family Guy* because of it! Stewie [the evil baby] beams in *The Next Generation* into his bedroom and there I am," she blushes. "I met Seth MacFarlane and found out he was a huge *Trek* fan! It's amazing who is watching this stuff. A lot of guys who grew up watching *The Next Gen* are now making the stuff.

"It's so funny to play Tasha as drawn MacFarlane Style. It's funny, because I look at Stewie and I say, 'He's just a baby' and Stewie snaps at me, 'That's right, Denise Crosby, I'm just a baby!' *Family Guy* was the most fun working environment. Seth and those guys are gloriously nuts!"

As a wife, mother and working actress, Denise Crosby has stayed busy with a recent role in serial killer drama *Dexter*. "I'm happy to maintain my connection to *Star Trek* through things like [the documentary she produced] *Trekkies*. I was sad to leave the show, but like I said, you've got to stay true to yourself. I have to be honest, I had no idea that my leaving the show was going to make such an impact! But if I hadn't, I wouldn't have been able to do *Pet Sematary* with Mary Lambert or some of the other roles, which I really enjoyed." ▲

Crosby's early departure as a regular on *The Next Generation* opened opportunities for her to return as half-Romulan daughter Sela (top left), and as a version of Tasha from another timeline (above and bottom left).

"I WAS SAD TO LEAVE THE SHOW, BUT LIKE I SAID, YOU'VE GOT TO STAY TRUE TO YOURSELF. I HAVE TO BE HONEST, I HAD NO IDEA THAT MY LEAVING THE SHOW WAS GOING TO MAKE SUCH AN IMPACT!"

DENISE CROSBY

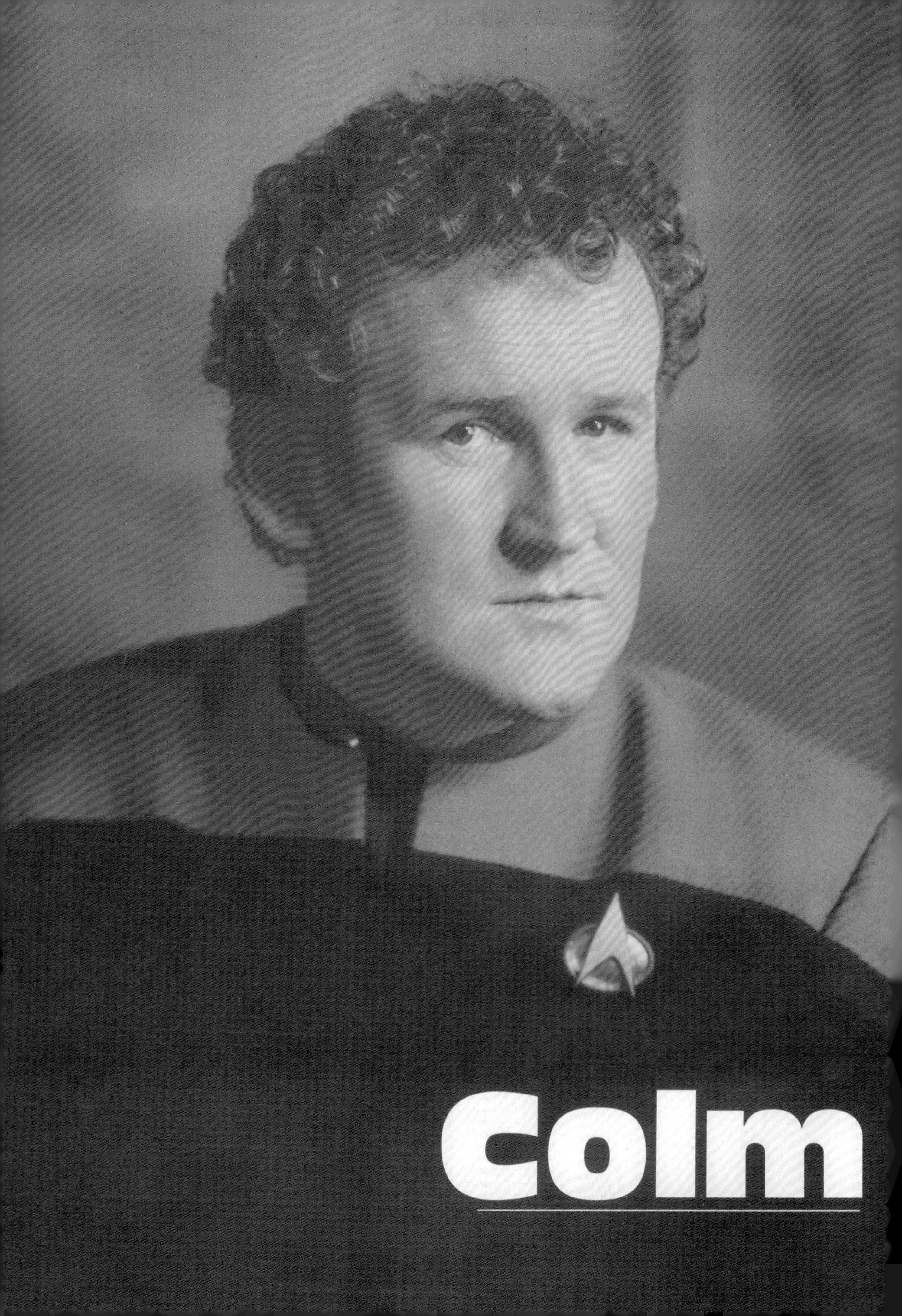
Colm

"I sit down here and think we've been at Star Trek: Deep Space Nine for four years now. It's flown by and we're still having a good time. It is hard to believe."

An Enlisted Man

He's the only major *Star Trek* crew man to marry, he's down to earth and never one to pull punches when he has something to complain about. Ian Spelling talks to perhaps the most Human of *Star Trek: Deep Space Nine*'s crew...

Growing up in Ireland, Colm Meaney never considered himself much of a science fiction fan. Nor was he at all a Trekker. "I was much more into history and, to some extent, comedy. Science fiction would not be a favourite of mine. I was always aware of *Star Trek*," remembers Meaney, "but *F-Troop* was more my kind of show."

Funny then, that Meaney has spent a good portion of his rather prolific career hurtling through Gene Roddenberry's legendary *Star Trek* Universe as *Chief Miles O'Brien*, first on *Star Trek: The Next Generation* and now on *Star Trek: Deep Space Nine*. The irony is not lost on the good-natured actor. "It is pretty strange, you know?" he acknowledges in that familiar accent of his. "I sit down here and think we've been at *ST:DS9* for four years now. It's flown by and we're still having a good time. It is hard to believe. Then, I think about how long I did *ST:TNG* and it gets even harder to believe. I still enjoy coming to work. We're still doing good work and we're still entertaining people. So it's great. Right now, we're all very pleased with where the show is, creatively and otherwise. We have good, strong storylines. Each of us in the cast gets our episodes. It's cyclical in that two or three times a season we'll each have a major episode. I think also that the writers have been incredibly inventive this season. So, I'm quite happy.

"O'Brien has continued to evolve. There are the obvious things, like the family situation with Miles, *Keiko* (Rosalind Chao) and *Molly* (Hana Hatae), which has been developed nicely, and the relationship between *Dr Julian Bashir*

(Alexander Siddig) and O'Brien shows us another dimension to both of these guys. We see them go out and be playful, in a sense. They compete and they're friends, and they've also had disagreements. I like that. We've seen them do the normal kinds of things that guys do, outside of their actual work situation. I think they've also done a nice job with O'Brien's relationship with *Captain Benjamin Sisko* (Avery Brooks). There's a loyalty between these two men that I like. I'd say O'Brien has been fleshed out here and there, more than can be revealed all at once, which is smart. His personality is being enhanced and filled in. As time goes on, there are more and more elements to be found in the character."

Due to Meaney's remarkably hectic schedule, which finds him leaving the *Paramount Pictures* lot to tackle roles in various television and film projects, the actor doesn't appear in every *ST:DS9* episode. Usually, he's either in just a scene here or there or featured quite heavily in a given hour. Over the past year or two, as Meaney toiled in such films as *The Road to Wellville*, *The Snapper* and *The Englishman Who Went Up a Hill and Came Down a Mountain*, as well as the upcoming *The Van* and *Last of the High Kings*, his *ST:DS9* presence has been noticeably low-profile.

Still, he's managed to squeeze in such O'Brien-centric episodes as *Paradise*, *Tribunal*, *Visionary*, *Facets*, *Hippocratic Oath*, *Accession*, *Hard Times* and *Shattered Mirror*, among others. The majority of these shows, not surprisingly, have paired Meaney with Siddig, Brooks, or Chao. "I suppose I've worked more with Sid than anyone else over that period of time. We have a lot of fun together, Sid and I. We do

Meaney

get a little worried sometimes," admits Meaney, "that the relationship between O'Brien and Bashir becomes a little too one-dimensional. So, we try to gear our performances to counter that as much as possible. I think people watching the show see that there's a good relationship going between the actors playing the characters.

"I also love getting to work with Avery. Unfortunately I haven't been doing too much of it this season and I've missed it. We only have a scene together every so often. Actually, I just did a scene with him today, and it was like we hadn't seen each other in months! So that was great.

"Avery has also directed a few episode of the show, as you know. Working with Avery as a director is so great. He's got an amazing mind and he always makes his episodes exciting to do and to look at. Roz is another one I haven't worked with nearly enough in the last year or two. She's actually been back for the last two episodes we've recorded and it's been like meeting a long-lost pal. We kind of know instinctively what the other is going to do in a scene, with a line. It's just a joy to work with Roz, and we have such a good time. Everyone else here in the cast is really great, but most of my scenes, as I've said, are with Sid, Avery, and Roz."

Nearly two years ago, O'Brien found himself back aboard the *U.S.S. Enterprise*, surrounded by all of his old friends, in the *ST:TNG* final episode, *All Good Things*. Meaney remembers being both excited and feeling a sense of *déja vu* as he slipped into a vintage, first season *ST:TNG* costume and joined his former cast mates one last time. "It was strange, very nostalgic. I thought it was a very powerful way for *ST:TNG* to go out," he notes. "I thought it was a great story and a terrific episode. It covered a lot of ground and left you thinking. I'd seen most of the guys on a fairly regular basis because *ST:DS9* and *ST:TNG* were just across the street from each other. Now, I still see some of them. LeVar (Burton) has directed a couple of our episodes, so I've seen a lot of him. Michael (Dorn), of course, is with us full-time now on *ST:DS9*. Jonathan (Frakes) is around all the time, too. He's directed a number of *Star Trek: Voyager* episodes and he's just set up an office around the corner here to prepare for the (upcoming *ST:TNG* film. We've all got our own, different things going on, our own families and our own lives, but we see each other fairly regularly, which is nice."

While Meaney has indeed been put through his paces by such actors-turned-directors as Brooks, Burton, Frakes, and René Auberjonois, he himself harbours no aspirations to beam behind the camera. "I won't be directing anything any time soon," he promises. "I don't know that I'd be very good at it and I don't see the point of trying when I don't have any kind of unique, visionary brain towards it. You never say never," he states, "but I was asked to direct in the theatre and didn't think that was a good idea. What I do is act. I am an actor and I try to do that well. I'm happy with that. I get enough satisfaction out of the acting to keep me happy."

From here, the conversation moves onto some of those 'other things' Meaney has going on in his professional life. First, there is *The Van*. "That's the third book in Roddy

> *"So much of one's acting depends on the writing. It's like being a musician. If you get a good score, you can play great music."*

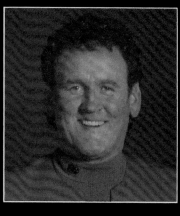

Colm Meaney PROFILE

Colm Meaney PROFILE

BIRTHDAY: 30 May
BIRTHPLACE: Ireland

Selected Credits:

FILM
Omega Syndrome (1987)
The Dead (1987) – Mr Bergin
Perfect Witness (1989, TV)
Die Hard 2 (1990)
– Pilot (Windsor Plane)
Dick Tracy (1990) – Cop at Tess'
Come See the Paradise (1990)
The Commitments (1991) – Mr Rabbitte
Under Siege (1992) – Doumer
The Last of the Mohicans (1992)
– Major Ambrose
Into the West (1992) – Barreller
Far and Away (1992) – Kelly
Dr Quinn, Medicine Woman (1992)
The Snapper (1993) – Dessie Curley
(Nominated for a Golden Globe award for Best Actor)
War of the Buttons (1994)
– Geronimo's Dad
The Road to Wellville (1994)

– Dr Lionel Badger
The Englishman Who Went Up a Hill, But Came Down a Mountain (1995)
– Morgan the Goat
The Van (1996)

TELEVISION
One Life to Live (1968)
Kenny Rogers as The Gambler, Part III - The Legend Continues (1987, TV)
– Tinkerer
Star Trek: The Next Generation (1987)
– Chief Miles Edward O'Brien (1987-93)
Star Trek: Deep Space Nine (1993-)
– Chief Miles O'Brien
Scarlett (1994, mini-series)
– Father Colum O'Hara

Doyle's trilogy, and it brings *The Commitments* story to an end," he reveals. "It actually takes place before *The Snapper*, but it's the third book, which makes it the finale. It's a prequel, I guess. Basically, it's the story of the dad, who was Jimmy Rabbite, Sr. in *The Commitments* and had another name in *The Snapper*. Believe it or not, they've changed his name again for *The Van*. While there were copyright reasons involved in changing his name for *The Commitments*, they were actually such different films. There was an effort to distance *The Snapper* from *The Commitments* because we didn't want people to think they were going to see *The Commitments II*. People can be so obsessive about sequels. So, we're just doing that distancing thing again. Word is that the film is terrific."

And what of *Last of the High Kings*? "I did a cameo in that one, sort of an extended cameo. Stephen Rea and I both have these small parts in the film, which was written and produced by Gabriel Byrne, who's a friend of mine and who I worked with on *Into the West*. It's a basic coming-of-age story about a young man (Jared Leto) just about to graduate from high school. It's about the summer of graduation, this young boy growing into manhood, and his memories of all that," explains the actor. "It's a lovely story. I play a politician. The boy's mother (Catherine O'Hara of *Beetlejuice* fame) is very active politically and she swoons at the mention of my name. A general action takes place and I come to visit her family's house the night of the election. Everyone is very impressed with me, of course, except for the kid and his friends. They think I'm a boring old fart."

Meaney also takes a few minutes to reflect on *The Englishman Who Went Up a Hill and Came Down a Mountain*, the charming Christopher Monger-directed film in which he portrays Morgan the Goat, an entrepreneurial innkeeper who tries to both make a buck and convince map makers Hugh Grant and Ian McNiece not to reclassi-

fy a Welsh town's mountain as a mere hill. "I'd read that script a year, a year and a half before we ever did it. From the moment I read it I really wanted to do it," enthuses Meaney, who lives in Los Angeles but spends as much free time as possible with some of his family in Ireland. "So much of one's acting depends on the writing. It's like being a musician. If you get a good score, you can play great music. In a sense, Morgan the Goat was effortless to play

Opposite page:
Top left: *Conversation, flirtation and a damn fine cup of coffee*
Centre left: *Captain Picard meets Miles O'Brien for the first time – again – in ST:TNG All Good Things*
Bottom left: *Another first as O'Brien tries to make sense of Data's peculiar understanding of the Human language*
This page:
Far left: *Miles and Keiko share a tender moment – or at least Keiko does*
Left: *Smiley by name...*

because he was so well written, so honestly written. We also had a good time making the film, and I quite enjoyed working with Hugh. I'm glad it finally came together, because it was something we all really believed in, and rightly so, you know?"

So busy is Meaney these days, that one can't help but wonder if he ever tires of *ST:DS9*, or whether or not the show might be deterring him from acting in more feature films or pursuing other television opportunities. The answer, he replies with virtually no hesitation, is no. O'Brien remains a challenge to him, what with episodes

> *"I won't be directing anything any time soon – I don't know that I'd be very good at it..."*

that find O'Brien being tortured by *Cardassians*, watching his own death, or even not quite being O'Brien, as when he's been *Falcon*, a Shapeshifter delivering a message to Sisko, or *Smiley*.

"All of these different, interesting things keep happening to O'Brien," says Meaney, "Each new episode brings something new for him and for me. I often compare the situation of being here on the show to being in the theatre, in weekly rep, where you do a new show every week. One week you play the lead and the next week you're hardly in it. That helps to keep it fresh, at least for me," reasons

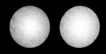

A QUESTION OF RANK...

Many *STAR TREK Monthly* readers have asked about *Chief Miles O'Brien's* rank, given that he seems to have been demoted when transferred to the DEEP SPACE NINE space station from the *U.S.S. Enterprise NCC-1701-D*. It appears the situation may originally have been due to a wardrobe error, although Jeri Taylor argues that the error existed in *Star Trek: The Next Generation* and was simply being corrected when he transferred.

The quest to discover O'Brien's true rank within Starfleet begins all the way back in 1987 in *ST:TNG's Encounter at Farpoint*, when he appears as the conn officer. He was next seen as a Transporter Chief, wearing two solid gold pips on his collar. But later in *ST:TNG's* run, Worf's foster father refers to O'Brien being a Chief Petty Officer – so, do Starfleet use the same rank insignia to donate officers and non-commissioned officers?

At some point a member of the *ST:TNG* production team must have realised this lack of distinction was a problem and changed O'Brien's insignia to one hollow pip at the beginning of season six, before he left for DEEP SPACE NINE. Unfortunately, O'Brien's two gold pips returned in the *Star Trek: Deep Space Nine* pilot *The Emissary*, then reverted to the hollow pip in time for *Past Prologue*. Is it any wonder confusion has reigned...

Thankfully, the recent *ST:DS9* episode *Hippocratic Oath* should have cleared up all this confusion once and for all, when O'Brien's status as a Chief Petty Officer was confirmed by a Jem'Hadar. It appears Starfleet does not consist solely of full officers but also of personnel who have undergone specialised training in particular areas. In O'Brien's case these would be transporter operation and, since he was once tactical officer of the *U.S.S. Rutledge*, tactical operations.

The existence of unenlisted officers was confirmed in *ST:TNG's The Drumhead*, when Simon Tarsis is asked by Picard why he did not study to become a full officer. Perhaps all non-commissioned officers are usually given the hollow insignia to distinguish themselves from ordinary enlisted personnel. Looking back as far as *Where No One Has Gone Before*, Specialist Kosinski had two square or rectangular gold pips, and, although they were never seen again, it could be possible that the producers were attempting to institutionalise insignia for non-coms.

Incidentally, *Tuvok's* rank is Lieutenant, and it has been since *The Caretaker*, but he was mistakenly given a Commander's insignia for the first few episodes of *Star Trek: Voyager*. Another debate in the making... ▪

Compiled with the assistance of Andrew Darling and reader Ciaran Creedon

Opposite page:
Top left: *A fine display of Klingon bashing in* The Way of the Warrior...
Top right: *...offset by yet another fine display of deep feeling*
Bottom: *Miles is about to lose more than just his shirt in* ST:DS9 Tribunal
This page:
Below: *The feisty engineer takes the helm of the U.S.S. Defiant in* For The Cause

"I don't want to be the lead every week, just as I don't want to not be the lead every week."

Colm Meaney. "I don't want to be the lead every week, just as I don't want to not be the lead every week. Also, the fact that the producers here have let me get away so often to do other things kind of keeps my head in it. Since I came onto *ST:DS9*, I haven't actually been here for an entire season straight through. That's helped. But, as I say, O'Brien is still interesting, I enjoy the company I keep here, and we're still doing work we can be very proud of. It's a nice mix, a very nice mix. I'll probably be around as long as all of that continues!" ▪

from Ba'ku to Broadway

Star Trek: Insurrection's **Dr Beverly Crusher** takes time out to talk to **Ian Spelling** and *STAR TREK Monthly* about life with and without *Star Trek*

"My son was talking to me about *Star Trek* just this morning," Gates McFadden begins, referring to her young son, James Cleveland McFadden Talbot – also known as Jack – who's now seven. "He's never seen an episode of *Star Trek: The Next Generation*, but he grew up on the set. He learned, literally, how to walk on the Bridge of the *Enterprise*. He loved to play with the medical props. Uncle Brent [Spiner, *Data*] was just this weird godfather who was painted gold. *Worf* was scarier when he was Michael Dorn. But he's just now getting into *Star Trek*. He knew that I had done *Star Trek: Insurrection* and that it was going to be coming out. He said, 'So, this is like a big movie. Are you going to be famous?'

"It was such a weird question from him because he's usually not into any of that. I said, 'I don't think so.' Then he said this morning, 'So, what is *Star Trek* about?' I said, 'Sweetie, I had 70 [television] interviews yesterday and I'm going to do more today, all day. We'll talk about it next week.' He got it. He laughed and said, 'OK, OK, no more questions.' But he asked *the* question we all always get. He said, 'What is *Star Trek*?' I couldn't believe it. I guess that's one of the questions everyone wants the answer to."

McFadden, relaxing in a suite at a Los Angeles hotel, smiles. "This is the year that I'll let him see *ST:TNG*," she continues. "I wanted to wait until he was seven or eight years old. Developmentally, kids can make up their own minds about whether or not they like something at that age. He seems to have really impeccable taste for movies. He doesn't watch television. He sees movies. He sees videos. He sees a lot of theatre. He knows about *Star Trek* because he has been on the set, because we have an unplugged *ST:TNG* pinball machine in the house.

Gates **McFadden**

"If 11 years ago you had asked me, 'Do you think this will go for a year?' I would have said, 'Probably not.'"

He's seen the *Dr Crusher* action figure, but to him it's his Mommy doll. He thought everybody's mom had a doll. I think he will make up his own mind about *Star Trek*.

"It's been uncomfortable for him at times, when people have taken pictures and things like that. That can be scary. Now, as he gets older, he's not as frightened of it. He knows that people will not take his mother away from him. I think he's secure in the amount of attention he gets. Right after I'm done here today, I've got to go straight over to his soccer game. I've got my priorities."

As Dr Beverly Crusher, McFadden has been a part of *ST:TNG* from day one and has appeared in all three *ST:TNG* features, although she skipped the second season of the series and was replaced by Diana Muldaur as *Dr Katherine Pulaski* that year. The high-point of McFadden's television voyage aboard the *U.S.S. Enterprise NCC-1701-D* was, arguably, directing the earthquake-interrupted seventh-season episode *Genesis*. As for the doctor, she has had her ups and downs saving and losing lives, her assorted and aborted romances (in *The Host*, *Attached* and *Evolution*) and a good many moments as devoted mom (to Wil Wheaton as *Wesley Crusher*). It's been argued, and it would be hard for anyone to disagree, that the character has been given short shrift in the feature films, particularly in *Star Trek: Insurrection*.

"You enjoy what you have and I had a great time filming *Insurrection*," the actresses stresses. "Ask [Executive Producer] Rick Berman about screen time. Ask [*Paramount Pictures* boss] Sherry Lansing about it. For me, I am given something, and it's already a gift to be a part of this whole franchise. I do what I can with the role. I had been in this dark little theatre doing a play about everyone trying to murder me. To go and do *Insurrection* and to be in these beautiful mountains, where it was so breathtaking, and on the *Ba'ku* village set, was like being on vacation.

"Also, it's always fun to get back together with everyone,"

she admits. "We have a very good time and we can pick up right where we left off with the characters. I actually see a number of the actors a lot. It depends where everybody is and what they're up to. No one was seeing much of Patrick [Stewart] when he was off in Australia doing a mini-series [*Moby Dick*], but we all keep in touch one way or another when we're not doing the movies. We like each other. I couldn't imagine saying, 'I'd like to come back and do another one,' if we hated each other. It would be like, 'Oh, we have to do *another* one.' Thankfully, it's not like that at all."

At one point in the development of *Star Trek: Insurrection*, Dr Crusher figured into a nifty comic story thread that survived several script drafts before screenwriter Michael Piller finally dropped it. In it, all of the Ba'ku were still 300 years old but they looked as if they were about 12. One male Ba'ku, the alien equivalent of a dirty old man, fancied Dr Crusher, and the good doctor spent much of her time eluding the would-be paramour. "I heard something like that, but I hadn't heard it in that much detail," McFadden says, laughing. "I love comedy. That sounds funny, but it might not have worked well within the movie. The people making our movies know what they're doing, and if they felt that that storyline didn't work, I understand it."

In a perfect world, one wonders, what might McFadden want to learn about Dr Crusher? What would she like to see the character do? "I'd like to go further into ethical medical deci-sions she has to make," she responds. "Everything we're dealing with now, like cloning, is fascinating to think about. I'd love to see Beverly dealing with ethical medical issues of the future. It would be so appropriate for *Star Trek*, which always tries to reflect what's going on now. In the same way, I'd love to see more of the argument over the Prime Directive versus a doctor's oath to end suffering and cure disease, which we did address in the series at the time. Actually, *Insurrection* looked at some of those Prime Directive versus saving people issues, but not so much from a medical perspective and not really from Beverly's perspective."

Sitting just a few feet from McFadden, on a table, is a pile of *Star Trek* memorabilia – posters and copies of the *Insurrection* script – that she's asking her *ST:TNG* co-stars to autograph. McFadden provides the signed items to charities of her choosing, which then auction the pieces at fund-raising events. That people are still so interested in *Star Trek*, so willing to pay top dollars for a small piece of history, such as a scribbled-upon script, never ceases to amaze the actress. "If 11 years ago you had asked me, 'Do you think this will go for a year?' I would have said, 'Probably not,'" she says. "I thought *The Next Generation* would be a short-term job. *Star Trek*, however, is very important to people. Of course, we wonder about a saturation point, but it's not a personal concern of mine.

"There are so many things going on in my life that I don't at all feel my life is over-whelmed by *Star Trek*. *Star Trek* has been a

Above: *Crusher with* Enterprise *medical crew member Nurse Alyssa Ogawa*
Above right: *Crusher, Hawk and Worf ready themselves to shoot upon any possible adversary in* Star Trek: First Contact

"I'd love to see Beverly dealing with ethical medical issues of the future. It would be so appropriate for Star Trek, which always tries to reflect what's going on now."

springboard for many things that are very meaningful to me. I will always be working, in one way or another. Even if it's not a job I want, I'll be doing something that interests me on some level. I love spending time with my family. I wanted to have a family. I waited and it's even more fabulous than I expected. I have a lot of other things I want to do in the theatre. I'd love to do more choreography and directing. I'd love to do some writing."

McFadden pauses, segueing into another thought obviously on her mind. "I love *Star Trek*, and it *is* a great part of my life, but it's not something I'm obsessed with," she notes. "I don't go home and watch *Star Trek: Voyager* or *Star Trek: Deep Space Nine*. I don't sit there on the computer and write back to all of my fans. In fact, I've had to risk a lot of anger from the

"I've had to risk a lot of anger from the fans and say, 'Look, I don't have enough time in the day to spend with my son as it is. I can't sit here and sign pictures of my face all day.'"

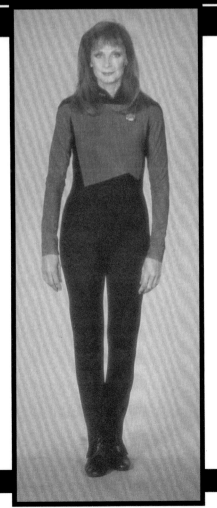

fans and say, 'Look, I don't have enough time in the day to spend with my son as it is. I can't sit here and sign pictures of my face all day.' It's not my priority. When I have a lot of time on my hands I am more than happy to do it, because some people really care about it for one reason or another. One day many years ago I was signing my pictures and my son said, 'Why won't you play with me?' And I said, 'That's it.' It was a choice that was very easy to make."

Then, as the conversation comes to a close, McFadden returns to the future of her career, to what she hopes to do next. After all, after *Star Trek: First Contact*, she appeared in two plays, *Voices in the Dark* and *This Town*, and in the TV movie *Broken Crown* with Yasmine Bleeth and Jill Clayburgh. "In a funny way I don't even think in those terms anymore," McFadden says. "I just try to be in the moment. I don't know what's going to happen with *Voices in the Dark*, which I've been involved with for a while. We're hoping there will be a New York production, and there's a good chance there will be.

"It's a scary murder-mystery show, the one I mentioned before in which everyone's trying to kill me. There's comedy in it and there are also incredible stage fights, some of the best I've ever been involved in. People really gasped when they saw the fights, and I'd bet they'd gasp if they saw them on Broadway. Nevertheless, if the show doesn't go to Broadway, I won't be worried. My attitude is that something always comes along." ∎

Fo

Just as *Geordi La Forge* started off as the *U.S.S. Enterprise*'s helmsman before finding his true vocation as the ship's Chief Engineer, LeVar Burton has been spending less and less time in front of the camera to work as a writer, producer and director. In conversation with David Bassom, Burton reveals the logic of his career change, and discusses his long-awaited appearances in *Star Trek: Insurrection* and *Star Trek: Voyager*'s 100th episode, *Timeless*

resight

The adventures of Lieutenant Commander Geordi La Forge may largely be confined to the *Star Trek* movies these days, but that hasn't stopped LeVar Burton from continuing to explore new frontiers as an artiste. In the four and a half years since *Star Trek: The Next Generation* ceased production as a weekly series, Burton has successfully established himself as a respected writer, producer and director to the extent that the Emmy Award-winning actor now believes that his future lies more behind the camera than in front of it.

"Producing and directing is really where the focus of my life is right now," Burton tells *STAR TREK Monthly*. "I started this part of my career about 10 or 12 years ago, when I first produced episodes of *Reading Rainbow*, and formed my production company, *Eagle Nation Films*. I then moved into directing while I was with *ST:TNG*, and my first episode, *Second Chances*, was a baptism by fire, because it was such an incredibly challenging story. But when it was over, I was convinced that I had made the right decision in asking to sit in the director's chair.

"So I feel that the past 20 years of my life as well as my career have been about figuring out who I am and what I have to offer. As part of that journey, I've discovered where my talents lie, developed new skills and nurtured certain abilities. I now believe that I'm standing on the threshold of

"I'm enormously proud of [Timeless]. I think that [it] represents Star Trek *at its absolute best."*

the next major chapter of my life, in which I intend to speak my piece as a filmmaker, a writer, a director, a producer *and* as an actor. Acting is last on the list now.

"When I started out as an actor 20 years ago, I would never have expected my career to have gone in this direction," he admits. "But life is a continuous series of surprises, and I'm really just awfully thankful to be on this journey."

While writing, producing and directing currently occupy most of Burton's attention, readers shouldn't think for one second that they've seen the last of his *ST:TNG* alter-ego, Geordi La Forge, just yet. On the contrary, Burton remains committed to playing the *Enterprise*'s blind Chief Engineer, and has actually reprised the role on no less than two separate occasions in the past 12 months.

The first of these occasions came, of course, in the ninth *Star Trek* film, *Star Trek: Insurrection*, which sees the crew of the *Enterprise* disobeying the orders of their superiors to protect the people of *Ba'ku* from a conspiracy involving both the treacherous *Son'a* and a high-ranking member of Starfleet itself. Although the film promises all the action, drama and special effects that made *Star Trek: First Contact* such an enormous hit, Burton feels that it actually owes more to *Star Trek IV: The Voyage Home* than to the *ST:TNG* cast's first solo outing.

"It's a very different movie from *First Contact*, and I think necessarily so," he explains. "It would have been a mistake to duplicate the tone and feeling of *First Contact*, which was a very intense,

white-knuckle action-adventure picture. *Star Trek: Insurrection* is more open, more romantic and has a lot more humour in it. I think this movie is a lot more emotional in content than *First Contact*, and it's in the tradition of the best *Star Trek* movies, in that it's about something.

"Like *The Voyage Home*, we discuss a lot of issues that I believe are absolutely relevant to today's world, and there a number of messages and meanings to be derived from the film. Personally, I think it's about the potential that exists for us all to find eternity in a single moment, and how important that quest is to Humanity. However, I think everybody will find different meanings in the film.

"People will also get to see us explore the ever-deepening relationship of the *ST:TNG* characters, who so obviously care for one another. It was great to be back with everyone again, and I truly believe

that the feelings we all have for each other as friends and as castmates gets translated to the screen in *Insurrection*."

Another similarity *Insurrection* shares with *The Voyage Home* is the film's attempt to utilise its main cast as fully as possible, and give everyone their moment under the spotlight. While Burton readily acknowledges that his character's screen time is still limited in the new movie, he is quick to point out that he was more than satisfied with the nature of Geordi's role from day one.

"When I first read the screenplay, there was a scene that is still in the movie and has survived every draft of the screenplay, and I feel that it's one of the more memorable moments of the picture. It's the scene where Geordi sees the sunrise with Human eyes for the first time. I was very happy with that scene and that entire story arc about Geordi's sight.

"I also got a lot to do in Engineering. *Riker* and Geordi are left in charge of the *U.S.S. Enterprise* while the rest of the crew are down on the planet. There was lots of running and jumping, and Jonathan [Frakes] and I got to do some fun stuff."

To many viewers, the resolution of Geordi's story arc in *Star Trek: Insurrection* might seem a little downbeat, as it leaves him dependent on his artificial eye implants for sight once again. However, Geordi's real-life alter ego not only supports the story arc's conclusion, but actually spoke to the film's producers to ensure that his character reverted back to his artificial sight.

"Geordi, more than any of the other *ST:TNG* characters, is at peace with who he is," Burton points out. "He has the least *angst* or anxiety of any of the characters. The way Geordi sees is a big part of him, so I wanted him to revert to his normal

Above left: *The Ba'ku planet's fountain of youth-like properties restore Geordi's sight in* Insurrection
Above: *LeVar Burton directs Nicole de Boer in the final mirror universe story* The Emperor's New Cloak
Below left: *Geordi and Riker dodge the attacks of two Son'a ships as they return to Federation space*

vision at the end of the picture. I think Geordi gaining Human eyes would be a bit like me getting the opportunity to walk around as a white man for a few days. I guarantee that at the end of that time, I would want to go back to being a black man because that's who I am."

Coming hot on the heels of *Star Trek Generations* and the exceptionally well-received *First Contact*, *Star Trek: Insurrection* has a lot to live up to, both artistically and commercially. Burton feels confident that the new film has a lot to offer cinemagoers, but insists that history will be the ultimate judge of how well it stands up to its predecessors. "*First Contact* raised the bar, without question," he admits. "*Generations*, I felt, had to serve too many masters and was too much of a hybrid, so I tend to discount that one. But *First Contact* was definitely one of the best of the *Star Trek* movies. It set a new high watermark for the franchise.

"Nevertheless, I was only able to say that about *First Contact* after feeling the response to it. The suc-

"... I'm standing on the threshold of the next major chapter of my life, in which I intend to speak my piece as a filmmaker, a writer, a director, a producer and as an actor. Acting is last on the list now."

"Geordi, more than any of the other ST:TNG characters, is at peace with who he is... The way Geordi sees is a big part of him, so I wanted him to revert to his normal vision at the end of the picture."

cess of *Insurrection* will, to a large part, be determined by the audience and how they respond to the movie. I do believe that the experience of making this movie was a very high one for all of us. We all enjoyed it, we all had a great time and we all felt like we were doing our best. Whether or not it's deemed a success is out of our control."

Once *Star Trek: Insurrection* ceased production, Burton resumed his career as a writer/producer/director, and promptly landed the plum assignment of helming *Star Trek: Voyager*'s much-

touted 100th instalment, *Timeless*. Set 15 years into the show's future, *Timeless* follows *Harry Kim*'s desperate bid to change history and save the lives of his former crewmates, all of whom are destined to die during a return trip to the Alpha Quadrant. The fifth season episode received rave reviews when it premièred in the US last November, and has been widely hailed as one of *ST:VOY*'s finest hours to date.

"I'm enormously proud of the episode," Burton enthuses. "I think that *Timeless* represents *Star Trek* at its absolute best. First of all, it offers crackerjack story-telling. I mean from the opening moments, we're on an adventure; we're on a journey. What's wonderful about *Star Trek* is that we have an opportunity to go on these journeys and adventures with characters that are totally engaging, and in the process, we get to witness their continuing unfolding as characters. I think that the journey we go on in *Timeless*, particularly with Harry Kim, is a very moving and emotional one."

As the episode unfolds, Harry Kim finds himself pursued by a certain Captain Geordi La Forge of the *U.S.S. Challenger*, who is assigned to stop him from altering the timeline. Although Burton's sec-

Above left: *A frozen Seven of Nine poses for the cameras to publicise the 100th episode of* **Star Trek: Voyager**, Timeless, *directed by Burton*
Below: *Garak also has his turn in the alternate universe in* **The Emperor's New Cloak**
Below right: *Harry Kim becomes a bitter man determined to rectify a mistake made long ago in* **Timeless**

ond stint of the year as Geordi proved to be one of *Timeless*' many highlights, it was actually a surprisingly late addition to the episode.

"It was not planned at the beginning," he reveals. "The idea came to Brannon [Braga, the series' executive producer] very late. Originally, we planned to use Whoopi [Goldberg as *Guinan*] in the episode, but they couldn't really get it to work. Then, just as we were about to start filming, Brannon called me at home, on a Sunday, and asked me how I would feel about being in the episode.

"At that point, I felt that I had my hands full just directing the thing. It was a huge show: the bridge, sickbay and a large section of corridor were all completely frozen over, and also had to be redressed as normal to be used in the same episode. So, there were a lot of challenges inherent in making sure that we were going to be able to do the best job we could, and I certainly wasn't thinking of putting on a space suit and acting in it as well!

"But I told Brannon, 'Look, you write it, and we'll take a look at it and talk about it once we've got it on the page.' And when I read it, it not only suited the story, but I thought it would also be really nice for the fans. It just seemed like a nice way to tie those two universes together, especially as I don't know that we've had that much crossover between *ST:TNG* and *ST:VOY*. So I just thought it would be a good thing, and that it would be our gift to the loyal fans."

Apart from *Timeless*, Burton points to three other episodes as the highlights of his directorial work on *Star Trek*. "I'm proud of *The Raven*," he

"I can't see that far into the future," he grins. "But sure, if there is another one of these and they come to me and say, 'LeVar, we're interested in you directing', I'd certainly be willing to have that conversation. It would depend on a lot of things, most notably the other projects I had going on at that time of my life and whether or not it fits and makes sense. But all things being equal, one of the things I have learned during my 11 year association with *Star Trek* is that anything is possible. So who knows?"

In the meantime, Burton certainly isn't short of work, and has two non-*Star Trek* directorial outings ready to roll. The first is a family comedy for Disney, while the second is a Columbia Tri-Star movie which is slated to star *ST:TNG*'s Whoopi Goldberg and *First Contact*'s Alfre Woodard. Beyond that, there are a host of projects on the drawing board, including a further film to direct entitled *Masters of the Far East*, and a television series for *Paramount Pictures* called *John Smith*, which the former *ST:TNG* star not only intends to produce but is also considering playing the lead role in.

All in all, LeVar Burton has absolutely no complaints about the direction his career is taking these days. And he is convinced that the future has never looked brighter.

"I am really happy doing what I'm doing now, which is developing projects as a producer and director," he declares. "And it's been made possible, in large measure, by my time on *Star Trek*. So I am enormously grateful to *Star Trek* for starting my career as a director, and for helping me to enter this new phase of my life." ∎

reveals, "because it was my first introduction to Jeri Ryan [*Seven of Nine*] and I find her truly delightful. She's a really terrific actor and is very, very easy to work with. I was just really pleased with the way that episode came out.

"I've had a lot of really fine episodes of *ST:DS9* to direct. Most notable among them was the *Worf* on trial episode [*Rule of Engagement*]. I saw that not so long ago, watched it right through and thought 'Wow, that really worked!' I thought Avery [Brooks, *Captain Sisko*] in particular gave one of the best performances I've seen him do. I thought he was really involved.

"Then there's *Indiscretion*, which is a favourite of mine because it was a two-hander. It was mostly Nana [Visitor, *Major Kira*] and Marc Alaimo [*Gul Dukat*]. It's not easy to have two actors in pretty much every scene and make it interesting and engaging, but those two are just terrific. You just turn the camera on and let them go and you've got it."

Burton hopes that his most recent episode of *ST:DS9* will live up to the high standards set by

Top and above: *Burton displays his helming abilities on the set of* **The Emperor's New Cloak,** *pointing Jeffrey Combs, Andrew Robinson, Alexander Siddig, Nana Visitor and others in the right direction*

Rules of Engagement and *Indiscretion*. Entitled *The Emperor's New Cloak*, this seventh season instalment marks the long-awaited return to the show's ongoing mirror universe storyline.

"I loved doing that one," he says. "I'd been in the mirror universe before with *Bareil*, Kira and the Intendent [in *Resurrection*], so *The Emperor's New Cloak* was a return to the alternate universe for me, and a really fun trip."

With 15 episodes of the franchise now under his director's belt, LeVar Burton would seem like a logical choice to direct a *Star Trek* film in the not-too-distant future. However, while he fully expects to play Geordi La Forge again in future instalments, Burton is far less sure if he will ever get to helm a *Star Trek* feature.

"I'm proud of **The Raven,** because it was my first introduction to Jeri Ryan and I find her truly delightful. She's a really terrific actor and is very, very easy to work with."

Geordi La Forge (LeVar Burton) joined the *Enterprise* crew as helmsman, before becoming its Chief of Engineering

NUMBER ONE
JONATHAN FRAKES

As first officer of the *Enterprise*-D, Commander Will Riker was always at the center of the action, and behind-the-scenes so was the man who portrayed him. Jonathan Frakes took time out of his busy schedule for an exclusive interview with *Star Trek Magazine*'s Tara Bennett, to talk about the impact *Trek* has had on his creative life, what he admires most about the Riker character, and how he feels about where *Star Trek* is headed now.

In the pantheon of *Star Trek* characters, William Thomas Riker has always managed to stand out from the Starfleet pack as a reliable officer, a brash strategizer, and a loyal friend. Even assessing him on shallower terms, Riker's got a smile that rivals Captain Kirk's on the charm-o-meter and, frankly, no one's rocked any *Enterprise* Bridge with a beard as bad-ass as his.

Of course, the smile and beard are just two of many, many assets that actor Jonathan Frakes brought to his portrayal of Riker over the span of 18 years, four different *Trek* series, and four *Star Trek: The Next Generation* films. But playing Riker also shifted Frakes towards a new career as a director, where he made a huge impact on helping to successfully transition, and then keep, epic *Star Trek* stories featuring the *Next Generation* cast viable on the big screen.

Now a frequent director on the TNT dramedy series, *Leverage*, Frakes took a break from prepping his upcoming episode to reminisce with us. Recently back from a *Star Trek* convention appearance in Australia, Frakes opened with genuine warmth and surprise in regards to the reception he and his fellow *Trek* colleagues received Down Under. "I was just in Adelaide, Australia where there were 19,000 people at a comic book convention for the first time there ever," he says with awe. "My show is 25 years old! The original show is 45 years old! It's just insanity. It's fabulous!"

Jonathan Frakes as Commander William T. Riker

"WE WERE GOING INTO A WORLD WHERE EVERYONE WAS SO SKEPTICAL ABOUT US."

Frakes says this with the benefit of hindsight, remembering when the idea of a new *Star Trek* series appearing on television wasn't welcomed with open arms by critics or fans. "We were going into a world where everyone was so skeptical about us because of the success of the 'Kirk, Spock, Bones' *Star Trek*. I'm not sure they wanted us to succeed, or let anyone else into the family," Frakes muses.

Already a successful TV actor for a decade when he auditioned for *Star Trek: The Next Generation* in 1987, Frakes says no one in the cast was prepared for how *Trek* would impact their careers and lives when they first signed up. "The only people who really knew *Star Trek* were Michael Dorn [Worf] and Wil Wheaton [Wesley Crusher]," the actor admits. "And the only people who were famous were LeVar Burton [Geordi La Forge] and Wil Wheaton. I don't think we were aware until we got into it and then we were lucky to become this phenomenon of pop culture that's the world of *Star Trek*."

Playing Commander William Riker, the first officer to Captain Jean-Luc Picard (Patrick Stewart) on the *U.S.S. Enterprise*-D, Frakes' character started the show as a fresh-faced, confident, ladies' man. While Picard was the steady, erudite Captain, Riker initially got to fill the quasi-Kirk roll, going on away missions and being more aggressive with off-book strategy. Asked if the producers nudged him to

Director and *Star Trek* actor Jonathan Frakes gives fans a Vulcan salute

Photo courtesy of Paradigm Agency

the same energy because I knew that when I got there, not only were we going to do some great storytelling, but we were going to have a ball. It was the most wonderful, funny, irreverent, clever group of friends."

URBAN LEGEND

It's been seven years since Frakes last played Riker on-screen, but he admits that certain topics still come up often when he speaks to fans. "The beard!" he laughs. As fans know, Riker came back in season two with a new beard and it immediately became a signature look for Picard's "Number One." Explaining its birth, Frakes says, "It happened that [Gene] Roddenberry liked it very much. He thought it would be great for the character to have what he referred to as a 'nautical and decorative beard,' so that's why the beard became so distinctly shaped. I still have it, even though it's white now," the actor chuckles.

He continues, "You know, I got the greatest news from one of our writers on *Leverage*. There's an Urban Dictionary reference that says Riker's beard is equivalent to the opposite of 'Jumping the Shark' when you're making a TV show. It means when you make a cool choice, it's a 'Riker's Beard'. Come on! What kind of privilege is that?" he enthuses.

A regret the actor has never had is being a part of the *Trek* world in the first place. While the support of the *Trek* fandom can be incredible for actors, close association with the *Trek* franchise itself can be tough on actors trying to move on to other projects in their career. For that reason, plenty of actors have walked away from *Trek* and declined to return. However Frakes has never distanced himself from *Trek*, and in fact he's appeared as Riker on four

put more Kirk in his character, Frakes affably demurs. "No, they didn't put that pressure on me. Part of Kirk's charm was that he had an alien in every port and they tried that for a while with Riker, which was great fun, but I was never Kirk. Also with Marina [Sirtis] and me, it was established in the Pilot that Riker and Deanna Troi had a relationship, even though the writers chose to neglect it until we convinced them otherwise – or maybe they saw the light," he laughs. "We got married during *Star Trek: Nemesis*, and that relationship informed the way the two of us behaved with each other and other people. Neither of us was as free as Kirk to just go out and have these affairs, although both characters sort of did."

Frakes says the bond between him and Sirtis is indicative of all the relationships he formed on *TNG*, a very rare thing in Hollywood. "As

"IT'S NO SECRET THAT BEING A *STAR TREK* ACTOR IS A DOUBLE-EDGED SWORD."

you've read and probably know, we're all still friends. We're so fortunate. Other shows are not like that," Frakes explains about the tensions that eventually arise on most long-running shows. "I've done a lot of shows since *Star Trek*, and I see what the cast feels like in the fourth season or the sixth season or the fifth season. But my memory of the 182 episodes and the seven seasons that we did – and I don't know if it's shaded by distance – but my memory is that I looked forward to going to work every day with

Great beards of the galaxy reunited, in *Star Trek: First Contact* (Left to right: Michael Dorn as Worf, with Frakes as Riker)

New voyages beckon for
Captain Riker in *Star Trek Nemesis*

to have learned another craft, because now I'm flat out [booked] until the end of the year."

That other craft he speaks of is directing; a calling that didn't manifest itself until Frakes was working on *TNG*. He reveals to us the reasons why he started to look outside of acting for creative fulfillment: "I hated waiting around in my dressing room at Paramount, and that feeling started to motivate me. So I looked around the set for the most interesting and engaging job, and that was obviously the director. It felt like something I knew about because, as an actor, I knew how to communicate with other actors and break down the beats of a scene. You learn a lot about that in drama school, and that applies to a lot of directing. By voicing an interest, I'm sure my friend [*Star Trek* producer] Rick Berman just cringed and he said, 'No, you have to learn more than that.'"

Instead of walking away, Frakes says he jumped right into on-the-job training. "I went to what we refer to as Paramount University, where I was able to shadow all the directors on the show. I spent about 300 hours in the editing room with all the editors, who were very generous with their time, and where I learned

different series: *TNG*, *DS9*, *Star Trek: Voyager*, and *Enterprise*. "I always said yes, because by that point the die had already been cast, for better or for worse," Frakes explains about his choices. "It's no secret that being a *Star Trek* actor is a double-edged sword. Patrick seems to

have dodged a bullet, and Shatner has reinvented himself to a certain degree, especially in the last few years. As actors, when we're dead they'll say, 'You knew him best as Riker' or 'You knew him best as Data' and that's great. But still it's another reason I feel so lucky

DATACORE

Not content with his duties as Starfleet's number one Number One, Jonathan Frakes took command of 16 *Star Trek* adventures as Director:

STAR TREK: THE NEXT GENERATION
"The Offspring"
"Reunion"
"The Drumhead"
"Cause and Effect"
"The Quality of Life"
"The Chase"
"Attached"
"Sub Rosa"

STAR TREK: DEEP SPACE NINE
"The Search, Part II"
"Meridian"
"Past Tense, Part II"

STAR TREK: VOYAGER
"Projections"
"Parturition"
"Prototype"

STAR TREK: FIRST CONTACT

STAR TREK: INSURRECTION

Will Riker continues his tour of duty aboard the *Enterprise*-D in the fourth season of *Star Trek: The Next Generation*

what you need to give an editor to put a scene together. I did a lot of post-production in terms of the mix, the sound, and the scoring. And then I got involved in pre-production where I learned about casting and budgeting. Oddly, by virtue of Rick being reticent and my lovely wife, Genie Francis, encouraging me to persevere, by the time they finally relinquished a *TNG* episode, I was so over-prepared it was insane," he laughs.

THE A-LIST

In 1996, Frakes earned the opportunity to direct *Star Trek: First Contact*, the first to feature just the *TNG* cast. It was his first major motion picture directorial effort, and Frakes chuckles when he admits, "I was naïve enough to be confident. Also, it became clear that the A-list sci-fi directors were not going to do *Star Trek* 8. The Ridley Scotts of the world were not interested. Sherry Lansing, who was running [Paramount] at the time, said to Rick [Berman] that she didn't understand *Star Trek* as well as everybody else. She told him to make the decisions and make the movie the way they had been, which was very generous. So we put our hats in the ring [to direct] and I was the lucky guy who won the lottery with that one."

"I LOOKED AROUND THE SET FOR THE MOST INTERESTING AND ENGAGING JOB, AND THAT WAS OBVIOUSLY THE DIRECTOR."

Frakes made a final appearance as Riker in *Enterprise* finale, "These Are the Voyages"

Jonathan Frakes directed the hit *TNG* movie, *Star Trek: First Contact*

Captain Picard (Patrick Stewart) congratulates Will Riker and Deanna Troi (Marina Sirtis) on their marriage in *Star Trek Nemesis*

Star Trek: First Contact ended up being a very positive experience for Frakes all around. The film was a critical and a commercial hit, earning $146 million worldwide, the best international box office performance by a *Trek* film ever until 2009's *Star Trek*. In 1998, Frakes was back to direct *Star Trek: Insurrection*, another solid hit for the franchise.

Frakes says he learned about directing a TV episode as opposed to a theatrical film. "The real difference is in the size of the toys and the amount of time. You can do all those things on TV if you have the time and the money to do them. Also, I was lucky enough to get this big brother figure in Matthew Leonetti, who was the director of photography on *First Contact*. He'd worked with a lot of first-time directors before, and he was so generous and fabulous with his team. Matt helped me discover what it took to make a movie. Also there was Terry Frazee, who was the special effects guy who blew everything up for me, and he made the scope of the movie huge. What I really learned was that you're really as good as the people you hire to work with you. Those guys were part of the team that included the brilliant Herman Zimmerman, the production designer, and the brilliant Michael Westmore, who was the king of make-up. Another part of the *Star Trek* movies was that we had John Knoll, the Academy Award winner from ILM, who did special effects for *First Contact*, and then we had Jim Rygiel, who ultimately won the Academy Award for *The Lord of the Rings*, who did *Insurrection*. We had the cream of the crop." He pauses, then adds with glee, "I'm so blessed. I'm so friggin' blessed!"

Now a respected and in-demand television drama director who moonlights occasionally as an actor, Frakes admits he's really comfortable now assuming command of any show that hires him. "It's something I enjoy, and as you do it, you get a little more confident with it. When you do the shows that I do, which are established television shows –when you do the *Burn Notice*,

the *Leverage*, the *NCIS: LA*, and *Castle*, your responsibility is to make their show. You don't go in and reinvent the wheel. You don't go in and shoot it in a style the audience is uncomfortable with. I do try to inject small things, keeping an eye on the acting and keeping the pace and telling the story clearly, so I'm thrilled when people respond to my directing."

Asked what it is about directing that appeals to his creative self, Frakes considers his answer for a moment. "That's a really good question. I really actively like shooting much more than prep. I like to go to work in the morning, shoot all day and at the end of the day you know you have accomplished, let's say, eight pages of the story you want to tell. I like being in the factory working with other people making something together. When I was an actor, you really just wait. There's a famous old quote that says, "They pay me to wait. I act for free." That's really what happens, especially if you're not the lead."

DREAM JOB

Since watching TV is now research for a possible next gig, or at least a potential add to his directorial wish-list, Frakes now has a whole host of current shows which he admires. "I think *Homeland* is the best show I've seen in five years. Genie and I would wait with baited breath for it to come on, and I haven't felt that way about television in a long time. I just watched some *Sons of Anarchy*, which I think is spectacular. We watch *Modern Family*, which I think is genius. A friend of ours turned us on to *Downton Abbey*. And the sense of humor on *Leverage* is fabulous."

In the near future, Frakes says his ultimate goal is to become a director/executive producer on a series where he guides the visual aesthetic for the entire series and mentors guest directors that come to the show. "I'm still looking for that job!" he exhales wistfully. "It gets harder and harder because there are so few of them, because there are so few scripted shows. Plus, there are so many movie guys making television now. It used to be that people who made movies didn't think about making television, but now everyone is making the move, and especially with pilots. So I'm actively looking for my own show, but in the meantime I'm very happy to have the places where I can hang my hat for a few weeks at a time."

Frakes admits the closest situation he's had to that dream director job was at the helm of TNT's popular *The Librarian* adventure TV movies starring Noah Wyle (*ER*, *Falling Skies*). "I feel great ownership of those with Dean [Devlin] and Noah [Wyle]. I think we are

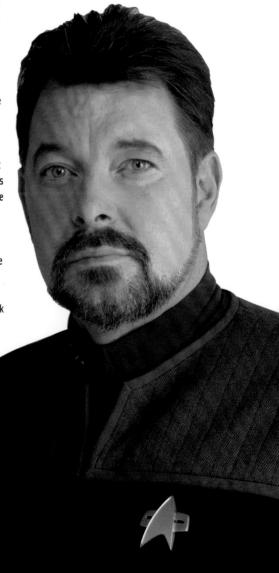

Riker hunts down the enemy in *Star Trek: Nemesis*

Commander Riker in *Star Trek: Generations*

"LEVAR BURTON WILL GO INTO A TOWN AND ANNOUNCE HE IS LOOKING FOR A PLACE TO HAVE A BEER, AND 70 FANS WILL SHOW UP."

joined at the hip with *The Librarian* movies and we're hoping to do another one. I think [the delay] is a function of timing, because even TNT would like to get the team back together again. I love them, and I love Noah."

Bringing the conversation back to fandom and *Trek*, we talk about how the world has changed incredibly since Frakes started on *Trek*, especially in regards to the Internet and social media engagement directly with fans. Frakes has a Twitter account (@jonathansfrakes) but he admits, "I'm a reluctant Twitterer. I had my arm twisted by Jeri Ryan, who is a massive Tweeter, and Beth Riesgraf, who plays Parker on *Leverage*, pressured me when we were doing a show together. Then friggin' Beth signed me up on my iPhone without putting any screening on, so when I got back to my hotel room there were

thousands of f*****g emails! I had to delete thousands of emails and put the filter on so I didn't get email notices," he laughs.

Still uncomfortable with how much to engage or not, Frakes chuckles that social media "goes from the mundane to weird. It's a good tool to promote what you're doing but, interestingly, I get the impression that that's not what Twitter followers want. They don't want to hear that you're doing another episode of *Leverage*. They want to hear where you're having a drink or what your favorite foods are. I just don't roll that way. Wil Wheaton is a great Tweeter. LeVar [Burton] will go into a town and announce he is looking for a place to have a beer, and 70 fans will show up and join him in a pub. He's got like a million seven followers! Yet Brent [Spiner], who also has a million five followers, is as shy as LeVar is out there."

As for *Trek*, it's been seven years since *Enterprise* was cancelled, and there've been no serious moves towards developing a new television series. Asked if he thinks it's time for a new show, Frakes answers with a smile, "It's still on TV every night, somewhere, and the fans watch it with the same loyalty. Really, the fact there is no new *Star Trek*, from what I'm told, is a very conscious effort on behalf of J.J. Abrams, CBS, and Paramount. What happened with *Star Trek: Nemesis* was that greed drove them to the well too much. It really did." With lessons learned, Frakes thinks *Star Trek* on the big screen is enough for now.

"I'm a huge J.J. fan, and he's been great for the franchise. J.J.'s reboot was so sensational. As a matter of fact, I was just on the set [of *Star Trek* 2] where Benedict Cumberbatch (*Sherlock*) is the bad guy in the movie, and he's spectacular!"

Rounding out our conversation, Frakes says William Riker will always remain a character near and dear to his heart. "One of the things that Patrick and I always said about both Picard and Riker was that we wished we could be as clever, diplomatic, appropriate, and intelligent as those two characters were. I think the character that the writers gave me to play is the man I wish I was able to be." ▲

The *Enterprise*-E crew depart the planet Ba'ku in *Star Trek: Insurrection*

A MATCH MADE IN SPACE

Relationships. Even in the 24th Century, they're complicated. Picard's affection for Beverly Crusher seemed destined to go unspoken, while Will Riker and Deanna Troi's history was a rollercoaster ride right from the start. But in *Star Trek*, relationships aren't always about people – just as Kirk's love for his *Enterprise* was life-long, Riker's connection to the *Enterprise*-D and its crew could easily have held him back forever...

ALWAYS THE

Despite many opportunities, why wouldn't Commander William T. Riker man up and take the center seat? We look at three key moments where the *Enterprise*-D's first officer balked at the prospect of his own command – and ask why, in the end, "family" was more important... Words: Rich Matthews

Pity poor Riker. You knew the *Enterprise*-D's first officer was getting short shrift when growing a beard was the biggest moment of character development he got across seven seasons and four movies, (and why shaving it off in *Insurrection* was such a big deal too). It's no wonder Jonathan Frakes started directing – he wasn't asked to do much else while Patrick Stewart, Brent Spiner, Michael Dorn and even Marina Sirtis got all the juicy storylines. You can imagine Frakes sitting at craft services with Gates McFadden, bemoaning the lack of "going mad" or "stranded alone on the ship" bottle episodes for them to get their teeth into.

We exaggerate, of course, but there is a kernel of truth here, best exemplified by the show's inability to resolve Riker's natural career trajectory towards the captain's chair. The TV era of *The Next Generation* meant each episode had to largely stand alone, so story arcs and character paths tended to be brief, and most actors had to repeat similar tropes over and over again. So Riker – who by rights should have been promoted after his "Best Of Both Worlds" quadrant-saving brilliance – had to tread water, just to keep him on the bridge beside Picard. This inevitably meant that Riker tended to be banished to the B-story, sidelined somewhat by his android/alien/follically-challenged colleagues. Roddenberry, Berman et al did too good a job at making Riker the new Kirk, but you can't have two captains.

The *U.S. Army Handbook*'s definition of leadership is based on beliefs, values, skills, and traits like honesty, competency, intelligence, fair-mindedness, broad-mindedness, courage, imagination, vision, decisiveness, and inspiration. Add "making beards cool in space" and that's the

A clean-shaven look for Number One (Jonathan Frakes), in *Next Generation* pilot episode, "Encounter at Farpoint"

Riker (Jonathan Frakes) flexes his whiskers against a Klingon foe

BRIDESMAID

Riker (Frakes), Data (Brent Spiner) and Tasha (Denise Crosby) find themselves stranded on a dangerous planet ("The Arsenal of Freedom")

Picard and Crusher get close, in "The Arsenal of Freedom"

DATACORE
"THE ARSENAL OF FREEDOM"
SEASON 1, EPISODE 21

When a rogue automated weapons platform traps an away team on the planet Minos, Geordi La Forge assumes command and leads the crew into battle.

FIRST AIRED:	11 APRIL 1988
EPISODE ORDER:	20TH OF 176
WRITTEN BY:	RICHARD MANNING, HANS BEIMLER, MAURICE HURLEY AND ROBERT LEWIN
DIRECTED BY:	LES LANDAU

- This was *TNG* veteran Les Landau's first directing gig on the show, and it was a baptism by fire: "The episode was in creative turmoil, going through massive, last-minute rewrites. In five years, it was the only time that we had to shut down because there was no shooting script ready to be shot." Chaos reigned because Robert Lewin's story more fully explored the burgeoning romance between Picard and Crusher – which was vetoed by Gene Roddenberry. The result was a scramble to restructure the episode (Crusher took over as the injured party from Picard), and Lewin left the show, frustrated at Roddenberry's alleged lack of interest in character development.

- Shots of a young, clean-shaven Riker during a scene with Rice in this episode

were reused in the series finale, "All Good Things," to depict Riker in the past. The beard would only go (well, temporarily anyway) when Deanna Troi shaves him in the hot-tub in "Insurrection."

- The unfortunate *Enterprise*-D was still in search of a permanent chief engineer at this point, with Geordi stationed at the helm (although he does captain the *Enterprise* for a second – and last – time during this episode). Lieutenant Logan is apparently the chief, although in previous episodes we'd already seen both Argyle ("Where No One Has Gone Before" and "Datalore") and Sarah MacDougal ("The Naked Now") in charge – the absence of Wesley from this episode at least meant Logan could get on with the job without being made to look stupid.

definition of Will Riker. Given that we'd had decades of pro-Kirk programming, is it any wonder that we expected Riker to become captain, and when he didn't – and seemingly refused to – he came across as a bit of a... (ahem) *loser*?
So what reasons did the writers concoct to keep Riker from accepting command, just to maintain the undeniable Stewart/Frakes chemistry? Let's take a quick slingshot round the sun to the moments when Riker was offered a captaincy, and examine why he just couldn't/wouldn't/wasn't allowed to climb aboard...

BEAMS CAN COME TRUE
SHIP OFFERED: *U.S.S. DRAKE (NCC-20381)*

It turns out that Riker rejected his first command BEFORE he was even on the *Enterprise*. He's also subjected to a particularly cruel and ironic narrative device in "The Arsenal of Freedom," namely a stasis beam that "freezes" him for a large chunk of the episode, leaving the way open for Jean-Luc and Beverly (stranded on the planet), and Geordi (back on the ship), to dominate the action. Even though the premise of the episode – the search for the *U.S.S. Drake* – is predicated on Riker's own past refusal of the *Drake*'s center seat, meaning Riker's Academy pal Paul Rice was in the chair when the ship was destroyed by a self-upgrading defense system. Riker's reasons seem reasonably justified – with a maximum warp of 3, would you want to captain "the slowest ship in all of Starfleet?" That's how the Minosian Echo Papa 607 drone (disguised as the unlucky Captain Rice) describes the *U.S.S. Drake*. No thanks!

Riker's ambition was clearly grounded not solely in rank, but also prestige – like a magpie to a bar of well-polished gold-pressed latinum. Already XO of the *U.S.S. Hood*, Riker had his sights set on a more illustrious commission, aboard a bigger, bolder ship like the *Enterprise*. Being First Officer of the flagship would garner him more attention than the paltry *Drake*. This marked the first instance of the writers making Riker's *Enterprise*-tethered decisions seem correct by destroying the ship he'd turned down. "See, Riker

DATACORE
"THE ICARUS FACTOR"
SEASON 2, EPISODE 14

Riker is forced to think about who he is, and what he wants from life, when he is offered the captaincy of the *U.S.S. Aries*, and Starfleet sends his father, Kyle, to brief him. All the while, Worf gets some help from his shipmates with the Klingon Rite of Ascension.

FIRST AIRED:
EPISODE ORDER:
WRITTEN BY:

DIRECTED BY:

24 APRIL 1989
39TH OF 176
DAVID ASSAEL AND
ROBERT MCCULLOUGH
ROBERT ISCOVE

- Riker's father not only neglected his son for 25 years, but also appears to have a very "close" relationship with Dr Pulaski – who we discover has been married three times, and prides herself on remaining good friends with all her exes.

- In what was by now a recurring theme, director Robert Iscove found his first *TNG* assignment stymied by Roddenberry's edict that humankind has outgrown negative attitudes. Iscove tried to inject a level of emotion that he associated with the original series, which he loved, but even though the director had the support of Rick Berman, he was overruled by the Great Bird. This led to him turning down further work, saying, "If you can't deal with the emotion, what's the point?"

- The filming of the Rite of Ascension was chronicled by the popular magazine show, "Entertainment Tonight", with longtime host John Tesh playing a Klingon who jabs Worf with a painstick. The presenter eventually got his own trading card, where his cameo garnered the Klingon name of K'Tesh.

Father and son sort out their family differences, in "The Icarus Factor"

would have DIED if he'd taken *that* commission!" Rice took command instead, and expired at the hands of Echo Papa 607, annihilated while orbiting uninhabited Minos, previously home to the long-extinct builders of the deadly defense system that probably killed them too. Not that we're given much time to ruminate on Riker's role in all this, when there's so much sexual tension bubbling betwixt Picard and Crusher, and you've got a blind guy battling a probe in the outer atmosphere! (Yes, it was still early enough in the series for La Forge's main hook to be his hair-barrette-covered peepers).

As a side note, the ship Riker turned down was named after Sir Francis Drake, the charismatic English explorer who circumnavigated the globe, and successfully fought off the Spanish Armada's attack on 16th-Century England. It's safe to say that Jonathan Frakes could easily have played Drake, and that Riker, like Kirk, had something of Sir Francis' privateer twinkle in his eye. When he isn't trapped in a stasis beam that is…

DADDY ISSUES
SHIP OFFERED: *U.S.S. ARIES (NCC-45167)*

At last, a promotion! Not to Captain – nope, Riker says no again – but at least to the main story of the episode! It did get a bit messy for poor old Will, though, what with his estranged daddy getting all up in his forward deflector array!

In 2365, the *U.S.S. Aries* detected intelligent life in the Vego-Omicron sector, and needed a commanding officer to lead the investigative mission ("The Icarus Factor"). Here's where Riker is undermined from the get-go. We know that Starfleet officers are rounded, erudite individuals, but does Riker strike anyone as the prime candidate for a *scientific* mission? Not to be unfair, but if you line up the *Enterprise* crew in your mind – Picard, Riker, Data, Geordi, Beverly Crusher, Worf, Troi, Wesley, Tasha Yar – and rank them in order of scientific acumen (even if it's just to get Tribbles out of the anti-matter matrix), we reckon Riker would rank fifth, at best. Putting a positive spin on the commission, Picard tells his first officer that the *Aries* may be "a relatively insignificant ship, in an obscure corner of the galaxy, but it will be *your* ship." No doubt the words "insignificant" and "obscure" were the ones Riker heard – and maybe Picard chose them carefully, hoping they might dissuade his Number One from jumping ship?

Then, to make matters worse, Riker is emasculated by comparison to his brusque, over-achieving father, Kyle, while simultaneously having his dirty laundry aired all over the ship, causing him to act like a petulant teenager. The

A game of poker, in "The Best of Both Worlds"

Picard's assimilation by the Borg puts Riker in command of the *Enterprise*

DATACORE
"THE BEST OF BOTH WORLDS — PART ONE"
SEASON 3, EPISODE 26

The Borg attack the Alpha Quadrant, decimating Starfleet on its course towards Earth. To aid in the assimilation of humankind, the hive-minded, biomechanical race kidnap Picard and transform him into a drone called Locutus. With Riker in command (hooray!), the *Enterprise* attempts to stop the invasion, even if the cost is killing Picard in the process...

FIRST AIRED:	18 JUNE 1990
EPISODE ORDER:	73RD OF 176
WRITTEN BY:	MICHAEL PILLER
DIRECTED BY:	CLIFF BOLE

- Michael Piller famously wrote this cliffhanger without knowing how he was going to conclude it later that year. The writing team had struggled since the second season's "Q Who" to reintroduce the Borg, due to their monolithic hive-mind. However, Piller reworked a previously rejected "Queen Bee" idea to make Picard the face of the Borg, while the Borg Queen would eventually surface in *First Contact*. Paramount allowed them to spend more money than usual, to make "The Best Of Both Worlds" one of the most epic stories of the entire run. It was also the series' first two-parter — its success guaranteed more!

- Eventually dropped due to problems resolving storytelling logic, an early draft of the script had Picard being combined with Data to create Locutus — which would

have been truly terrifying, and perhaps too devastating for fans.

- Wolf 359, perhaps one of *Star Trek*'s most famous locations, is a real star that lies approximately 7.8 light years from Earth. A very faint red dwarf, it is the fifth closest star to our own sun.

- In a wonderful example of creative thinking, one of the episode's most indelible visuals was entirely unplanned. Michael Westmore's son found a cheap, inch-long laser in their workshop, and decided to incorporate it into Locutus' headpiece. Westmore Sr. admits that they had no idea how the laser would look on camera, but when the rushes were first screened, Rick Berman declared, "Oh my god — what a great effect!"

Rikers had become estranged after the death of Will's mother, and career was an obvious escape for Kyle, and for Will too. But here's where Will finally gets some proper character development. By specifically *choosing* not to become captain, it became clear Riker wasn't Kirk, and with Picard slowly loosening up and getting more "romantic," Riker was also allowed to change course. This may simply have been a need to justify his remaining on the *Enterprise*, but nonetheless his outlook on life was changing. The *Enterprise* crew was the catalyst for a shift in attitude away from career and towards a more rounded sense of purpose. He wasn't ready to settle down with Deanna when they first met, but working next to people of character, surrounded by families, and with a paternal/fraternal surrogate in Picard, and an avuncular relationship with Wesley Crusher, Riker's sense of self was (gradually – we're talking impulse power) redefined. His father followed career and ambition over family. Riker, in contrast, found that rare balance of life and work. Reconciliation with Kyle and acknowledging the events surrounding his mother's death allows Riker to recognize the change. "Right now, the best place for me is here," he says, describing his decision as "motivated self-interest."

And maybe because this decision was rooted in a genuine progression for the character, they didn't blow the *Aries* to bits just to make the choice seem valid, making it the only ship turned down by Riker that didn't end up as so much atomized space dust.

RESISTANCE IS FUTILE
SHIP OFFERED: *U.S.S. MELBOURNE (NCC-62043)*

The poor *Melbourne* wasn't so lucky. Although, to be fair, it was one of dozens of ships to buy the dilithium farm. By the end of the third season, Riker's career woes fell back to the B-story (or C-story, if we're honest), but at least it's in the Single Best Episode of *Star Trek* Ever Made (TM)!

This was the biggie. Starfleet *really* wanted Riker to take command of the *Melbourne* in 2366. Two words: The Borg. Yep, the future of the entire Alpha Quadrant hung in the balance, and Starfleet was throwing everything they could at the Collective badasses. And with eager young bloods like Lt. Commander Shelby (ice-perfect Elizabeth Dennehy) taking full advantage – if they survived, of course – the time was ripe for Riker.

It seemed like everyone above him in the chain of command was telling him to do his business or get off the pot – including Picard: "She's a fine ship, Will." "Yes, but she's not the *Enterprise*," was Will's reply. Was his attachment to his home and Starfleet family now so strong

Rising star Lt. Commander Shelby
(Elizabeth Dennehy) outshines Riker, in
The Best of Both Worlds

that nothing could prise him away? Was he waiting for Picard to move on, get promoted, or retire? Had he swapped one prodigal father for a sterner-yet-warmer surrogate, from whom he wanted to inherit the family business?

So here was the great fake-out. For a moment, *The Next Generation* had us convinced that Patrick Stewart might actually leave the series and make way for Frakes. How else could the Picard-assimilated-into-the-Borg-as-Locutus storyline finish? Riker, finally in charge, gave the order to "Fire!" at Picard on the Borg cube. The irony was lost on no-one that Riker's first true test as captain was against his mentor – a test that he sailed through with flying colors, saving Earth from those pasty-faced, cybernetic assimilators. And saving his captain too. But once Picard was back (after only one episode of recovery, episodic TV fans), Riker was forever relegated. The series couldn't play that hand again without sacrificing dramatic credibility, so Riker's change became the new normal, leading him back into Troi's loving embrace (once Worf had been transferred to *Deep Space 9*, of course...)

And guess what became of the *Melbourne? KER-BLOOEY!* Annihilated at Wolf 359. In this case, there can be no doubt that, had Riker taken command, he would have perished. Instead, he saved the entire quadrant. Can you think of *anyone* else in Starfleet who wouldn't have been made captain – Admiral even! – for doing as much?

Eventually Riker did get his own command, stepping up to captain the *U.S.S. Titan* in the franchise's literary expanded universe, but was the final screen Riker a more rounded and balanced individual than the man we'd first encountered at Farpoint? Perhaps – and that's why he began to seem somewhat bland. He was too content for good drama, the embodiment of Roddenberry's 24th-Century human, unbothered by petty emotions or self-doubt. He had a cosy arc, a very human arc, one that many adults can identify with and aspire to. Whether or not that arc was fair to the genesis of the character or the ambition of the actor is irrelevant. He could never leave. It wouldn't have been the *Enterprise* without him. ▲

Jean-Luc Picard (Patrick Stewart) and
Beverly Crusher (Gates McFadden) at
the wedding of Riker and Troi

"DID I MISS SOMETHING?"
- RIKER (NEMESIS)

PICARD & CRUSHER

DON'T MISS

○ **"Attached"** from the show's final season, which allows Patrick Stewart and Gates McFadden to focus entirely on the Picard/Crusher relationship.

Star Trek: Insurrection

One particular character-based plotline was never adequately resolved on *Star Trek: The Next Generation*. Over the years, Worf was discommended from his people and eventually reinstated; Data learned how to dream and got his emotion chip; Riker and Troi got married; Wesley fulfilled his potential by becoming a Traveler. But despite its presence as a subtext of the show from the very first episode, there was never an adequate resolution to the romantic and sexual tension between Captain Jean-Luc Picard and Dr. Beverly Crusher.

The relationship got a great deal of play in the first season. "Encounter at Farpoint" provided backstory: Picard and Jack Crusher were best friends, and Beverly was Jack's wife. But Jack died on a mission under Picard's command. Picard is concerned about Crusher serving under the command of the man who ordered her late husband to his death, and the tension between them is thick.

In "The Naked Now," the mutated form of the Psi 2000 virus allows Picard and Crusher to make eyes at each other and smile goofily, and Picard even skips a step with glee. In "We'll Always Have Paris," Crusher seems jealous of Picard's former love Jenice Mannheim. In "The Big Goodbye," Picard is obviously (and understandably) wowed by Crusher in her 1940s attire. And in "The Arsenal of Freedom," Picard helps Crusher through an injury in a very tender set of scenes.

After Crusher returns following her one-year absence during the second season, the relationship grows more subtle. The two are seen sharing breakfast together regularly, and become comfortable as friends. But between the third and seventh seasons, the only time we saw any indications of movement past the friendship stage was in "Allegiance." Sadly, that turned out to be a false start, as it was a doppelgänger of Picard who started flirting more aggressively with Crusher (and also acting generally bizarre).

Twice during the show's run ("The High Ground," "Remember Me"), Crusher started to tell Picard (or, at the very least, someone she thought was Picard) something important only to be interrupted. That was enough for it to become a running joke among *Star Trek* fans.

Each side shows sparks of jealousy, but also support and affection, when the other becomes romantically involved with someone else (Crusher falling for Odan in "The Host," Picard for Nella Daren in "Lessons"), which modulates into concern when there's danger in the relationship (Picard's unintended fling with the empathic metamorph Kamala in "The Perfect Mate," Crusher's being mind-controlled by Ronin in "Sub-Rosa").

However, Crusher's jealousy/concern tends to be more overt than Picard's. A notable exception is in "The Child," when Picard discusses Crusher's departure with her son, Wesley, and is very obviously hurting at her decision to leave the *Enterprise*. Part of that is the nature of the two characters – the captain is far less emotional than the doctor – but the true reasons for Picard's reticence with Crusher become clear in the seventh season's "Attached."

A holodeck date for Beverly (McFadden) and Jean-Luc (Stewart) in "The Big Goodbye"

An intimate moment – albeit under the influence of an alien virus – in "The Naked Now"

Beverly was a close confidante to Jean-Luc, hinting at their mutual and deep regard for one another.

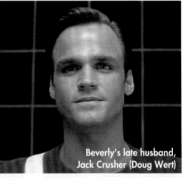
Beverly's late husband, Jack Crusher (Doug Wert)

> "Picard is finally forced to admit that he's been in love with Crusher since they first met, but she was his best friend's wife."

MOST ROMANTIC MOMENT

When Crusher, looking absolutely adorable in pink pajamas and with a ribbon in her hair, hears odd voices in her quarters in "Cause and Effect," she goes to Picard, and the captain provides his aunt Adele's tonic of warm milk with nutmeg as a sleep aid. The two of them sitting and chatting and smiling in the captain's ready room enjoying each others' company while Crusher grips the warm milk is a simply beautiful little scene.

CORNIEST DIALOGUE

"Now that we know how each of us feels, perhaps we should not be afraid to explore those feelings."

"Or perhaps we *should* be afraid."
— Jean-Luc Picard and Beverly Crusher, "Attached"

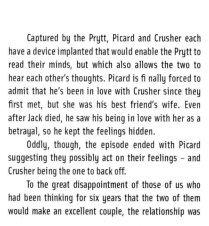

Captured by the Prytt, Picard and Crusher each have a device implanted that would enable the Prytt to read their minds, but which also allows the two to hear each other's thoughts. Picard is finally forced to admit that he's been in love with Crusher since they first met, but she was his best friend's wife. Even after Jack died, he saw his being in love with her as a betrayal, so he kept the feelings hidden.

Oddly, though, the episode ended with Picard suggesting they possibly act on their feelings – and Crusher being the one to back off.

To the great disappointment of those of us who had been thinking for six years that the two of them would make an excellent couple, the relationship was only really dealt with once more after that episode: in the alternate future of the television finale "All Good Things...," in which Picard and Crusher had married and divorced in the ensuing 25 years. The possibility of a romance was never even hinted at in the movies, which instead focused on Picard's relationships with Jim Kirk, Lily Sloane, Anij (the only romantic encounter Picard had in the films), and Shinzon. Especially disappointing was that *Star Trek Generations* had a great opportunity to use Crusher, given Picard's character arc in the film regarding family, and *Star Trek Nemesis* chose to resolve one of the cast's other will-they-won't-they couples rather than these two. A

Keith R.A. DeCandido

A rare on-screen kiss for Picard and Crusher

Beverly Crusher (Gates McFadden) goes all-action, in *Star Trek: Insurrection*

NOW READ ON:

In the novels, starting with *Death In Winter*, Picard and Crusher do get together in the aftermath of *Star Trek Nemesis*, eventually getting married and, after some considerable debate, particularly in the light of the Borg invasion charted in the *Destiny* trilogy, starting a family.

RIKER & TROI

Troi (Marina Sirtis) and Riker (Jonathan Frakes) enjoy a brush with history, in *Star Trek: First Contact*

Commander William T. Riker and Deanna Troi formed *Star Trek: The Next Generation*'s emotional core. Throughout the seven seasons, we watched the *Enterprise*-D's first officer and the ship's counselor struggle with their strong feelings for one another. The circumstances around their romance and their breakup were revealed in bits and pieces.

We know they met when Riker, then a Lieutenant Commander, was temporarily assigned as the Starfleet liaison to the Federation Embassy on Betazed. While attending a wedding, he spotted Deanna, a bridesmaid, and was smitten. When they first made love, Will heard her voice in his mind, a single word "Imzadi," meaning he was the first to touch her mind, soul, and body. We do know that when the romance ended, neither could say "goodbye."

When we first met the characters in "Encounter at Farpoint," we knew that there was a history between them but the facts were slowly doled out over the subsequent seasons. Both quickly assured Captain Picard they could work together and privately agreed that while they each had feelings for the other, they would maintain a purely professional relationship.

They remained relaxed best friends, teasing one another regardless of the circumstances. Still, the underlying sexual tension between them remained close to the surface as seen when Deanna tried to seduce Riker during "The Naked Now."

During their time together on board the ship, though, they watched each other get involved with other people and the sting was keenly felt time and again. Riker was the first to exhibit signs of jealousy, demonstrating the depth of his feelings, when Dr.

DON'T MISS

○ **"Second Chances"** from the fifth season, not only for the insights it gives into William Thomas Riker but for Jonathan Frakes's assured playing of two identical yet vastly different characters, and Marina Sirtis showing a deeper side to Troi.

The happy couple finally make it official, in *Star Trek Nemesis*

STAR TREK

STAR TREK MOVIES

STAR TREK
THE NEXT GENERATION®

STAR TREK
THE NEXT GENERATION®
MOVIES

STAR TREK
DEEP SPACE NINE

STAR TREK
VOYAGER

STAR TREK
ENTERPRISE

STAR TREK

"DEANNA, JUST BECAUSE THINGS TURNED OUT THE WAY THEY DID BETWEEN YOU AND COMMANDER RIKER, DOESN'T MEAN YOU SHOULDN'T LET THINGS BETWEEN YOU AND LIEUTENANT RIKER TAKE THEIR OWN COURSE."
– DR. CRUSHER

Wyatt Miller arrived on board to fulfill his arranged marriage to Deanna in "Haven." Miller broke things off, to Deanna's (and Riker's) relief, when he realized she was not the woman of his dreams.

Interestingly, it was Troi who usually had to back off; displaying her maturity by repeatedly declaring their friendship would endure, regardless of who Riker chose to be with. She did this in "The Vengeance Factor", "A Matter of Perspective", and "The Outcast" among other incidents.

It was Riker's happy memories of Deanna that helped keep him from dying after picking up a predatory plant on Surata IV during the "Shades of Gray" clip episode that closed out season two.

Complicating their relationship was the presence of that force of nature, Lwaxana Troi. When the two did try to renew their romance on Betazed in "Ménage à Troi," Lwaxana wound up getting mixed up with the couple as all three were kidnapped by the Ferengi. Later on, she told Riker it was his fault Deanna had yet to marry.

Lwaxana (Majel Barrett-Roddenberry) plays gooseberry to Will and Deanna.

Troi (Marina Sirtis) gives Riker (Jonathan Frakes) a close shave, in *Star Trek: Insurrection*

By this point, though, the two had given in to their simmering feelings after one of the ship's regular poker nights, a fact revealed in "Violations" but which was considered a one-off.

When Riker's transporter duplicate, Thomas, turned up five years into the *Enterprise's* voyage in "Second Chances," his passion for Deanna remained unabated and awakened in Will the desires he had too long suppressed.

Riker backed off when life threw them a significant change. Worf encountered many different universes

> **"When they first made love, Will heard her voice in his mind, a single word "Imzadi," meaning he was the first to touch her mind, soul and body."**

MOST ROMANTIC MOMENT
"STAR TREK: INSURRECTION"

Ironically, most of these happened off-screen, but the playful scene between Riker and Troi in the *Enterprise*-E's library during *Star Trek: Insurrection* best exhibited their affection for one another.

CORNIEST DIALOGUE
"HAVEN"

Sadly, for a couple whose love helped center the series, there are precious good or bad memorable quotes. The silliest, and most obvious may be, Troi's comment to Riker in "Haven", who certainly knew "Humans...young human males particularly...have difficulty separating platonic love and physical love."

in "Parallels," several showing him married to Deanna, a prospect he had never previously considered. As their romance blossomed, Riker tried to put a game face on, but it was clear to Worf this would remain an issue between the friends. By the series' final episode, the two agreed they needed to talk.

However, when the characters shifted to film, the romance between Worf and Deanna was over. Nothing was said or indicated how things changed. Despite her having previously accepted the Klingon's marriage proposal, Deanna seemed ready to move on. Riker and Troi were helped along the way during a visit to the Ba'ku world in *Star Trek: Insurrection*. The planet's unique metaphasic radiation rekindled the spark that never really died out in either of their hearts.

In guest appearances on *Star Trek: Voyager*, Deanna made comments that indicated she and Riker remained a couple, even offering to fix up Reg Barclay with a mutual acquaintance. As a result, things reached their natural conclusion with the wedding, parts of which helped open the final on-screen appearance of the full *Enterprise* crew in *Star Trek Nemesis*. Both would then honeymoon before Will finally took the center seat aboard the *U.S.S. Titan*.

It's interesting to note that for such a grand romance, it fell to the novels to fill in key gaps, such as what transpired on Betazed when they first met (Peter David's *Imzadi*), how the relationship with Worf ended (David's *Triangle: Imzadi II*), and when a marriage proposal was made (*A Time to Hate*). ▲
Robert Greenberger

Troi helped Dr. Pulaski (Diana Muldar) save Riker's life in *TNG* Season 2 episode, "Shades of Gray"

NOW READ ON:

In the *Star Trek: Titan* novel series, Riker and Deanna took command of the *U.S.S. Titan* as a married couple and struggled to manage its crew and the rigors that came with being a couple, including the long-delayed matter of children. Their relationship was tested in the books, right up to and including the birth of their child, Natasha Miana Riker-Troi in *Over a Torrent Sea*. Deanna had miscarried previously, and when she conceived in 2381, it took all of CMO Dr. Ree's medical know-how to ensure that the fetus would grow to term and be safely delivered. The *Star Trek Online* tie-in *The Needs of the Many* indicates that the two remained a bonded couple as of 2409, producing a total of three grandchildren.

Marina Sirtis as ship's counselor, Deanna Troi

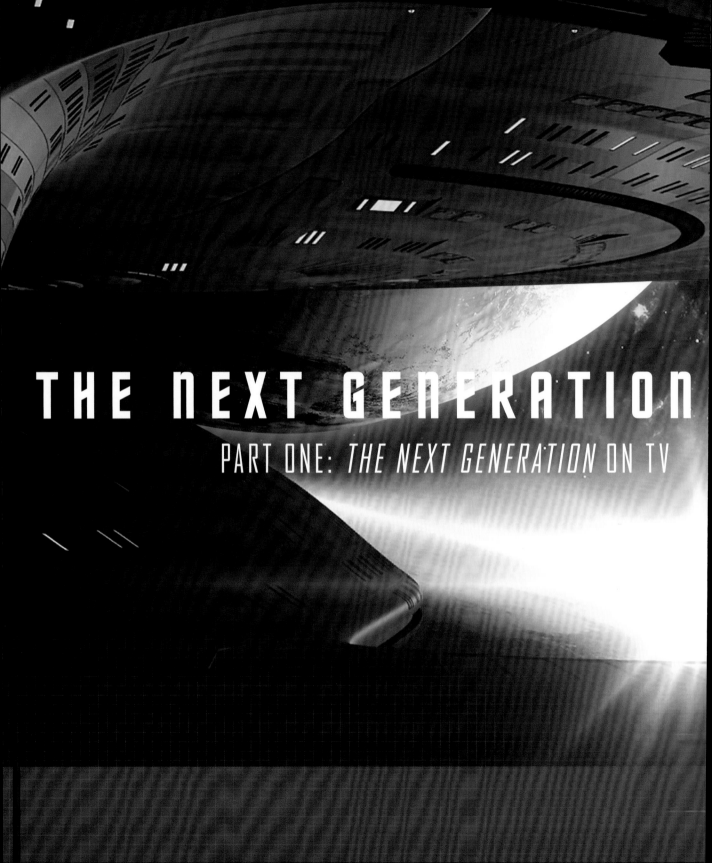

THE NEXT GENERATION

PART ONE: *THE NEXT GENERATION* ON TV

GUIDE

As Data might explain, while the likelihood of lightning striking the same coordinates twice is statistically improbable, it is not theoretically impossible. *Star Trek: The Next Generation* was televisual proof of this, defying critics who claimed a revival without the original cast would never work. However, with old hands returning to craft the new show, and many more talented creatives joining the series over subsequent years, *The Next Generation* became the template for an 18-year, unbroken run of *Star Trek* on TV...

STAR TREK SCRAPBOOK

IT COULD WRECK YOUR CAREER

Strange planets created by stray dogs; scorpions, snakes and fleas on the attack; and an underwater plunge for brave co-stars Patrick Stewart and Brent Spiner. All part of television's biggest ever gamble – bringing *Star Trek* back to the small screen. Thankfully, everything worked out okay... Mark Phillips scans the news media archives to discover how Gene Roddenberry "made it so" for *Star Trek: The Next Generation*.

"It could wreck your career. Don't take it." That was the warning from Sir Ian McKellen to Patrick Stewart over dinner in 1986. Stewart considered his friend's advice carefully before accepting the role of *Star Trek: The Next Generation*'s indomitable Captain Jean-Luc Picard, although he didn't imagine the show would last more than 13 weeks. Two years later, Stewart had to admit to *Copley News* that, "Now I don't know where Patrick Stewart ends and the role of Jean-Luc Picard begins."

Casting Picard was not an easy process, with Gene Roddenberry initially wanting Stephen Macht (who would later appear in two episodes of *Deep Space Nine*), or Patrick Bauchau (Bond villain Scarpine, in *A View to a Kill*), but producer Robert Justman pushed hard for Stewart, having been convinced the British actor was perfect for the role after seeing him reading Shakespeare at UCLA.

Another contender had been Roy Thinnes, the former star of the 1960s alien invasion

Patrick Stewart takes command

Dr. Beverly Crusher (Gates McFadden) left the crew for Season 2, but the popular character returned the following season

because his hands were covered with delicate powder to simulate android skin. "Fame is tough on my face," he quipped.

He found it remarkable that he was rarely recognized in public, and didn't understand press comparisons between Data and Mr. Spock. "Data wants to enhance his humanity, Spock rejects his humanity," Spiner told *The Observer Reporter*. "Data is accessible. Spock is remote and mystical." Off-set, Spiner helped Patrick Stewart overcome his life-long fear of water by agreeing to take scuba diving lessons with him. "We'll hold hands and jump into the water together," Stewart said.

"THE ONLY WAY FOR US TO SUCCEED WAS TO START FRESH."

A RATINGS MONSTER

Marina Sirtis (Deanna Troi) echoed the same fears that DeForest Kelley (McCoy) had expressed before his *Star Trek* debuted in 1966. "This series will either be a huge hit or a bomb," she said. Thankfully, the former proved to be the case, making Sirtis a well-known television face, and she was happy to accept invitations to various functions during the series' run. However, since she looked so different in reality from her Betazoid character, "When I would show up, people didn't know who I was, which was embarrassing." Sirtis told Jerry Buck of *Associate Press* that she and Jonathan Frakes would try to play up the romance between their characters, "but a lot of the stuff between us ended up on the cutting room floor." She noted the producers didn't like the relationship and wanted both Troi and Riker to be free "to have dalliances with aliens instead."

LeVar Burton (Geordi La Forge) was excited by the show's premise, props, and sets. "Look at all of these great toys we can play with," he told writer Lewis Beale. Beale predicted mega-success for the series, saying, "It is practically guaranteed to be a ratings monster."

series, *The Invaders*. This was the second time Thinnes had missed out on *Star Trek*, having previously been in the running for the role of James T. Kirk in 1965.

Stewart would soon become fiercely protective of his show. While waiting to be interviewed on ABC's *Good Morning, America* talk show, he noticed their weatherman was reading the national forecast while wearing a *Star Trek* uniform. Furious, Stewart stormed off the set. "I thought that was disrespectful," he recalled to *The News Sentinel*. "They were doing shtick in our costumes. It was demeaning to our show." Nevertheless, he regretted his flash of temper. Back in his early days as captain, he admitted to Luaine Lee of *The Herald Journal*, "I was very pompous," and that he would sternly forbid people from sitting in his captain's chair. He credited his fellow cast members for "loosening him up." Part of his insecurity was fear, he said. He was "terrified" Picard would typecast him forever.

ALIAS GEORDI AND DATA
Casting for the other regular cast was no less eventful. During *Star Trek*'s wilderness years, Gene Roddenberry wrote an episode for TV western *Alias Smith and Jones*, starring Ben Murphy as Kid Curry (alias Jones) and Pete Duel (a huge *Star Trek* fan) as Hanibal Heyes/John Smith. Murphy would later be considered for the role of Commander William Riker, while Jenny Agutter (*Logan's Run* and more recently *Captain America: The Winter Solider*) read for ship's doctor Beverly Crusher. Former basketball player Kevin Peter Hall was considered for both Geordi La Forge and Data.

Brent Spiner meanwhile would eventually win the role of the friendly android who often provided comedy relief. "Brent was the true acting find of *The Next Generation*," said director Corey Allen. "He was excellent in that role, and wonderful to work with." It took an hour to put on Spiner's makeup and adjust his yellow contact lenses. The actor couldn't scratch his face

STAR TRIVIA
One of the original *Star Trek* cast, James Doohan (Montgomery Scott), wasn't initially happy with the direction the new show was taking, finding it all a little too familiar. "They were doing shows we had already done," he complained, pointing to episodes like "The Naked Now." He called up his old friend Roddenberry. "I said, 'What's the matter, Gene? Are you running out of ideas?'" But Doohan soon grew to respect the series, and enjoyed reprising his iconic role of Scotty in the season six episode, "Relics."

Original series veteran James Doohan reprised his role as Scotty, in "Relics"

A new *Enterprise* for a new crew

"THE ONLY WAY FOR US TO SUCCEED WAS TO START FRESH."

John de Lancie as Q, in "Encounter at Farpoint"

Kelsey Grammer guest-starred in the episode "Cause and Effect"

Worf (Michael Dorn), on the *Enterprise*-D battle-bridge

Michael Dorn (Worf) enjoyed reading through the Klingon dictionary on set, and bravely endured the two-hour makeup sessions required for the role. He had paid his dues to get on *The Next Generation*, having begun his acting career as one of the silent reporters seen in the background in the WJM newsroom on the 1970s comedy hit *The Mary Tyler Moore Show*. In fact, it was Edward Asner (whose character, Lou Grant, went on to star in his own spin-off show) who encouraged Dorn to expand his acting talents.

Meanwhile, Roddenberry himself was nervous over the show's fate. "Listen, I'd be a damned fool if I wasn't. I'm still bruised from the battles I had with NBC," he commented. He decided to re-watch many of the original *Trek* episodes in 1986, and while they were getting "quainter and quainter-looking" with the passage of time, he was still pleased with them. "The characters and stories will prevent them from becoming laughable," he said, "The human condition doesn't age."

STAR TRIVIA

"You will never beat that teaser," writer Ronald D. Moore proclaimed of Brannon Braga's shocking opening of "Cause and Effect," where the *Enterprise* and her crew perished in a mighty explosion. Perhaps he was too young to recall how audiences were shocked, when the very last episode of *Voyage to the Bottom of the Sea* (1968's "No Way Back") opened with its famous submarine and heroes being blown to bits in a mighty explosion...

Still, he wanted less gunplay and more harmony with *The Next Generation*, stressing that, "If we can't get along here on Earth, we don't belong in space." He also wanted the new series to avoid what had happened to *Star Trek: The Motion Picture*, "where the special effects were highlighted over our people." Indeed, when one fan asked columnist Betty Lou Peterson in 1980 about the chances of a new *Star Trek* TV series, she replied, "Sorry, but the prognosis is not good. The expense of *Star Trek: The Motion Picture* has really hurt that idea."

The Next Generation continued to linger under Captain Kirk's shadow for some time. "The original *Star Trek* was a giant," said director Rob Bowman. "You couldn't compete. The only way for us to succeed was to start fresh."

BAD, BETTER, OR BEST

The original *Star Trek*'s modestly budgeted 79 episodes had sustained fan interest throughout the 1970s and into the early 1980s, and its record-breaking sales in syndication had paved the way for *The Next Generation*'s syndicated success, but the series would stand or fall by its own merits. The first year was "dreadful," said critic John Peel, but by the third year he acknowledged, "It is now as good as the old show ever was."

bald head!" Producers knew the series had achieved mainstream success when *MAD* magazine ran a typically deranged spoof entitled *Star Blecch: the Next Degradation.*

The Free Press stated that most journalists were secret trekkers. When *Knight Ridder*'s Steve Sonsky visited the set in 1987, he revealed he snuck into the transporter room set and whipped out his wallet to say, "Beam me up Scotty!" Other reporters played it cool – until they began taking turns swiveling around in Picard's command chair, barking "Phaser one, fire!"

Picard finds himself playing doctor, in "The Arsenal of Freedom"

Viewers remained curious about the new crew. A. F. of Salt Lake City asked *The Panama City News*, "Marina Sirtis seems to be trying to suppress some kind of foreign accent on the show, but we can't determine what it is." The paper replied, "She's British – born and raised in London." On the other hand, some viewers were just plain confused. T. W. of Texas insisted award-winning journalist Barbara Walters played Dr. Beverly Crusher, not Gates McFadden, to which columnist Dick Kleiner replied, "Walters is a woman of many talents, but acting on *Star Trek* is not one of them."

"IF WE CAN'T GET ALONG HERE ON EARTH, WE DON'T BELONG IN SPACE."

"I think we are more realistic than the original," producer Rick Berman told *The Associated Press* in 1991. "Television has become a bit more sophisticated since then." But Berman stressed, "I don't see a reason for the two shows to compete with one another. I see them as father and son."

"*The Next Generation* doesn't have the bite of the original, and it sacrifices social significance for lavish special effects," said *TV Guide*, but added, "The cast skillfully and convincingly delivers the intelligent and often eloquent dialog." J. K. Malmgren of Canada's *TV Week* said the series "marked a major turning point in TV space exploration. The debut show, 'Encounter at Farpoint,' had plot complexity and thought-provoking writing." *Sassy* magazine loved *The Next Generation* and was grateful that, "there are no lame paper maché boulders being hurled around." In praising the multi-dimensional characters, the magazine's reviewer admitted she yearned "to stroke Picard's hot

MUCH A DOGGY-DOO ABOUT NOTHING

Filming *The Next Generation* could be fun, but the set could also be a dangerous place to visit. Writer Richard Manning recalled seeing deadly snakes and scorpions while filming "Who Watches the Watchers" in the desert, and vicious sand fleas attacked Patrick Stewart and Gates McFadden as they huddled in the sandpit in "Arsenal of Freedom." Most bizarrely, somewhere in the vast universe of 178 episodes of *The Next Generation* resides a celestial body that owes its existence to a dog's dinner, revealed visual effects producer Dan Curry. A pile of dog faecal matter, left steaming on a sidewalk, was scooped up by the special effects people and rushed to

Diana Muldaur joined the show in its second year, as Dr. Katherine Pulaski

disagreed. "Wesley needs a parent to guide his development," said a fan named Stefan. "Besides, while Muldaur was excellent, she was as brittle and abrupt as Picard. When you rub two crusty people together, you don't get sparks, you get breadcrumbs." A woman named Joyce said Picard was far too aloof and solitary, "and McFadden's character can do something about that."

"WHEN YOU RUB TWO CRUSTY PEOPLE TOGETHER, YOU DON'T GET SPARKS, YOU GET BREADCRUMBS."

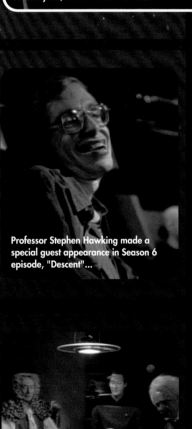

Professor Stephen Hawking made a special guest appearance in Season 6 episode, "Descent"...

Paramount Studios, where "a close-macro shot," transformed the dog's deposit into "a cool-looking planet!"

Such cheeky behind-the-scenes revelations make bigger on set controversies seem out of proportion in retrospect, but they raged at the time. Gates McFadden had turned down the role of Dr. Beverly Crusher twice, "and by the time I started to enjoy the role, they didn't want me anymore," she said. She was replaced in season two by Dr. Katherine Pulaski (Diana Muldaur) for a year. When McFadden was brought back for season three, *The Baltimore Evening News* conducted a poll as to which doctor the fans preferred. "The votes were too close to call," the paper said. The editors preferred Muldaur's character, admitting they liked her way back in 1968 when she appeared as Miranda in "Is There In Truth No Beauty?" Some readers

There were endless Kirk vs. Picard debates too, over who was better. *The Fort Worth Star-Telegram* voted for Captain Kirk, on the basis of his "camp appeal," calling him, "an icon who will survive the ages." The paper couldn't imagine any of Picard's lines being quoted 30 years from now. However, *The Los Angeles Times* chose Picard, saying Stewart's interpretation brought "a thoughtful, mature masculinity to the role," praising *The Next Generation* for showing *Star Trek* "had grown up gracefully."

Mick Fleetwood, of legendary rock group Fleetwood Mac, made a cameo appearance as a piscine alien

STAR TRIVIA

The props department created a little *Lost in Space* robot chessman for the episode "Conundrum," in homage to *Star Trek*'s 1960s competition.

All good things must come to an end, including *The Next Generation*, after seven seasons. John de Lancie reprised his role as Q for the series' 1994 finale

NOT GUEST STARRING

The late actor and comedian Robin Williams was a big fan of the series, as were Mel Brooks, actress Jean Simmons, and General Colin Powell. The *L.A.Times* reported that Stevie Wonder, Kiss bassist Gene Simmons, Sean Young and Adrienne Barbeau were all interested in making guest appearances. While they never made it into the show, musician Mick Fleetwood of Fleetwood Mac did, and he enjoyed having "to drool and slurp gelatin," playing "a naughty fish alien" in "Manhunt" – despite having to shave off his famous beard. In 1993, 70 renowned scientists gathered with physicist Stephen Hawking to watch his acting debut (playing poker with Isaac Newton and Albert Einstein) in the episode "Descent."

The Next Generation's seventh and final year grabbed its first Emmy nomination as Best Dramatic series. The last episode, "All Good Things," was a critically acclaimed two-hour finale that sent Picard forward and backward in his life, with encounters with the God-like being Q (John de Lancie). Scott Williams of *The Associated Press* said the concluding moments of the episode "were spectacular, deft and fitting... it does honor to the series, its characters and to the *Star Trek* universe."

"Some found *The Next Generation* marginally less fun than the original," said author John Clute. "But that was because *Star Trek* had grown up." Bruce Westbrook of *The Houston Chronicle* had a differing view." That fine cast had to grapple for years with

plots laden with stuffy idealism and tedious technical talk." But *TV Guide*, in a 2002 issue, ranked the series as the 46th best television show of all time. "Even die-hard Trekkers came to acknowledge that it not only equaled but surpassed the original." As the curtain closed on the series, Eric Schmuckler of *The NY Times* revealed that Paramount wanted to cancel the show "while it was at the height of its popularity," and the characters made their move to the silver screen.

For Gene Roddenberry, the high ratings and good reviews garnered by the show in 1989 were a vindication of his vision. He had achieved the near impossible by bringing *Star Trek* back to life for a new generation, saying, with characteristic humility, "I finally feel that I've become a philosopher – junior grade." ⋀

The *Enterprise*-D Bridge crew

Riker, with Wesley and Beverly Crusher

Q interupts the Farpoint mission

GIVING THE WAGON NEW WHEELS

Robert H. Justman, co-producer of the original *Star Trek* series, looks back at his part in bringing *The Next Generation* to the screen. Words: Joe Nazzaro.

It could be argued that without Robert H. Justman, the original *Star Trek* could have been a very different series. As the show's co-producer, Justman (who died on May 28, 2008 at age 81), was involved in just about every aspect of production, from casting to story ideas; a function he performed again two decades later on *Star Trek: The Next Generation*.

During production of the original series and for quite some time afterward, Justman largely kept a low profile, allowing more outspoken voices, such as series creator Gene Roddenberry, to lead the behind-the-scenes narrative. It wasn't until he teamed up with former production executive Herb Solow for their 1996 memoir "Inside *Star Trek*" that the

full scope of his contribution was spelled out. During the conversation that follows, which was conducted during promotion for that book, Justman looked back at his long and sometimes turbulent association with the franchise.

For Bob Justman, a career in show-business began as a lowly production assistant in the early 1950s, quickly moving up the ladder to

Justman was responsible
for suggesting that a Klingon
be part of the *Enterprise*-D crew

assistant director in features. "I actually started in motion pictures," he recalls, "and the very first film I did was *A Letter to Three Husbands*. I was a production assistant, a gofer. That was followed by *The Scarf*, directed by the famous hoofer director E.A. Dupont, and the most interesting thing I possibly ever worked on – not the best, but most interesting – was a remake of *M* [Fritz Lang's 1931 thriller about the search for a child killer in Berlin], which starred David Wayne, and was directed by Joseph Losey."

Other early credits included *Red Planet Mars* ["My first science fiction credit"], *Lady in the Iron Mask*, *The Moon is Blue*, *Abbot and Costello Meet Captain Kidd*, and *The Moonlighter*, which was shot in 3D and starred Barbara Stanwyck, who nicknamed the young Justman 'Killer.' "I didn't want to do something the associate producer wanted me to do and he got a bit pissy about it, so I tore off my glasses and said, 'Okay, you throw the first punch!' Barbara Stanwyck heard about that and from then on, I was 'Killer.'"

After logging dozens of films as PA and second assistant director, Justman moved into television as a first assistant director, thanks to veteran director Robert Aldrich with whom he'd worked as a production assistant on several early films. "In those days, I always had the philosophy of 'Take the first thing that comes along!' and I was never out of work. So when Bob called me and asked, 'Did you want to do this?' and I said 'sure', that was the first thing I did. Don Siegel was the other director, and they were both doing television because they weren't into features yet.

"From that, I went on to the *Superman* series, and did a full season of that, episodes of several different weekly series, and some

Justman wanted the new *Enterprise* to have families on board

"WE WERE NEVER ABLE TO FIND A HOME, AND WERE MOVED TO A TIME WHEN HALF OUR AUDIENCE WASN'T AVAILABLE"

pilots. I also did four episodes of *One Step Beyond*, six episodes of *The Mickey Mouse Club*, and a thing called *Man on the Moon* for Disney, where we took a spaceship to the moon, orbited, and then came back to Earth. It was a very interesting experience. Then I did a series with Leslie Stevens called *Stoney Burke*, and

both seasons of *The Outer Limits*. That's where I first met James Goldstone, who directed the second *Star Trek* pilot.

Although *The Outer Limits* couldn't have been more different from *Star Trek*, it was Justman's first real foray in 1960s SF television. "There wasn't a lot of money on *Star Trek*," he elaborates, "so in a way, [*The Outer Limits*] prepared me with resources that I could tap. The assistant director's tenet is, 'How can we make this as good as possible, as cheap as possible?' I didn't exactly learn to save money on *The Outer Limits*, but I learned things about optical special FX and certain resources. On *Star Trek*, I was able to hire Wah Chang, who I knew from my days on *The Outer Limits*, and I knew Fred Philips the make-up man from my days on *Stoney Burke* and the other shows."

MISSION IMPOSSIBLE?

Justman originally turned down an invitation to work on the original *Star Trek* pilot but, as luck would have it, NBC had reservations about "The Cage", ordering a second pilot that they hoped would address their concerns. When the opportunity to work on the new show came up again, he was keen to accept the challenge. "As an assistant director in television, you know how long it takes to get a set-up shot and the seat of your pants tells you how long it will take. The amount of work you have left to do will just fill up the amount of time you have left to do it in, so we worked as hard as we could on the second pilot.

"On the last day of production when we were a day over, we did two days' work in a day. That's the day that Lucy [legendary comedienne

The *Enterprise*-D boldly goes "Where No One Has Gone Before"

and owner of Desilu Studios, Lucille Ball] came on the stage, because we were supposed to have an end-of-picture party and we were still shooting. So in between set-ups, she helped Herb and me sweep out the stage and get the sand out of the way of the camera dolly. I think she just did that for effect, because she wanted to get the party started, but we worked hard, and we wouldn't have done the second pilot in that short a time if Jimmy Goldstone and I hadn't worked so well together before on *The Outer Limits.* We had a method in our madness. I always knew what set-ups Jimmy had planned to cover the work we had to do that day, and I'd arranged them so that no time would be lost, so if we'd point the camera in one direction and lit in that direction for the most part, we would shoot everything that needed to be shot that day in that direction before we turned around and shot the opposing angle."

Star Trek may have subsequently been picked up as a series, but as Rodney Dangerfield probably would have pointed out, it never really got any respect. Ratings were never very high and the budget was relatively low for the kind of material that was being produced. Meanwhile, *Mission Impossible*, the show's neighbor on the Desilu lot, was winning awards and being recognized as a compelling drama series. "It wasn't their fault that they got the Emmys, and we didn't," Justman reflects, "so there wasn't really a rivalry between us. There was kind of a wistfulness at times, a 'Gee whiz, you'd think we'd get something!' but we didn't get anything, ever on the original series – make-up, special FX, we had the most complicated sound FX, which had to be created and built – and we never got any recognition for them.

"To this day, no one from any of the *Star Trek* series has won an Emmy for acting. Patrick Stewart never got one, and I don't think he even got nominated. To me, Patrick was the best actor on nightly television at that time, but *Star Trek: The Next Generation* wasn't shown on a major network. It was syndicated, and wasn't considered a major prime-time show, so he didn't get any of the respect to which he was so richly entitled.

"The regret about the original *Star Trek* versus *Mission Impossible* is that I knew what both shows cost, having been heavily involved in each of them. Each of the three seasons that *Star Trek* was on, it made its series budget; it never went over its average budget. *Mission Impossible* was constantly over-budget, and it cost a lot more than *Star Trek* did, but CBS was a different beast than NBC; they made some extra money, and

Robert H. Justman (center, second from left) stands with Gene Roddenberry, Rick Berman, and the *Star Trek: The Next Generation* cast

"I WANTED TO SHOW THAT WE COULD MAKE *STAR TREK* SUCCESSFUL RIGHT OUT OF THE BOX"

they were more tolerant of their hit show, but we were on Thursday night at 8:30 for the first season, Friday night at 8:30 for the second season and 10:00 for the third season. We were never able to find a home, and were moved to a time when half our audience wasn't available to watch the show."

A PASSING PHASE

When the proposed *Star Trek: Phase II* was abandoned in favor of a feature-length motion picture, Justman found himself excluded from the project, and admits he had mixed emotions about starting it up all over again for *Star Trek: The Next Generation.* One of his strongest motivations for returning was to prove that a

successful *Trek* series could be made. "I wanted to work with Gene again because overall I was still his friend, but it was still stuck in the back of my mind, and I did bring the subject up. Ed Milkis was our associate producer in charge of post-production, and was working with Gene as they began to prepare *Star Trek: The Next Generation,* and I told Ed of my disappointment with Gene, about the time that he had called me when he was just about to do that first feature. I told Eddie 'Gene broke my heart,' and he told that to Gene, who as Herb has said, always found it difficult to take responsibility or to tell people things they didn't want to hear. I don't think that he didn't want me to work on the movie.

The challenge that gripped me so hard was that I wanted to show that we could make *Star Trek* successful right out of the box, and that we could make it better. I was inspired to prove so many things. That's where some of the creative ideas for the new show came about."

Just as he had a couple of decades earlier, Justman produced countless memos covering just about every aspect of the series. "There were certain things I suggested, such as having families on board, for instance. I wrote an impassioned memo to Gene about that. I also created the back-story for Captain Picard and Dr. Crusher and what happened in the past between them.

"I talked Gene into going with a Klingon, and he was utterly opposed to it. I remember him saying, 'No, we've done all that, and I don't want to repeat myself,' and I said, 'But Gene, think of the possibilities, think of what it means!' He thought about it, and the next thing you know, we had a Klingon on board.

"There were a number of things I created on *The Next Generation*, and in fact during that first season, Gene's business manager Leonard came to me and said, 'We want you to know that we appreciate everything that you've done on this show, and we're going to see to it that you get a piece of the show.' Well, I'm still looking for that piece."

MAKE IT SO

There is one contribution of which Justman was justifiably glad to have made, and that was the 'discovery' of Patrick Stewart for the lead role. "I've told this story before and Patrick would confirm it if you ever corral him, but my wife and I were attending a UCLA extension class on humor, where there was a class every couple of weeks and there would be guests who discussed their kind of humor, whatever that was. One night, there was going to be a cold reading by two actors who were going to read from Noel Coward and the Shakespeare comedies. There was a woman and a man who came out, and that man was Patrick Stewart. He looked familiar, but I hadn't placed him from *I, Claudius* or *Tinker, Tailor* and shows like that.

"Patrick sat down, pushed up his jacket sleeves to display his massive forearms and commenced to read, and after just a few sentences, I was thunderstruck. I turned to my wife Jackie, and I said, 'I think I found our new captain!'

"That was November or December of 1986, and I'd been back at Paramount preparing the show for a month or two at the most, but I was so impressed with what I saw and heard that night, I called SAG [the Screen Actor's Guild] the next day and found out who Patrick's agent was here in town, and made arrangements for Patrick to visit with Gene and me at Gene's house the following Monday. Patrick came in his rental car, and we sat around for 30-40 minutes, and then he made his good-byes and left to fly back to England.

"After he drove away, Gene closed the door and turned to me – and I will quote him exactly

The first season of *The Next Generation* featured planetary landscapes that were not disimilar to those seen in the original series

"The Naked Now" was the first regular episode of *The Next Generation* to be filmed after the pilot, and was an homage to original series episode, "The Naked Time"

Chief Engineer Argyle (Biff Yeager, center) was another short-lived addition to the rolling roster of *Enterprise*-D engineers ("Where No One Has Gone Before")

Patrick Stewart:
definitely not a hairy frenchman

– he said, 'I won't have him!' No matter what I said, he was adamant, and the reason was because the character he had created in his mind was a hairy Frenchman. So, we embarked upon a campaign that lasted for some months, and when Rick Berman came on the show and became supervising producer with me, Rick jumped all over it too and said, 'He's perfect!' Our casting director was for it, everyone was for it except Gene. We went through everybody in town, and in foreign countries, trying to find the right person to play the captain and couldn't.

"Finally, our last candidate came in, read for us and after he left, we were sitting there – the casting director, Rick, Gene and myself – and Gene finally turned around and said, 'All right, I'll go with Patrick' and that was it. I've never been surer of anything in my life, at least in the business, than casting Patrick in that role. He was everything that a captain ought to be."

NEW FRONTIERS

Justman stayed until the end of *The Next Generation*'s first season before deciding it was time to move on. "I was suffering from hypertension, overwork; I wasn't as young as I had been, I was still working 16-hour days, and it was taking its toll on me. My blood pressure rose, because I was having problems with Gene's business manager, who was interfering in what Rick Berman and I considered to be our producer functions, and it just drove me crazy. It was the only time I ever had harsh words with Gene.

"One day, I drove over to his house after Leonard Maizlish fell asleep in the middle of a casting session, right in full view of the actor who was reading for us. I was furious, and

Security Chief Tasha Yar (Denise Crosby) gets iced by Q, in "Encounter at Farpoint"

"I'VE NEVER BEEN SURER OF ANYTHING IN MY LIFE, AT LEAST IN THE BUSINESS, THAN CASTING PATRICK"

stopped the casting session, jumped in my car and rode over to Gene's house and screamed at him. It wasn't long after that I decided, 'Wait a second, I can't let this happen!' I knew the show was going to be successful, it was a terrific show, but I was lucky that I didn't have to remain at work there. I gave away a lot of money by not

coming back, but I think I also kept some hold of what little sanity remains to me, and physically, it was my salvation. I just decided to be happier and have less."

That final season marked the end of Bob Justman's participation in the franchise, and while he had mixed feelings about the various *Trek* spin-offs that followed over the years, he's proud of the foundation he helped create. "I thought *Deep Space Nine* was a very good show, but I think there were casting problems, or there weren't necessarily cast problems, but a role problem; Sisko was a role that really didn't make anything happen. It's a tough role, and [Avery Brooks] was an actor who displayed such flash and fire in [*Spencer: for Hire*] when he played a guy named Hawk. He's a marvelous actor, and has a lot of power and energy and anger, but he was playing against himself, and the character wasn't as proactive as, say, Bill Shatner had been. I felt there was a problem there, but some of the other casting choices were very good, and I thought the show was excellent. With *Voyager*, I never really watched. I kind of felt that they were over-milking it, and they never should have overlapped the series. They should have done one and then gone on to the next one. Certainly I considered *The Next Generation* one hell of a show, and every time I saw any part of an episode in any of the succeeding seasons, I was mightily impressed.

"I think the reason why *Star Trek* became popular after they started 'stripping' it, running it five nights a week, is because of its inherent message: it's a really neat thing to live a proper moral life, and to do unto others as they would do unto you, to do the right thing."

The Ferengi make their debut in *TNG*'s "The Last Outpost"

STAR TREK
THE NEXT GENERATION

SEASON 1
September 1987-May 1988

1987-88

1966
1967
1968
1969
1970
1971
1972
1973
1974
1975
1976
1977
1978
1979
1980
1981
1982
1983
1984
1985
1986
1987
1988
1989
1990
1991
1992
1993
1994
1995
1996
1997
1998
1999
2000
2001
2002
2003
2004
2005
2006
2007
2008
2009
2010
2011

1st

Encounter at Farpoint ▲▲▲▲

Writers: D. C. Fontana and Gene Roddenberry
Director: Corey Allen
September 28, 1987
Investigating the mysterious, advanced Farpoint Station, Captain Picard encounters Q, an all-powerful being who puts mankind on trial.

Though achingly slow and clunky in places, the pilot succeeds in introducing a new and interesting cast of characters, and in convincing us, despite the less-than-stellar episodes that follow, to keep tuning in week after week.

BEST MOMENT

Data escorting Admiral Leonard McCoy to the shuttlebay. A touching passing-of-the-torch scene that no doubt served to win over a significant number of classic *Trek* fans to the new series.

On January 28, 1986, the Space Shuttle *Challenger* exploded 73 seconds after liftoff, killing all seven crewmembers, including a civilian schoolteacher. The United States' space program was put on hold indefinitely and, the Space Race having long since been won, some posed the question of whether putting humans into space was really worth the risk anymore.

Just over a year and a half later, the *U.S.S. Enterprise*-D was launched on our television screens, a starship carrying over 1000 crew, including civilians and children. Within the first minutes of the pilot, "Encounter at Farpoint," the new captain, Jean-Luc Picard, and his crew are threatened by an omnipotent being called Q, who tells them mankind has ventured far enough into space, and they need to turn back. At one point he even presents himself as a contemporary U.S. Marine Corps officer to insist there are more important Earth-bound matters for them to deal with.

Needless to say, the new captain rejects this kind of talk, and before the credits roll, he and his new crew have demonstrated that they are more than worthy of continuing the previous generation's mission – not only to Q, but also to millions who would continue to tune in over the course of *Star Trek: The Next Generation*'s inaugural year.

Doing an all-new *Star Trek* series had seemed like a risk until then. Given the uproar that followed the death of Spock in *Star Trek II*, how would fans react to the lack of any familiar faces whatsoever in the new show? For that matter, how would new viewers, used to hour dramas like *Dallas* and *Hill Street Blues*, respond to this 1960s revival?

As it turned out, there was little reason to worry. Picard and Data quickly became fan favorites, despite the fact that the new captain could scarcely be more different from Kirk, and the android who wanted to be human was Spock flipped on his head. The reception given to the rest of the cast of characters was more mixed, ranging from the unexpected popularity of Worf (originally a mere background figure) to the overblown derision heaped upon boy genius Wesley Crusher. Unfortunately, the female characters got the short shrift, to such a degree that Denise Crosby asked to be released from her contract (leading to the pointless death of her character, Tasha Yar, in "Skin of Evil"), and Beverly Crusher was given an off-camera transfer during the summer hiatus.

The new series was set a century after the original, and thanks to a budget of $1 million per episode (boosted to $1.5 million by season's end), it looked a hundred years more advanced than its 20-year-old predecessor. Numerous veterans of the first four *Trek* films brought their talents to the small screen, and Industrial Light and Magic was hired to create the visual effects, including what would become the trademark "rubber band" warp

effect. These investments paid off when *TNG* received seven Emmy Award nominations, winning for costume design, sound editing, and makeup.

Where the new series was most lacking, sadly, was in the quality of its writing. Creator Gene Roddenberry had decided that 24th Century humans had evolved beyond interpersonal conflict – a premise that did not lend itself to dramatic storytelling. Roddenberry also reviewed all the scripts, and would often rewrite them without input from, or knowledge of, the original writers. But, at age 66 and in declining health, he couldn't take on the day-to-day responsibilities of running a weekly series, giving rise to power struggles and office politics among the rest of the writing staff... whoever they were any given week. Only five of the 28 writers receiving screen credit during season one (excluding Roddenberry) would return during season two.

Despite this rocky road, *TNG* enjoyed consistently strong ratings throughout its freshman year. Not only did it beat out its network competition in several U.S. markets, but Paramount was also able to rake in another $2 million in video cassette sales in foreign markets where they hadn't been able to make broadcast deals. While there was some tweaking to be done, a solid foundation had been laid, not only for the continuation of this series, but that of the *Star Trek* franchise as a whole. **William Leisner**

The Naked Now ▲▲
Teleplay: J. Michael Bingham (D. C. Fontana)
Story: John D.F. Black and J. Michael Bingham
Director: Paul Lynch
October 5, 1987
The *Enterprise* crew are infected with a virus that sees them lose their inhibitions, endangering the ship.

Code of Honor ▲▲
Writers: Katharyn Powers & Michael Baron
Director: Russ Mayberry
October 12, 1987
An alien kidnaps *Enterprise* security officer Tasha Yar to make her his wife!

The Last Outpost ▲▲
Teleplay: Herbert Wright
Story: Richard Krzemien
Director: Richard Colla
October 19, 1987
Along with a Ferengi vessel they are pursing, the *Enterprise* is trapped by an ancient alien energy beam.

Where No One Has Gone Before ▲▲
Writers: Diane Duane & Michael Reaves
Director: Rob Bowman
October 26, 1987
Breaking the warp barrier causes weird side effects for the crew of the *Enterprise*.

Lonely Among Us ▲
Worst Episode ✕
Teleplay: D. C. Fontana
Story: Michael Halperin
Director: Cliff Bole
November 2, 1987
The *Enterprise* crew must negotiate entry to the Federation for two mutually hostile races.

A lost energy bolt wanders around the *Enterprise* searching for a plot, then convinces Picard to beam into a space cloud and give up his physical existence permanently... until he decides to beam back. Plus, alien peace envoys kill and eat each other, to the consternation of no one. This episode makes even the following episode "Justice" look like a Peabody winner in comparison.

Justice ▲
Teleplay: Worley Thorne
Story: Ralph Wills (John D. F. Black) and Worley Thorne
Director: James L. Conway
November 9, 1987
Visiting a seemingly idyllic planet, the *Enterprise* crew fall foul of their harsh justice system.

2nd

The Battle ▲▲▲▲
Teleplay: Herbert Wright
Story: Larry Forrester
Director: Rob Bowman
November 16, 1987
Picard is led to his old ship, the *Stargazer*, and finds himself reliving a past battle.

Picard's backstory gets fleshed out, and the Ferengi improve from "totally ridiculous" (in "The Last Outpost") to merely "a bit silly." Patrick Stewart's performance, conveying a tumult of emotions both genuine and induced, is simply outstanding.

Hide and Q ▲▲▲
Teleplay: C. J. Holland and Gene Roddenberry
Story: C. J. Holland
Director: Cliff Bole
November 23, 1987
First Officer Riker is given the powers of the Q Continuum, causing friction with his crewmates.

John de Lancie, who in his two appearances as Q (in "Encounter at Farpoint" and "Hide and Q") manages to mix impish irreverence and dangerous arrogance in perfect proportions, quickly establishing himself as one the fans' favorite villains.

Best Guest Star

Haven ▲▲
Teleplay: Tracy Tormé
Story: Tracy Tormé and Lan O'Kun
Director: Richard Compton
November 30, 1987
Betazed tradition sees Counselor Troi take part in an arranged marriage, but her would-be husband declares she's not the woman of his dreams...

5th

The Big Goodbye ▲▲▲
Writer: Tracy Tormé
Director: Joseph L. Scanlan
January 11, 1988
Relaxing on the holodeck, Picard is trapped within a malfunctioning 1930s pulp detective simulation.

The only *Star Trek* episode ever to win the George Foster Peabody Award for Excellence in Television Broadcasting. For this, we can forgive it for spawning the 5,218 holodeck malfunction tales that followed.

Datalore ▲▲▲
Teleplay: Robert Lewin and Gene Roddenberry
Story: Robert Lewin & Maurice Hurley
Director: Rob Bowman
January 18, 1988
Android Data discovers his 'brother', the misguided Lore, who tries to take over the *Enterprise*.

Angel One ▲▲
Writer: Patrick Barry
Director: Michael Rhodes
January 25, 1988
Riker helps rebels on a planet ruled by women.

11001001 ▲▲▲
Writers: Maurice Hurley & Robert Lewin
Director: Paul Lynch
February 1, 1988
When upgrading the ship's computer systems, the Bynars steal the *Enterprise* in an attempt to save their species.

Too Short a Season ▲▲▲
Teleplay: Michael Michaelian and D. C. Fontana
Story: Michael Michaelian
Director: Rob Bowman
February 8, 1988
Picard takes an old Starfleet Admiral back to the scene of a diplomatic victory 40 years before, only to find all is not as it seems.

When the Bough Breaks ▲▲
Writer: Hannah Louise Shearer
Director: Kim Manners
February 15, 1988
The *Enterprise* discovers a mythical planet whose barren inhabitants offer to swap their technology for the ship's children...

Home Soil ▲▲▲
Teleplay: Robert Sabaroff
Story: Karl Geurs & Ralph Sanchez and Robert Sabaroff
Director: Corey Allen
February 22, 1988
A terraforming project threatens a newly discovered life-form, which uses the *Enterprise* to declare war on humanity.

Coming of Age ▲▲▲
Writer: Sandy Fries
Director: Mike Vejar
March 14, 1988
Wesley sits his Starfleet entrance exam, while Picard is investigated for violating the Prime Directive.

Heart of Glory ▲▲▲
Teleplay: Maurice Hurley
Story: Maurice Hurley and Herbert Wright & D.C. Fontana
Director: Rob Bowman
March 21, 1988
Rebel Klingons, who fear their alliance with the Federation is sapping their warrior spirit, try to co-opt Worf to their cause.

MOST VALUED PERFORMANCE

Picard could have been a stiff old stick-in-the-mud who sat on the bridge while his young first officer beamed off into adventure every week. Patrick Stewart not only brought a tremendous degree of gravitas to the role, but also was able to bring depth and nuances to the character that elevated even the worst stories and dialogue. Had a lesser actor taken the role, the question "Kirk or Picard?" would likely never even have been asked, let alone seriously debated.

3rd

The Arsenal of Freedom ▲▲▲▲
Teleplay: Richard Manning & Hans Beimler
Story: Maurice Hurley & Robert Lewin
Director: Les Landau
April 11, 1988
The *Enterprise* faces an alien weapon that wiped out its creators.

TNG takes on the global weapons trade in the vein of classic *Trek*, with an elegantly simple and surprising resolution, plus some very good building of the Picard-Crusher relationship and backstory.

Symbiosis ▲▲▲▲
Teleplay: Robert Lewin and Richard Manning & Hans Beimler
Story: Robert Lewin
Director: Win Phelps
April 18, 1988
Two groups battling over an addictive drug are helped by the crew of the *Enterprise*.

Skin of Evil ▲▲
Teleplay: Joseph Stefano and Hannah Louise Shearer
Story: Joseph Stefano
Director: Joseph L. Scanlan
April 25, 1988
A pool of living oil – a kind of concentrated evil – kills a key member of the *Enterprise* bridge crew.

We'll Always Have Paris ▲▲▲
Writers: Deborah Dean Davis & Hannah Louise Shearer
Director: Robert Becker
May 2, 1988
Picard encounters a former lover and has to deal with her husband's disruptive time experiments.

4th

Conspiracy ▲▲▲▲
Teleplay: Tracy Tormé
Story: Robert Sabaroff
Director: Cliff Bole
May 9, 1988
The *Enterprise* uncovers a conspiracy that is controlling senior Starfleet personnel through alien parasites.

The darkest *Trek* episode to date, and the first hint that the new series was willing and able to push the limits of what could be done within the confines of Gene Roddenberry's universe.

The Neutral Zone ▲▲▲
Television Story and Teleplay: Maurice Hurley
From a Story by: Deborah McIntyre & Mona Clee
Director: James L. Conway
May 16, 1988
Picard faces a new Romulan threat, while revived frozen humans from the 20th Century cause problems on the *Enterprise*.

Amidst the chaos and fallout of the 1988 Writers Guild of America strike, the second season of *Star Trek: The Next Generation* premiered.

The show's producers and writer-producers struggled to write (yet not write) scripts for the young show that was still finding its way. Last-minute solutions to the lack of available scripts prompted the staff to mine old, previously purchased scripts for the developed, but never produced, series *Star Trek: Phase II*. The first script of the season, "The Child," was one of these 're-name the characters and shoot it' re-purposed scripts. The transposal was not as difficult as it seemed, as the *Phase II* scripts were based on *Star Trek: The Motion Picture* characters including Will Decker and Ilia, which translated reasonably well to *Next Generation* characters Will Riker and Deanna Troi. Yet the dearth of completed scripts ultimately resulted in not only a later start to the season (November, rather than September), but the shortest season of the show's run – 22 episodes instead of the usual 26. And it prompted a season finale with that last-ditch filler effort that every show tries to avoid: a clip show, re-running the highlights of previous episodes in an attempt to fill time.

Though the show had started out of the gate with strong ratings, the producers felt there was still room for improvement in the formula, so during the break between seasons one and two, Gates McFadden's Dr. Beverly Crusher character was dropped. And in an attempt to bring more of an original series feeling to the show, the character of an irascible but highly-skilled doctor, original series guest star Diana Muldaur's Dr. Katherine Pulaski, was brought in to replace Crusher, whose character was mentioned in passing as being promoted to run Starfleet Medical. Pulaski's human vs. android ongoing conflict with Data was seen as an attempt to recreate the Dr. McCoy/Spock squabbling-but-fond relationship.

Other changes to the status quo in the second season included a new hairstyle for Deanna Troi and a settling into her look for much of the rest of the series with off-color jumpsuits, while Security Chief Worf and new Chief Engineer Geordi La Forge moved into their gold uniforms and Will Riker grew a beard.

Budgeting for the new season allowed for a new standing set to be built, a place for the crew to gather socially, called Ten Forward. This also brought the introduction of a recurring character who would quickly become a fan favorite, Whoopi Goldberg's wise alien bartender, Guinan. Her mysterious past and history with Captain Jean-Luc Picard added a welcome ongoing arc to the show and gave Picard the closest thing he had to a friend and confidante outside of the ship's command staff. Guinan quickly became not only Picard's sounding board, but the rest of the crew grew to rely on her age-old perspective as well.

Still, it was overall a transition season. Between the writers' strike challenges and the still-not-quite-there chemistry among the characters, the show had not quite found its way yet. So the stories of this shortened season seemed like a mix of lesser-quality season one holdovers, with a few sparkling gems that showed the promise of what the show would ultimately become, as it continued to capitalize on the popularity of and fascination with the character of Data.

One major hallmark of the season however, would be the introduction of what would become one of the *Star Trek* universe's most dreaded foes: the Borg. In an episode that featured the return of that omnipotent troublemaker, Q, the *Enterprise*-D crew was inadvertently made aware of, and therefore given a chance to prepare for, a foe that would provoke a conflict that would tear its way across multiple shows, crews, and quadrants of the galaxy and would eventually feature strongly in the hit *TNG* film *Star Trek: First Contact*.

In all, a mixed bag of a season, but one that would at least be appreciated for introducing some of the show's most popular guest characters including Worf's love interest K'Ehleyr and Data's Sherlockian foe, Moriarty.

Jill Sherwin

STAR TREK
THE NEXT GENERATION
SEASON 2
November 1988-July 1989

1988-89

1966
1967
1968
1969
1970
1971
1972
1973
1974
1975
1976
1977
1978
1979
1980
1981
1982
1983
1984
1985
1986
1987
1988
1989
1990
1991
1992
1993
1994
1995
1996
1997
1998
1999
2000
2001
2002
2003
2004
2005
2006
2007
2008
2009
2010
2011

The Child ^^
Writers: Jaron Summers & Jon Povill and Maurice Hurley
Director: Rob Bowman
November 21, 1988
Counselor Troi is suddenly pregnant – and the baby will be born in 36 hours!

Where Silence Has Lease ^^
Writer: Jack B. Sowards
Director: Winrich Kolbe
November 28, 1988
An all-powerful being threatens to kill half the *Enterprise* crew, all in the interest of a science experiment.

2nd

Elementary, Dear Data ^^^^^
Writer: Brian Alan Lane
Director: Rob Bowman
December 5, 1988
Data plays Sherlock Holmes on the holodeck, but will Moriarty prove to be smarter?

Building on the first season's "The Big Goodbye" fish out of water/trapped in the holodeck story, "Elementary, Dear Data" adds wonderful character interaction between La Forge and Data, the spice of Pulaski's goading commentary and a tour-de-force, deadly yet sympathetic and ultimately tragic turn by Daniel Davis as Moriarty. This mystery to challenge Data is not only one of the most entertaining episodes of the season, but of the series itself.

Best Guest Star

This is a tough call in a season that introduced both Diana Muldaur's Pulaski and Whoopi Goldberg's Guinan as regular recurring guest stars, not to mention Suzie Plakson's terrific turn as K'Ehleyr in "The Emissary." But if there was one character who stole viewers' hearts with great dignity and menace intact, it was **Daniel Davis'** Moriarty.

The Outrageous Okona ^^^
Teleplay: Burton Armus
Story: Les Menchen & Lance Dickson and David Landsberg
Director: Robert Becker
December 12, 1988
A larger-than-life rogue arrives on the *Enterprise* with two alien ships in hot pursuit.

Loud As A Whisper ^^^^
Writer: Jacqueline Zambrano
Director: Larry Shaw
January 9, 1989
A diplomatic mission is threatened when a negotiator's translators are killed.

The Schizoid Man ^^^^
Teleplay: Tracy Tormé
Story: Richard Manning & Hans Beimler
Director: Les Landau
January 23, 1989
A dying android specialist uploads his consciousness into Data.

Unnatural Selection ^^^
Writers: John Mason & Mike Gray
Director: Paul Lynch
January 30, 1989
Dr. Pulaski tries to discover a cure to an aging disease, before she dies of old age!

A Matter Of Honor ^^^^
Teleplay: Burton Armus
Story: Wanda M. Haight & Gregory Amos and Burton Armus
Director: Rob Bowman
February 6, 1989
Riker serves on a Klingon ship only to find he's expected to lead an attack on the *Enterprise*.

1st

The Measure Of A Man ^^^^^
Writer: Melinda M. Snodgrass
Director: Robert Scheerer
February 13, 1989
A hearing must decide on the status of Data: is he a machine or a person?

While strong on Data episodes, season two also gave Riker a chance to shine as the smart military man ("A Matter Of Honor"), lawyer ("The Measure Of A Man"), lover ("The Dauphin", "Up The Long Ladder"), and leader ("Peak Performance") – this episode spotlights the strength in both characters as well as Picard. It manages to be a quintessential *Star Trek* episode that takes on one of the big questions: what is humanity? This story also starts the tradition of the crew playing poker together which would continue to the end of the series.

The Dauphin ^^
Writers: Scott Rubenstein & Leonard Mlodinow
Director: Rob Bowman
February 20, 1989
Wesley Crusher experiences first love, but what secret is she hiding?

Contagion ^^^
Writers: Steve Gerber & Beth Woods
Director: Joseph L. Scanlan
March 20, 1989
Investigating the destruction of the *Enterprise's* sister ship *Yamato*, Picard finds his own vessel malfunctioning in the same way...

The Royale ^^
Writer: Keith Mills
Director: Cliff Bole
March 27, 1989
A 21st-Century astronaut is discovered living out his afterlife in an alien-created environment based on a pulp novel.

Time Squared ▲▲▲
Teleplay: Maurice Hurley
Story: Kurt Michael Bensmiller
Director: Joseph L. Scanlan
April 3, 1989
The *Enterprise* faces destruction in six hours – or so claims a version of Captain Picard from the future!

The Icarus Factor ▲▲▲
Teleplay: David Assael and Robert L. McCullough
Story: David Assael
Director: Robert Iscove
April 24, 1989
Worf tries to resist the traditional 'ascension' ceremony, while Riker reunites with his competitive father.

Pen Pals ▲▲▲▲
Teleplay: Melinda M. Snodgrass
Story: Hannah Louise Shearer
Director: Winrich Kolbe
May 1, 1989
A planet facing destruction attracts the attention of Data, when an innocent young girl contacts him.

Like "The Measure Of A Man," this episode is a philosophic and practical questioning of the values of both humanity and Starfleet – in this case, through a choice between saving a life and breaking the Prime Directive. In one of the better Wesley Crusher subplots, the acting ensign must face the challenges of his first command, confronting his own fears and self-doubts in the process.

5th

Q Who ▲▲▲▲▲ **3rd**
Writer: Maurice Hurley
Director: Rob Bowman
May 8, 1989
The mysterious Q reappears and zaps the *Enterprise* to a distant area of space where they encounter the cybernetic Borg.

A triple play of Q impishness, Guinan mystery, and the introduction of the greatest foe of the 24th Century – the Borg. Throw in some lessons in humility for our over-confident Starfleet crew who learn they are not as invincible as they thought, and this is one for the ages. It also follows up the mystery of the season one finale of what may have attacked the outposts along the Neutral Zone.

BEST MOMENT   Picard's realization that Q did them a favor by showing them they're not as strong or safe as they thought with the introduction of new enemy, the Borg. This was not only a turning point for the series, but would ultimately have repercussions across the entire franchise.

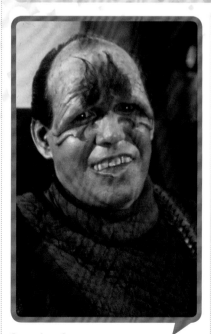

Samaritan Snare ▲
Writer: Robert L. McCullough
Director: Les Landau
May 15, 1989
Picard faces a serious operation, while aliens who need an engineer kidnap Geordi La Forge.

Up the Long Ladder ▲▲▲
Writer: Melinda M. Snodgrass
Director: Winrich Kolbe
May 22, 1989
A distress call brings the *Enterprise* to the wreckage of the long-lost *SS Mariposa* and an encounter with the descendants of the original crew.

Manhunt ▲
Writer: Terry Devereaux
Director: Rob Bowman
June 19, 1989
Troi's mother arrives on the *Enterprise* and sets her sights on Picard.

The Emissary ▲▲▲▲

4th

Television Story and Teleplay: Richard Manning & Hans Beimler

Based on an unpublished story by Thomas H. Calder

Director: Cliff Bole

June 29, 1989

A revived Klingon, who doesn't know the war with the Federation is over, is pursued by the *Enterprise*.

Featuring one of *TNG's* best guest stars as one of the strongest female characters in *Star Trek* with Suzie Plakson's K'Ehleyr, this episode and character managed to make Worf more than one-dimensional while wrapped around a plot with a good central moral dilemma – when faced with an enemy intent on killing you, is there an alternate solution beyond killing them? Snappy writing and a witty delivery by Plakson allow for several humorous moments amongst the dramatic tension.

MOST VALUED PERFORMANCE

Diana Muldaur brought a taste of original series flavor to a show still struggling to find its way. Ultimately, *TNG* discovered its own voice, but that push from a piece of its own history may have helped guide the way. Her caustic but loveable Dr. Katherine Pulaski may not have worked as a permanent part of the crew, but her humanity helped Data explore his own and her heart brought a new warmth to the still somewhat sterile sophomore season.

Peak Performance ▲▲▲

Writer: David Kemper

Director: Robert Scheerer

July 10, 1989

A war game goes wrong for the *Enterprise* when the Ferengi get involved.

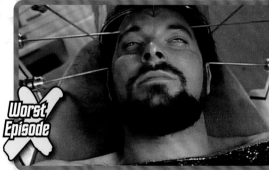

Worst Episode

Shades of Gray ▲

Teleplay by Maurice Hurley and Richard Manning & Hans Beimler

Story: Maurice Hurley

Director: Rob Bowman

July 17, 1989

Riker is attacked by an alien vine and the only way to save him is to review previous episodes.

There's just no way to make a good clip show – especially when a series has only been on the air for two seasons.

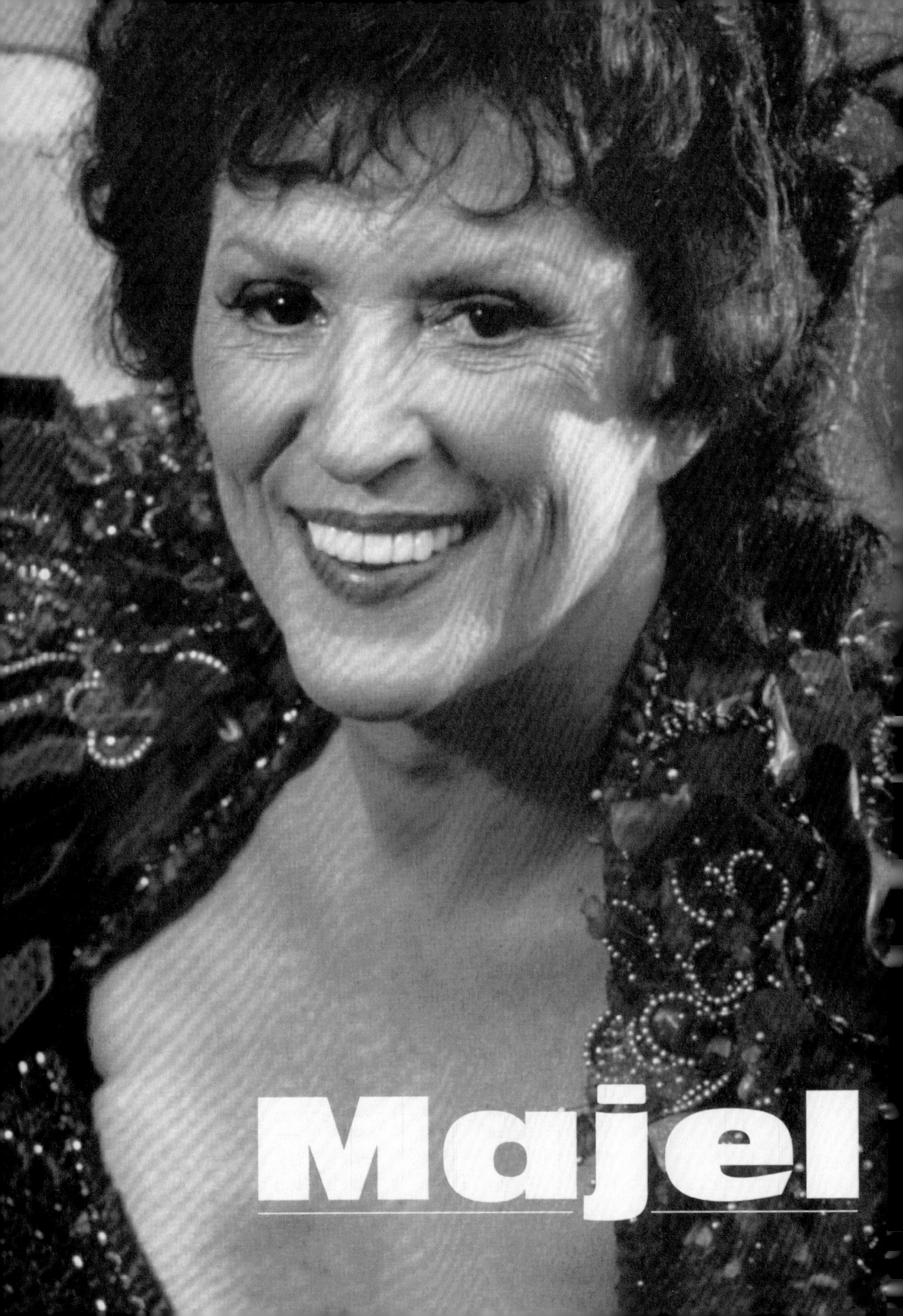
Majel

*"I've had women shout to me across parking lots things like:
'You've done more than anybody for women our age.'
I'm really glad when I hear people that appreciative."*

SPANNING GENERATIONS

**Justin Keay caught up with Majel Barrett during her whistle-stop tour
of Britain at London's *Forbidden Planet*...**

Throughout *Star Trek*'s **29 year mission Majel Barrett has been one of the few constants in the show.** Indeed, with the passing of her husband, the late Gene Roddenberry, many fans regard her as the leading 'keeper of the faith' - one reason, aside from her genuinely warm and outgoing personality, why she is always a favourite at conventions. (Indeed, Majel's concern for fans was demonstrated by the fact that

for many years she took much of the responsibility for answering the thousands of letters that started arriving soon after the original series was shelved, back in 1969.) Certainly she is unique in being the only cast member to have featured in all of the show's five incarnations. Following her appearance as Number One in *The Cage*, the pilot rejected by the studios as 'too cerebral', she found herself demoted to Nurse Chapel when the original series was finally shown a green light, a character who more than once expressed strong admiration for Mr Spock. She went on to play the same role – vocally – in the short-lived animated series of the early Seventies – which purists are often wont to ignore.

In *Star Trek: The Next Generation*, in a complete change of persona, Majel was – is – the inimitable Lwaxana Troi, Deanna Troi's often embarrassing, always outspoken, but fundamentally caring 'mother from hell.' And if she wasn't being seen as Lwaxana, she was being heard as the computer voice, something which she carried on to *Star Trek: Deep Space Nine* – where she also reprised her role as the person she describes as 'the Auntie Mame of the Universe' – and *Star Trek: Voyager*.

"Lwaxana is a great character, full of life, even if she is a little self-centred", says Barrett. "I think it is important that she is now becoming more real, more three-dimensional than she was in some of her earlier appearances." The actress feels this process began to happen during one of her own personal favourite *ST:TNG* episodes, *Half a Life*, with David Ogden-Stiers (of *M.A.S.H.* fame) playing Dr Timicin, a scientist sent onto the *U.S.S. Enterprise* to research stellar ignition theories that may help rescue the star circling his own planet. Dr Timicin is approaching 60, an age at which people of his race must commit suicide to save their children the burden of caring for them in old age. In *Half a Life*, Lwaxana reveals a more tender side to her personality; rather than being just a man-hunter she is seen as having concern for Dr Timicin's fate, in fact as being more than a little in love with him.

"It was important to show that Lwaxana wasn't just interested in chasing Picard", she jokes, admitting that that angle of Lwaxana was worked "about as hard as it could: they had nowhere else to go." She adds: "Lwaxana has feelings, she's a real person, with a heart of gold. And people like her, in spite of herself."

Majel admits to being delighted at the way viewers – not just fans – have taken to the character, particularly, she says, without really understanding why – including men aged between 18 and 30 and, more understandably, women over 40.

"God, I've had women shout to me across parking lots things like: 'You've done more than anybody for women our age.' I'm really glad when I hear people that appreciative."

Opposite: *The founding mother...*
Left: *With daughter in hand... Majel packs the house in a mini signing tour (Photo by Dick Jude)*

Barrett

Barrett's other two favourite *Star Trek: The Next Generation* episodes are *Cost of Living* and *Dark Page*. In the first, Lwaxana announces her engagement to a man she has never met and her decision to be married according to Betazoid custom – that is to say – *au naturel*. The episode also marks the start of her friendship with Worf's son, Alexander. In the other episode, she is haunted by the memory of another daughter, Kestra, who accidentally drowned when Deanna was but an infant.

Although Majel's memories of *Star Trek: The Next Generation* are positive - "Believe me", she says "it didn't feel like work at all" – some of her best memories go back to the show's early days.

"At the very start, *Star Trek* was something which Gene wanted as a vehicle for me, his wife: hence Number One", she recalls. "The show just went from there. People ask me whether I am surprised at the huge response that the show's had over the years, and I have

to say I am.

"You must remember that *Star Trek* only really became a hit in syndication; as far as the studio was concerned, at the time, those 79 episodes were just 79 opportunities to sell soap and toothpaste."

Asked what she feels it is that makes the *Star Trek* phenomenon so special, she says she has no doubt that it was Gene Roddenberry's vision which made possible a show of 'infinite diversity and infinite combinations.'

"It seems hard to believe now with what's on television, but back in those early days there were so many things that you were not allowed to discuss, or even hint at. Gene realised that you could get around that as long as the people involved were wearing strange colours and hairdos: in fact you could talk about anything as long as you covered it up like that!"

> *"People ask me whether I am surprised at the huge response that the show's had over the years, and I have to say I am... As far as the studio was concerned, at the time, those 79 episodes were just 79 opportunities to sell soap"*

Yet despite his satisfaction with the series, Majel admits that Roddenberry was unsettled with one aspect of his creation: the Klingons. She says he hated them when he introduced them in the original series but then came to realise that what he'd done was to invent a race of people that were wholly bad. That was not only improbable but, in many ways, out of keeping with the *Star Trek* ethos. When planning *Star Trek: The Next Generation*, Majel suggests that the original plan was to do away with them – until fans got to hear of it and Plan B was adopted: keep them, with their fierce 'guys, you've gotta watch out for' image, but have them join the Federation.

Conscious that she is, in many ways, the guardian of Gene Roddenberry's legacy (going so far as to co-ordinate publication of Roddenberry's quite separate creation, *Lost Universe*, for *Tekno Comics*), Majel has no complaints about the way *Star Trek* has developed under Executive Producers *Rick Berman* and *Michael Piller*. ST:TNG was a natural successor to the original series – and was monitored by Roddenberry right up to his death during its fifth year – while *Star Trek: Voyager* follows that legacy directly. But what about ST:DS9? Does she hold with any of the criticisms that have been made, that by being based in one place – the space-station *Deep Space Nine* – and concentrating on the soapier aspects of the inter-galactic relationships, it somehow broke away from Roddenberry's vision?

"I think with the third series things have been coming around nicely: there is a good combination of things going on. I guess in the early episodes, they did go off at a deep

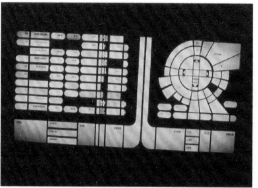

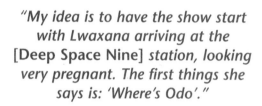

"My idea is to have the show start with Lwaxana arriving at the [Deep Space Nine] station, looking very pregnant. The first things she says is: 'Where's Odo'."

end and move away from Gene's thing, but that's come right around. Now they're giving what audiences want." Her personal favourite from that show is *The Forsaken*, when Lwaxana reveals her feelings for Odo after the Shapeshifter – desperate to return to liquid form – is obliged to 'morph' into the folds of her dress.

She feels *ST:DS9*'s new direction will continue as its fourth year develops, especially now that Michael Dorn is to be a regular on the show. The plan is to turn the Klingons into bad guys again, excepting Worf, of course.

As for the future, 'Lwaxana-like', Majel is holding her cards close to her chest. She has submitted a story idea for *ST:DS9*, the details of which she is reluctant to give out.

"Let's just say, my idea is to have the show start with Lwaxana arriving at the station, looking very pregnant. The first thing she says is: 'Where's Odo'."

She also admits that she has received a proposal to appear in another science fiction show – but can say no more. (Since this interview was written, we now know it will be *Babylon 5*, following on the heels of Walter Koenig in a role 'very different' to her *Star Trek* work – Ed.)

One thing she emphatically denies is the rumour that Lwaxana Troi dies in the new, forthcoming *Star Trek: The Next Generation* movie, which is still in the scripting stages, and about which only one thing appears to be known: that it features the Borg. As far as she is concerned, that is just another example of the *Star Trek* rumour-mill working overtime, and usually over the Internet.

"I was so upset when I heard that. Apparently, Lwaxana dies while trying to save the ship. I immediately rang Rick (Berman) and said 'Rick: what's all this? I don't wanna die.' He said ignore it: it was the first thing he'd heard about it. I gather there have been some script changes, though."

Of one thing there can be no doubt, however: *Star Trek* has not seen the back of Majel Barrett, a.k.a. Number One, a.k.a. Nurse Chapel, a.k.a. Lwaxana Troi, a.k.a. the voice of the computer. Indeed, it will probably only be a matter of time before she somehow makes an appearance in *Star Trek: Voyager*. Despite the difficulties of getting to the Delta Quadrant, if Q can do it, then it seems inevitable that Lwaxana will somehow find a way... ∎

MAJEL BARRETT IN STAR TREK

CLASSIC STAR TREK
Played Number One in The Cage
Played Nurse Christine Chapel from season one to three. Highlights include her passion for Spock, most in evidence in stories such as The Naked Time. *Her fiancé, Dr Roger Korby, was found on a planet run by androids in the episode* What Are Little Girls Made Of?

STAR TREK: THE ANIMATED SERIES
Played voice of Nurse Christine Chapel for seasons one and two, along with other voices such as Spock's mother, Amanda, in Yesteryear *and Lt. M'Ress in* The Survivor *(and others)*

STAR TREK FILMS
Dr Christine Chapel in Star Trek: The Motion Picture *and* Star Trek IV: The Voyage Home

STAR TREK: THE NEXT GENERATION
Guest-starred as Lwaxana Troi in Haven, Manhunt, Ménage à Troi, Half a Life, Cost of Living *and* Dark Page
Barrett also featured as the voice of the computer in many episodes, going uncredited in earlier shows

STAR TREK: DEEP SPACE NINE
So far, has guest-starred as Lwaxana Troi in The Forsaken *and* Fascination. *She's also featured as the voice of the computer in* Emissary *and other succeeding episodes*

STAR TREK: VOYAGER
Featured as the voice of the computer in The Caretaker *and other succeeding episodes*

Barrett has also provided the computer voice for the Star Trek Omnipedia, *the* ST:TNG Interactive Technical Manual *and the* Star Trek: Deep Space Nine *VoicePrint software. See this month's* The Most Toys *for further information on these products*

STAR TREK
THE NEXT GENERATION
SEASON 3
September 1989-June 1990

The behind-the-scenes turmoil that led to the first two seasons feeling incredibly inconsistent began to fade with the arrival of a new set of writers and producers. As Gene Roddenberry grew frailer and ceded more day-to-day control to producer Rick Berman, the show also bid farewell to the exhausted head writer Maurice Hurley. He was briefly replaced by Michael Wagner, but illness forced him to leave after just four episodes. However his recommended replacement, Michael Piller, proved to be the turning point in the show's fortunes. As Berman focused on the physical aspects, Piller took control of the writing staff, incorporating input from the actors, especially Patrick Stewart, who not only wanted to see Picard off the bridge more often, but running, shooting, fighting, and kissing babes.

The cast had also been complaining about the physical discomfort caused by the spandex uniforms. They were retooled by newly arrived costumer Bob Blackman, and made looser with the addition of the high collar. However, complaints continued, so during the season, the regulars received near-wool gabardine outfits, with the men welcoming the jackets while the women continued to wear one-piece outfits.

The most significant alteration to the writing staff was most likely the arrival of Ronald D. Moore, who submitted "The Bonding" as a spec script and was promptly hired on staff. His familiarity with the original series helped him tremendously, and

he also quickly grew to be the writer to focus most on the Klingon culture, which resulted in significant developments for Worf and the Federation's allies.

The show's evolution went beyond stronger scripts as the series truly lightened up with the elevation of Marvin V. Rush to cinematographer. The change meant the show went for brighter and bolder colors, establishing a look for the remainder of the series.

Another significant addition was the return of Gates McFadden as Beverly Crusher. Other character alterations saw Crusher's son Wesley receive a field promotion to ensign, while Geordi La Forge was promoted from lieutenant to lieutenant commander and Worf advanced from lieutenant j.g. to full lieutenant – none of which required walking the plank (as he would have to do in the later *Star Trek Generations*.)

All told, the changes on camera and behind it meant the show was maturing, and fast. We got a greater sense of cosmic politics through episodes like "The Defector" and "Sins of the Father." More character-centric shows allowed different members of the ensemble to shine, notably Brent Spiner in "The Offspring" and Dorn in "Sins" and "The Bonding." Jonathan Frakes began his directing career this season with the moving Data tale "The Offspring," making an impact away from Riker, a character that may have experienced the least challenges this season.

The ensemble was augmented with many returning guest stars led by the delightful John de

Lancie and Majel Barrett. We also welcomed back old friends in the moving "Yesterday's Enterprise" and Mark Lenard's turn as "Sarek." New additions to the canon included Reg Barclay (Dwight Schultz), who became a favorite and was brought back in subsequent seasons. Whoopi Goldberg made scant appearances as Guinan and Colm Meaney continued to man the transporters as O'Brien (who didn't get a first name yet).

The third season's most significant impact, perhaps, is the final episode, the series' first cliffhanger and a ratcheting up of the threat level. The Borg, introduced a season earlier with a warning from Q, finally arrived and wanted to add mankind to their diversity. Seeing Picard assimilated as Locutus, followed by Riker's order to fire phasers, meant fans had a very long summer of anticipation ahead of them. It was the first time a threat was introduced with lasting repercussions, unlike the thread introduced at the end of season one.

The year's ratings started strong but significantly grew as more stations added the syndicated series to their schedules. It was clear the improved series was not going to disappear, and it had a strong following. The producers' peers seemed to acknowledge the improvement, with six episodes receiving eight Emmy nominations, "Yesterday's Enterprise" receiving an award for Outstanding Sound Editing for a Series and "Sins of the Father" winning for Best Art Direction for a Series.

Robert Greenberger

Evolution ᴧᴧ
Writers: Michael Piller and Michael Wagner
Director: Winrich Kolbe
September 25, 1989
Wesley Crusher's genetics project infests the *Enterprise* with nanites.

The Ensigns of Command ᴧᴧᴧ
Writer: Melinda M. Snodgrass
Director: Cliff Bole
October 2, 1989
A colony under threat refuses to be evacuated, until Data intervenes.

The Survivors ᴧᴧ
Writer: Michael Wagner
Director: Les Landau
October 9, 1989
Picard investigates a pair of elderly humans who appear to have survived the destruction of a colony.

Who Watches the Watchers ᴧᴧ
Writer: Richard Manning and Hans Beimler
Director: Robert Wiemer
October 16, 1989
An accident reveals a Federation observation team to a feudal society...

The Bonding ᴧᴧᴧ
Writer: Ronald D. Moore
Director: Winrich Kolbe
October 23, 1989
When an *Enterprise* crewmember is killed in the field, Worf takes on responsibility for her young son.

Booby Trap ᴧᴧᴧ
Writers: Ron Roman, Michael Piller, and Richard Danus
Director: Gabrielle Beaumont
October 30, 1989
When the *Enterprise* is trapped, Geordi turns to a hologram of the ship's designer Dr. Leah Brahms for help, with unexpected consequences.

The Enemy ᴧᴧ
Writers: David Kemper and Michael Piller
Director: David Carson
November 6, 1989
Trapped on an alien world, Geordi has to work with a Romulan to save the *Enterprise*.

The Price ᴧᴧ
Writer: Hannah Louise Shearer
Director: Robert Scheerer
November 13, 1989
Troi is manipulated by a half-Betazoid, who seduces her to gain access to a stable wormhole.

The Vengeance Factor ᴧ
Writer: Sam Rolfe
Director: Timothy Bond
November 20, 1989
The *Enterprise* falls foul of space pirates, with Riker forced into a dreadful sacrifice.

The Defector ᴧᴧᴧ
Writer: Ronald D. Moore
Director: Robert Scheerer
January 1, 1990
A Romulan defector comes aboard the *Enterprise*.

The Hunted ᴧ
Writer: Robin Bernheim
Director: Cliff Bole
January 8, 1990
A super soldier who escapes from prison threatens a planet's entry to the Federation.

1989-90

Worst Episode

The High Ground ᴧ
Writer: Melinda M. Snodgrass
Director: Gabrielle Beaumont
January 29, 1990
Terrorists threaten the *Enterprise* as part of their fight for freedom.

One of the last scripts to show the interference of many hands, this tale of kidnapping and terrorism without a strong point of view leaves the crew and viewers extremely dissatisfied.

Déjà Q ᴧᴧᴧᴧ
Writer: Richard Danus
Director: Les Landau
February 5, 1990
There's only one person who can help Q when he loses his powers: Captain Picard!

BEST MOMENT

After attempting to understand human emotions for nearly three seasons, Q gifts Data with one taste, allowing the android to belly laugh at the conclusion of this episode.

1966
1967
1968
1969
1970
1971
1972
1973
1974
1975
1976
1977
1978
1979
1980
1981
1982
1983
1984
1985
1986
1987
1988
1989
1990
1991
1992
1993
1994
1995
1996
1997
1998
1999
2000
2001
2002
2003
2004
2005
2006
2007
2008
2009
2010
2011

A Matter of Perspective ▲▲
Writer: Ed Zuckerman
Director: Cliff Bole
February 12, 1990
Riker is arrested for murder; his only hope of proving his innocence is a holodeck recreation of events.

Yesterday's Enterprise ▲▲▲▲▲
Teleplay: Ira Steven Behr, Richard Manning, Hans Beimler, and Ronald D. Moore
Story: Trent Christopher Ganino & Eric A. Stillwell
Director: David Carson
February 19, 1990
A temporal rift finds an alternate *Enterprise* at war with the Klingons.

Not only does the show provide connective tissue between the original series and *TNG*, but it shows us a fascinating "What If" scenario for Tasha Yar (Denise Crosby).

Not since "Mirror, Mirror" had *Star Trek* ventured into an alternate reality as it did in "Yesterday's Enterprise." Audiences got to experience not merely the slightly altered versions of the *Enterprise*-D and her crew, but the immediate predecessor in the ship's lineage was also revealed, and Security Chief Natasha Yar, dead for nearly two years, made a surprise comeback.

The Offspring ▲▲▲▲
Writer: René Echevarria
Director: Jonathan Frakes
March 12, 1990
Data builds himself a daughter, called Lal, but will he get to keep her?

Sins of the Father ▲▲▲▲▲
Teleplay: Ronald D. Moore, and W. Reed Moran
Based on a Teleplay by: Drew Deighan
Director: Les Landau
March 19, 1990
Worf meets his brother and discovers his father has been branded a traitor.

Worf finally begins to develop his noble, distinctive personality in this story, that shows that he is more Klingon than his brethren, willing to accept discommendation from his people to preserve the peace.

Allegiance ▲
Writers: Richard Manning and Hans Beimler
Director: Winrich Kolbe
March 26, 1990
Picard is replaced by a duplicate by aliens exploring issues of leadership and individuality.

Captain's Holiday ▲▲▲
Writer: Ira Steven Behr
Director: Chip Chalmers
April 2, 1990
Even on holiday Picard can't avoid trouble, getting caught up in the quest for a mythical weapon.

The lighter side of Picard shines through in this episode, that also introduces us to Vash, one of the more interesting female foils for the captain.

Tin Man ▲▲
Writers: Dennis Putman Bailey and David Bischoff
Director: Robert Scheerer
April 23, 1990
The Romulans and the *Enterprise* race to uncover the nature of a strange life-form.

Hollow Pursuits ▲▲▲
Writer: Sally Caves
Director: Cliff Bole
April 30, 1990
Enterprise crewmember Reg Barclay hides from the real world in an elaborate holodeck simulation.

The Most Toys ▲▲
Writer: Shari Goodhartz
Director: Tim Bond
May 7, 1990
A collector of rare items snatches Data, leaving the *Enterprise* crew believing the android has been destroyed.

Sarek ▲▲▲▲

5th

Writer: Peter S. Beagle
Director: Les Landau
May 14, 1990
A terminally ill Ambassador Sarek – Spock's father – arrives on the *Enterprise* to lead a diplomatic mission.

Finally, the show embraces its past and gives Mark Lenard a great part, as the aged Sarek tries to complete his last ambassadorial task before illness robs him of his dignity.

The season was marked with several impressive and memorable performances but the nod has to go with **Mark Lenard**, returning as Sarek and succumbing to the emotions he eschewed for nearly two centuries. His scenes with Patrick Stewart remind us how talented the late but not forgotten Lenard was.

Best Guest Star

Ménage à Troi ▲▲▲

Writers: Fred Bronson and Susan Sackett
Director: Robert Legato
May 28, 1990
A Ferengi kidnaps Riker, Troi and her mother Lwaxana, hoping to use the Betazoid's telepathic abilities to his business advantage.

Transfigurations ▲▲

Writer: René Echevarria
Director: Tom Benko
June 4, 1990
A mysterious injured man found by the *Enterprise* heals extremely quickly, then kills Worf in an escape attempt...

3rd

The Best of Both Worlds ▲▲▲▲

Writer: Michael Piller
Director: Cliff Bole
June 18, 1990
The Borg invade Federation space, confronting the *Enterprise* and kidnapping Captain Picard.

We were warned a season previously the Borg were coming and here they are, scarier than promised. The first cliffhanger, it set the standard while giving the cast strong roles.

ULTIMATE TOP TEN #4

Having made an indelible impression with their debut a year earlier, the Borg returned to launch a direct attack on the heart of the Federation, starting with the complete dehumanization of Jean-Luc Picard. Coupled with the tale of Will Riker struggling with his own personal destiny, "The Best of Both Worlds" culminated with a cliffhanger confrontation of mythic proportions.

MOST VALUED PERFORMANCE

Brent Spiner's superbly nuanced Data saw some incredible highs and lows this season, such as commanding an away mission ("The Ensigns of Command"), seeing a former friend back from the dead ("Yesterday's Enterprise"), and becoming the object of a collector ("The Most Toys"). But his continued exploration of what it must mean to have emotions and be a human was touchingly demonstrated in "The Offspring", when he created a daughter, Lal (Hallie Todd).

STAR TREK
THE NEXT GENERATION

SEASON 4
September 1990-June 1991

How do you resolve one of the greatest ever TV cliffhangers? That was the question executive producer Michael Piller found himself wrestling with in the summer of 1990, as he attempted to write the series' heroes out of the crisis he had created for them in "The Best of Both Worlds."

Although the showdown between the *Enterprise* and the Borg cube fizzled, rather than exploded, the season quickly got up to speed as Piller injected a flurry of ideas into its opening episode. The result was an installment nominated for four Emmy Awards, and a show back on the air and in its prime; slick, confident, and energized. This was demonstrated in the bold decision to follow the premiere with a slow, subdued, and largely Earth-bound follow-up episode which would establish the overriding theme for much of the season – "Family."

Executive producer Rick Berman was wary of Piller's proposal, initially demanding the inclusion of a solid sci-fi B-story. Although it would prove the season's lowest-rated episode, he relented, and the first ever *Star Trek* episode not to feature an *Enterprise* bridge scene followed a damaged Captain Picard on a cathartic visit to his home village of La Barre, France.

Continuing the familial feel, "Brothers" saw Data reunited with his 'father', Dr. Noonian Soong, and 'sibling' Lore. It provided Brent Spiner with a memorable three-fold role and served as a worthy final bow for Rob Bowman, who had served as the series' lead director in its first two seasons.

However, *The Next Generation*'s own behind-the-scenes family was welcoming new blood. Jeri Taylor made her debut with "Suddenly Human," which saw Picard serve as father figure to a troubled teen, while Joe Menosky arrived with "Legacy," which introduced Tasha Yar's sister, Ishara. And having joined the show through an eight-week internship, Brannon Braga helped rewrite the script for the Klingon-themed episode "Reunion," which killed off Worf's mate K'Ehleyr,

introduced their son Alexander, as well as Robert O'Reilly's Gowron, and helped set up the season four finale. Riker gained a son in the false reality of "Future Imperfect," and Captain Picard lost an adopted son in "Final Mission" with Wesley Crusher's departure for Starfleet Academy. The episode marked Wil Wheaton's final appearance as a regular castmember, as he left to explore his career options, with the explanation for Wesley's exit proposed by his namesake and creator, Eugene Wesley Roddenberry.

Militaristic aliens the Cardassians were introduced in "The Wounded," which featured roles for an increasingly prominent Colm Meaney as Chief Miles O'Brien, one-time Tasha Yar candidate Rosalind Chao as his new bride, Keiko, and Marc Alaimo in his third *TNG* appearance. Alaimo would later appear alongside Meaney and Chao as the Cardassian Gul Dukat in *Star Trek* spin-off series *Deep Space Nine*.

Susan Gibney returned as the real Dr. Leah Brahms in "Galaxy's Child," before the Robin Hood-themed romp "Qpid" brought back Jennifer Hetrick as conwoman Vash and John de Lancie as omnipotent meddler Q. Writer Ira Steven Behr was lured back to pen "Qpid," with the original plan that Q would transport the crew to King Arthur's Camelot. It was Brannon Braga who suggested a

switch to Sherwood Forest, trading on the popularity of hit film *Robin Hood: Prince of Thieves*.

Ron Jones was fired as a composer by Rick Berman after "The Drumhead," critical of his tendency toward overly 'flamboyant' scores, while doomed relationships also appeared to be an on-screen theme towards the end of the season.

Lwaxana Troi fell for David Ogden Spiers' tortured scientist Timicin in "Half a Life," while Dr Crusher faced heartache in "The Host" – which introduced alien species the Trill, and prompted debate about the series' handling of homosexuality – while "In Theory" saw an officer develop an ill-fated romance with Data.

The Next Generation reached its landmark 100th episode with the season four finale "Redemption." Originally planned as the season three conclusion, it introduced Duras's sisters Lursa and B'Etor and his illegitimate son, Toral, challenging Gowron for control of the Klingon empire, and saw Denise Crosby return, this time as a mysterious blonde Romulan. Former President Ronald Reagan visited the set during production, picking up a cane dropped by Gene Roddenberry in what can now be seen as a poignant portent of the *Star Trek* creator's failing health.

Rod Edgar

1990-91

1966
1967
1968
1969
1970
1971
1972
1973
1974
1975
1976
1977
1978
1979
1980
1981
1982
1983
1984
1985
1986
1987
1988
1989
1990
1991
1992
1993
1994
1995
1996
1997
1998
1999
2000
2001
2002
2003
2004
2005
2006
2007
2008
2009
2010
2011

The Best of Both Worlds, Part II
▲▲▲▲

Writer: Michael Piller
Director: Cliff Bole
September 24, 1990

With Picard/Locutus leading the Borg attack on Starfleet, Riker must make some difficult choices to save his captain and the Earth.

Any resolution to season three's breathtaking finale was likely to prove a disappointment. But while Michael Piller was unable to deliver a great pay-off to the terrific cliffhanger, he compensated by stuffing an array of twists and turns into a frenetic and entertaining episode – from the epic and ingenious plan to rescue Picard through to the clever means by which the Borg threat is literally put to bed.

Brothers ▲▲▲

Writer: Rick Berman
Director: Rob Bowman
October 8, 1990

Data discovers his creator and re-encounters his 'brother' Lore, who offers him an emotion chip.

Suddenly Human ▲▲▲

Teleplay: John Whelpley & Jeri Taylor
Story: Ralph Phillips
Director: Gabrielle Beaumont
October 15, 1990

A young human boy raised by aliens is helped by Picard to discover his true heritage.

Legacy ▲▲

Writer: Joe Menosky
Director: Robert Scheerer
October 29, 1990

The *Enterprise* comes to the aid of Tasha Yar's sister in the search for survivors of the conflict of two warring factions.

Reunion ▲▲▲

Teleplay: Thomas Perry & Jo Perry and Brannon Braga & Ronald D. Moore
Story: Drew Deighan and Thomas Perry & Jo Perry
Director: Jonathan Frakes
November 5, 1990

Worf's son comes to the *Enterprise*, causing problems for the stoic Klingon.

Future Imperfect ▲▲▲

Writers: J Larry Carroll & David Bennett Carren
Director: Les Landau
November 12, 1990

Riker contracts a virus on an Away Team mission and awakens in Sickbay to discover 16 years have gone by...

Family ▲▲▲▲▲

Writer: Ronald D. Moore
Director: Les Landau
October 1, 1990

Recovering from his ordeal under Borg control, Picard returns to his family home.

He's been described as the Teflon-coated captain, but Jean-Luc Picard's human vulnerability is fully exposed for the first time in a slow, sensitive character-driven episode set in the aftermath of the Borg conflict at Wolf 359. There are no space battles or alien threats as Picard's guarded exterior is gradually worn down during a quiet visit with his brother's family on Earth; his crippling emotional wounds revealed in a riveting climax.

Remember Me ▲▲▲▲

Writer: Lee Sheldon
Director: Cliff Bole
October 22, 1990

Beverly Crusher discovers that *Enterprise* crewmembers have begun to disappear from the ship one-by-one.

A simple yet ingenious premise originally conceived as a B-story for "Family" results in a quirky and dramatically satisfying episode. And as the only person to remember they ever existed, the good doctor wrestles with her own sanity as she searches for a rational explanation to an increasingly unsettling mystery.

Final Mission ▲▲▲

Teleplay: Kacey Arnold-Ince and Jeri Taylor
Story: Kacey Arnold-Ince
Director: Corey Allen
November 19, 1990

Picard is injured and marooned on a hostile moon with only Wesley Crusher for company.

The Loss ∧∧
Teleplay: Hilary J. Bader and Alan J Adler & Vanessa Greene
Story: Hilary J. Bader
Director: Chip Chalmers
December 31, 1990
Troi's telepathic powers vanish when the *Enterprise* is dragged off course.

Data's Day ∧∧∧
Writer: Ronald D. Moore
Director: Robert Wiemer
January 7, 1991
A marriage and a death mark a day in the life of the android Data.

The Wounded ∧∧∧∧
Teleplay: Jeri Taylor
Story: Stuart Charno & Sara Charno and Cy Chermak
Director: Chip Chalmers
January 28, 1991
Peace negotiations between the Federation and the Cardassians are threatened by a rogue Starfleet captain.

4th

Devil's Due ∧∧∧∧
Teleplay: Phillip Lazebnik
Story: Phillip Lazebnik and William Douglas Lansford
Director: Tom Benko
February 4, 1991
An alien 'devil' drags the *Enterprise* crew into her dispute with a planet's inhabitants, with Data appointed as judge.

Comedy, suspense, sexual intrigue, and an appearance by the Klingon equivalent of Satan... what more could you ask for, as the *Enterprise* crew come to the aid of a planet in danger of losing everything thanks to a thousand-year-old deal with the devil? And what a devil she proves to be, as the alluring woman claiming to be the ancient demon sets her sights on an atypically flustered Captain Picard.

Best Guest Star

Tales of the Gold Monkey actress **Marta Dubois** edges out Jean Simmons from "The Drumhead" to claim this title with a delightfully vampish turn as the sultry and sinful Ardra in "Devil's Due." Dubois revels in the role of the crafty con artist who could give Harry Mudd a run for his money – effortlessly moving from intimidating, to alluring and arch, and generating great on-screen chemistry with Patrick Stewart.

Clues ∧∧∧∧
Teleplay: Bruce D. Arthurs and Joe Menosky
Story: Bruce D. Arthurs
Director: Les Landau
February 11, 1991
The *Enterprise* crew seems to have lost 24 hours; but why is Data lying?

First Contact ∧∧∧
Teleplay: Dennis Russell Bailey & David Bischoff and Joe Menosky & Ronald D. Moore and Michael Piller
Story: Marc Zicree
Director: Cliff Bole
February 18, 1991
On a first contact mission, Riker is injured and revealed to be an alien.

Galaxy's Child ∧∧∧
Teleplay: Maurice Hurley
Story: Thomas Kartozian
Director: Winrich Kolbe
March 11, 1991
Geordi meets the real Dr. Brahms, who is not at all like his holodeck recreation...

Night Terrors ∧∧
Teleplay: Pamela Douglas and Jeri Taylor
Story: Shari Goodhartz
Director: Les Landau
March 18, 1991
After discovering a derelict ship where the crew appear to have killed each other, Troi becomes concerned the *Enterprise* crew have been infected.

Identity Crisis ∧∧∧
Teleplay: Brannon Braga
Based on a Story by: Timothy De Haas
Director: Winrich Kolbe
March 25, 1991
Investigating the disappearance of his old crew, Geordi is transformed into an alien creature.

The Nth Degree ∧∧∧
Writer: Joe Menosky
Director: Rob Legato
April 1, 1991
Reclusive *Enterprise* crewmember Reg Barclay becomes a super genius thanks to the intervention of an alien race.

Qpid ∧∧∧

Teleplay: Ira Steven Behr
Story: Randee Russell and Ira Steven Behr
Director: Cliff Bole
April 22, 1991
Q, fascinated by Picard's romantic feelings for Vash, creates a Robin Hood fantasy for the *Enterprise* crew.

It may not be a classic episode, or even a particularly important scene, but a moment of televisual perfection is captured in the Robin Hood-themed "Qpid." Listening to Picard and his colleagues calmly analyzing their roles in Q's game, an infuriated Worf, dressed as Will Scarlet, exclaims, "Sir, I protest – I am *not* a merry man!" Never has a truer word been spoken than in this scene, now firmly embedded in the collective *Star Trek* psyche.

The Drumhead ∧∧∧∧

Writer: Jeri Taylor
Director: Jonathan Frakes
April 29, 1991
The loyalty of the crew comes under question when a retired admiral investigates an accident and a case of espionage, focusing her suspicions on Picard.

Star Trek doing what it does best – taking contemporary socio-political issues, placing them in a literally alien environment, then scrutinizing them via intelligent, powerful and beautifully-scripted drama. An investigation into a possible conspiracy on board the *Enterprise* gradually snowballs into a witch-hunt driven by fear and supposition, echoing McCarthyism and foreshadowing the political fall-out from 9/11. Picard has rarely been more noble or heroic than in his quiet courtroom confrontation.

Half a Life ∧∧

Teleplay: Peter Allan Fields
Story: Ted Roberts and Peter Allan Fields
Director: Les Landau
May 6, 1991
Troi's mother falls in love with a scientist, only to discover he has just a few days left to live...

The Host ∧∧∧

Writer: Michel Horvat
Director: Marvin Rush
May 13, 1991
Dr. Crusher starts a relationship with a man inhabited by a symbiotic life form called a Trill, but can't adjust when the Trill moves to inhabit a female body.

The Mind's Eye ∧∧∧

Teleplay: René Echevarria
Story: Ken Schafer and René Echevarria
Director: David Livingston
May 27, 1991
A brainwashed Geordi is used by the Romulans to sabotage a Federation alliance with the Klingons.

In Theory ∧∧

Writers: Joe Menosky & Ronald D. Moore
Director: Patrick Stewart
June 3, 1991
An emotionally-damaged crewmember forms a romantic bond with the android Data.

An appropriate title for an episode which, on paper, reads like a solid pitch. But in Patrick Stewart's directorial debut, scenes intended as being cute instead come across as either cloyingly mawkish or strangely sinister, and given the subject matter, it is perhaps no surprise that the resulting episode feels cold, sterile and void of emotion.

Redemption ∧∧∧∧

Writer: Ronald D. Moore
Director: Cliff Bole
June 17, 1991
Worf leaves Starfleet in order to return home and clear his family's name, as Gowron becomes leader of the High Council.

MOST VALUABLE PLAYER

He may only boast two writing credits in season four, but it was **Michael Piller** who proposed following up his strong season opener "The Best of Both Worlds Part II" with a slow, subdued tale exploring Picard's fragile emotions, resulting in the classic episode "Family"; Piller who suggested adding Lore to Rick Berman's script for "Brothers"; and Piller who advised killing off K'Ehleyr in "Reunion." Without him, *The Next Generation*'s fourth season would be missing many of its most memorable and important moments.

STAR TREK
THE NEXT GENERATION

SEASON 5
September 1991-June 1992

Going into its fifth season, *Star Trek: The Next Generation* was an established success, and was also the torch-bearer for a franchise celebrating its quarter-century.

The big anniversary element, of course, was the return of Spock in the "Unification" duology. Since Leonard Nimoy was only available for one episode, "Unification II" was written first, with Jeri Taylor then being left the task of writing an episode just to put the *TNG* characters where they needed to be. Nimoy wasn't the only returning guest from the beginning of *Trek*, as Malachi Throne, who played Commodore Mendez in "The Menagerie," joined him in "Unification." This was the first of the regular mid-season two-parters, but curiously eschews the word "Part."

Along with the usual aliens, Wesley Crusher also returned, in the latter case as a more flawed – and therefore interesting – character. In "The Game" there's actually good reason for him being the one person capable of saving the ship and crew. There is a glaring absence, though: in a season that celebrates both a quarter century of *Trek* as a whole, and a half-decade of *TNG* itself, the absence of *TNG*'s regular antagonist, Q, is astonishing. At least two Q stories were in development for the season, but neither made the cut.

Star Trek's creator, Gene Roddenberry, died during filming of the episode "Hero Worship." There's

a certain irony in this being an episode about an orphaned boy; now the series, the franchise, was orphaned. Although "The Game" was actually the first episode to air after Roddenberry's death, it was at too short notice to add a caption, and since "Unification" was the anniversary show, it was a more appropriate choice to carry the tribute caption, which was put up in front of both episodes.

The show also continued to move forward, with new developments and faces. An extra blue-trail flourish was added to the series' title in the opening credits, Picard got a new uniform design including a suede jacket, and, most importantly, there came the arrival of what was intended to be a new recurring regular, Ensign Ro Laren, played by the always-watchable Michelle Forbes, who would later go on to greater fame in *Homicide: Life On the Street* and *Battlestar Galactica*. Forbes makes an immediate impression, though Ro is written somewhat inconsistently. Other future faces to watch included Ashley Judd, future Bond and *X-Men* star Famke Janssen, and Robert Duncan MacNeill, who would go on to star as Tom Paris in *Voyager*.

Laren's addition to the show was an important step for two reasons; the obvious one being that it set up the Bajoran/Cardassian situation that wold provide the basis for *Deep Space Nine*, and the other one being that it showed that the *TNG* setup and crew had reached a

state of being stable enough to accept such changes and additions. In essence, the series had reached the age of maturity.

The series by this point was truly stretching its wings in the type of stories it told. Although ongoing story arcs weren't at the level later seen in *DS9*, there were threads that linked the year into a sort of cohesion, most notably the Romulan thread, running from "Redemption Part II" through "Unification" and into "The Next Phase" before continuing in season six. Even the Borg episode took a new direction, swapping the force-of-nature concept for the study of a single individual's mindset.

Overall, season five produced no sea-changes in the series, but it gave a broad range of episodes, from action thriller to comedy to domestic drama, and by now all centered around a cast the audience had become more than comfortable with. As always there were turkeys on this farm, but the closing four episodes in particular provide a consistent run of quality that only the best mini-arcs in *DS9* could match.

Whether the viewer was a longtime fan going back that quarter century and wanting to feel like the show they grew up with was still going, or a new viewer seeking out the best in TV SF, this was a season to deliver the goods.

David A McIntee

Redemption, Part II ^^^
Writer: Ronald D. Moore
Director: David Carson
September 23, 1991
The Klingon civil war threatens to draw in the Romulans, unless Picard can intervene.

3rd

Darmok ^^^^^
Teleplay: Joe Menosky
Story: Phillip LaZebnik and Joe Menosky
Director: Winrich Kolbe
September 30, 1991
Picard is trapped with an alien with whom he struggles to communicate.

One of the better "message episodes" of the franchise. At first glance it's a bit of a knock-off of the 1985 movie *Enemy Mine* (reptilian alien, human who can't understand him) but a sympathetic performance from Paul Winfield and the clever extra element of the nature of communication between cultures raise this on multiple levels.

Best Guest Star

Paul Winfield as Dathon has to contend not only with extensive makeup, but also dialog written in a highly unusual style and context. Despite having such apparent gibberish to say, he pulls it off magnificently, and makes the dialogue both comprehensible (at least on repeated viewings!) and gives us a memorable character.

Ensign Ro ^^^
Teleplay: Michael Piller
Story: Rick Berman & Michael Piller
Director: Les Landau
October 7, 1991
A crisis on a Federation colony sees an undisciplined Bajoran ensign join the *Enterprise*.

Silicon Avatar ^
Teleplay: Jeri Taylor
Story: Lawrence V. Conley
Director: Cliff Bole
October 14, 1991
The alien force that wiped out Data's home returns and threatens a new colony.

Disaster ^^^
Teleplay: Ronald D. Moore
Story: Ron Jarvis & Philip A. Scorza
Director: Gabrielle Beaumont
October 21, 1991
A strange phenomenon disables the *Enterprise*, trapping the crew away from the bridge, leaving Troi as captain.

The Game ^^^
Teleplay: Brannon Braga
Story: Susan Sackett & Fred Bronson and Brannon Braga
Director: Corey Allen
October 28, 1991
Returning to the *Enterprise*, Wesley Crusher finds the crew have fallen under the sway of an addictive computer game.

1991-92

Unification I ^^^
Teleplay: Jeri Taylor
Story: Rick Berman & Michael Piller
Director: Les Landau
November 4, 1991
Picard is ordered to find Ambassador Spock, who seems to have defected to the Romulans.

5th

Unification II ^^^^
Teleplay: Michael Piller
Story: Rick Berman & Michael Piller
Director: Cliff Bole
November 11, 1991
Picard becomes embroiled in Spock's efforts to reunite the Romulans and the Vulcans.

This bridges both the original *Star Trek* with *TNG*, and the movies, being directly linked to *The Undiscovered Country*. It has a somewhat abrupt ending, but the story is intriguing, and there's no denying the power of Leonard Nimoy's guest appearance as Spock.

A Matter of Time ^^^
Writer: Rick Berman
Director: Paul Lynch
November 18, 1991
A time traveler arrives to study the *Enterprise* and her crew.

New Ground ^^
Teleplay: Grant Rosenberg
Story: Sara Charno & Stuart Charno
Director: Robert Scheerer
January 6, 1992
A new propulsion system causes problems for the *Enterprise*, as Worf struggles with his son.

1966 1967 1968 1969 1970 1971 1972 1973 1974 1975 1976 1977 1978 1979 1980 1981 1982 1983 1984 1985 1986 1987 1988 1989 1990 **1991 1992** 1993 1994 1995 1996 1997 1998 1999 2000 2001 2002 2003 2004 2005 2006 2007 2008 2009 2010 2011

Hero Worship ᗅᗅ
Teleplay: Joe Menosky
Story: Hilary J. Bader
Director: Patrick Stewart
January 27, 1992
An orphaned young boy bonds with Data.

Violations ᗅᗅᗅ
Teleplay: Pamela Gray & Jeri Taylor
Story: Shari Goodhartz & T Michael and Pamela Gray
Director: Robert Wiemer
February 3, 1992
The *Enterprise* crew is subjected to nightmare experiences by a telepathic alien.

The Masterpiece Society ᗅᗅ
Teleplay: Adam Belanoff and Michael Piller
Story: James Kahn and Adam Belanoff
Director: Winrich Kolbe
February 10, 1992
Rebels from a planet of perfect people co-opt the *Enterprise* for help.

Conundrum ᗅᗅᗅ
Teleplay: Barry Schkolnick
Story: Paul Schiffer
Director: Les Landau
February 17, 1992
Having lost their memories, the *Enterprise* crew attempt to carry out a military mission...

Power Play ᗅᗅᗅᗅ
Teleplay: René Balcer and Herbert J. Wright & Brannon Braga
Story: Paul Ruben and Maurice Hurley
Director: David Livingston
February 24, 1992
Responding to a distress call, an *Enterprise* shuttle crew is possessed and attempts to hijack the ship.

Ethics ᗅ
Teleplay: Ronald D. Moore
Story: Sara Charno & Stuart Charno
Director: Chip Chalmers
March 2, 1992
Having lost the use of his legs following an accident, Worf decides he wants to die...

Worst Episode ✗

The Outcast ᗅ
Writer: Jeri Taylor
Director: Robert Scheerer
March 16, 1992
Riker falls in love with a scientist from a planet where male and female genders don't exist.

This sets out to be a lecturing episode with a labored moral – always a bad idea – and then gets it all horribly wrong. What can one say about an episode who's point is "let's do a story about tolerance of homosexuality by... having Riker fall for a girl"? If it had a decent B-story, or some good lines, or even chemistry between Jonathan Frakes and his love interest, perhaps something could have been salvaged from this. But it doesn't, and so nothing is.

2nd

Cause and Effect ᗅᗅᗅᗅᗅ
Writer: Brannon Braga
Director: Jonathan Frakes
March 23, 1992
...*prise* explodes. The *Enterprise* explodes. The *Enterprise* explodes. The *Enterprise* explod...

Braga give us an early and well-done example of one of his favorite types of story, the time travel episode. A bold teaser and clever resolution bookend one of the best time-paradox episodes in all of the franchise.

The First Duty ᗅᗅᗅ
Writers: Ronald D. Moore & Naren Shankar
Director: Paul Lynch
March 30, 1992
An accident at Starfleet Academy is covered up – by Wesley Crusher?

Cost of Living ᗅ
Writer: Peter Allan Fields
Director: Winrich Kolbe
April 20, 1992
The *Enterprise* is invaded by alien parasites, and Lwaxana Troi!

The Perfect Mate ᗅᗅ
Teleplay: Gary Perconte and Michael Piller
Story: René Echevarria and Gary Perconte
Director: Cliff Bole
April 27, 1992
Picard is seduced by a metamorph, an alien creature who can be anything the captain desires...

Imaginary Friend ▲
Teleplay: Edithe Swensen and Brannon Braga
Story: Jean Louise Matthias & Ronald Wilkerson and Richard Fliegel
Director: Gabrielle Beaumont
May 4, 1992
The imaginary friend of a child aboard the *Enterprise* puts the ship in danger.

I, Borg ▲▲▲▲
Writer: René Echevarria
Director: Robert Lederman
May 11, 1992
A single survivor is recovered from a crashed Borg ship and brought aboard the *Enterprise*.

This does something new with the Borg, and includes a winning guest appearance from the title character. It's the beginning of the weakening of the Borg, but it's done extremely well, and within the rules set out by previous episodes. Hugh isn't an assimilated person being rescued, but a native who doesn't know any other way. He's an intriguing character who tries to understand and adapt to new circumstances. This, more than the less-original questions about the morality of dehumanizing one's enemies, is what makes the episode such a standout.

The Next Phase ▲▲▲▲
Writer: Ronald D. Moore
Director: David Carson
May 18, 1992
Attempting to help a Romulan ship, Geordi and Ro suffer a transporter accident that makes them incorporeal.

The Inner Light ▲▲▲▲▲
Teleplay: Morgan Gendel and Peter Allan Fields
Story: Morgan Gendel
Director: Peter Lauritson
June 1, 1992
Knocked out by an alien probe, Captain Picard experiences a long life among the Ressikan people.

Not an original choice, but it's so highly regarded because it really is that good. Essentially it's Picard does *Quantum Leap*, but the emotional core of the story, following the aging of a devoted family man, is very affecting, and Patrick Stewart gives a pitch-perfect performance.

BEST MOMENT For emotional power nothing beats the moment when the dying Kamin/Picard is reunited with his dead wife in "The Inner Light." Patrick Stewart's reactions, the music, and the nature of the moment all combine to perfection. If that doesn't move you, then nothing will.

ULTIMATE TOP TEN #9 Touched by an alien probe, Jean-Luc Picard spends a subjective lifetime experiencing the life of Kamin, one of the last generation of a long-dead civilization doomed by a natural disaster. As Picard gradually accepts his new identity, complete with a wife, friends, and, eventually, children and grandchildren, his appreciation of his adopted culture and his sadness over its fate become ours, in one of the most emotionally powerful of all *Trek* episodes.

MOST VALUABLE PERFORMANCE

It's time to big up **Marina Sirtis**. She has evolved from the "I sense pain... pain..." performance of the early seasons, but hasn't dropped the accent. Better still, Troi is used well, except in "The Masterpiece Society," and she comes across as a professional counselor with a good "bedside manner" even in those episodes where she just has a brief cameo. That's valuable because, while Troi doesn't have any real *tour de force* moments, she is believable. This season, Troi seems to be the most real of the characters, doing a real job, and that's down to Sirtis. In fact, the actress even went so far as to do her own stunts when her face wouldn't be visible to confirm that it was her – though they didn't tell her that at the time! She also doesn't fall victim to the temptation to overact when possessed in "Power Play" and that's rare enough among actors to get her the nod.

Time's Arrow, Part I ▲▲▲▲
Teleplay: Joe Menosky and Michael Piller
Story: Joe Menosky
Director: Les Landau
June 15, 1992
Data's detached head is discovered buried on Earth, resulting in a journey back to the future for the *Enterprise*.

TO BOLDLY COMPOSE...

From *Star Trek: The Next Generation* to *Enterprise*, the music of Jay Chattaway accompanied many interplanetary adventures. The composer spoke to Calum Waddell about his 18-year musical odyssey.

Having plied his trade as a film composer for over 30 years, Jay Chattaway became a driving force in the symphonies of *Star Trek*, after beginning work on *The Next Generation* back in 1990. He would eventually steer the soundtracks of 42 episodes. Obviously satisfying the powers-that-be at Paramount, Chattaway would return to the *Star Trek* universe with *Deep Space Nine* (overseeing the music on 58 episodes), *Voyager* (54 episodes), and *Enterprise* (28 episodes). Outside of this impressive feat, the composer also boasts credits on such well-remembered B-flicks as the hit horror movie *Maniac* (1980), the Chuck Norris action outings

"Tin Man" was Chattaway's first *Next Generation* score

"YOU KNEW THAT MILLIONS OF PEOPLE WOULD BE WATCHING THE SHOW AND LISTENING TO YOUR SCORE. THAT PUTS A LOT OF PRESSURE ON YOU TO GET THINGS DONE."

The music for "A Fistful of Datas" is amongst Chattaway's favorite scores

Jay Chattaway conducts during a
Next Generation recording session

Missing in Action (1984) and The Delta Force (1986), and Dolph Lundgren's adventure romp Red Scorpion (1988). However, stepping out from the world of low-budget, independently-produced cinema and into a hit, prime-time television show such as The Next Generation was, for Chattaway, quite an imposing feat.

"You see, I came from a world where creative people worked with very little money to get things done – but there was a lot of freedom within that," admits the composer during an exclusive interview inside his spacious Malibu home. "But with Star Trek, it was a little different. There were lots of producers that you had to please and it never quite had the same sense of spontaneity as the films I had done. In fact, it was really quite scary when I began working on The Next Generation. Just to give you an idea – you can work for two months on a film and you never know what the outcome will be. It might last a week in cinemas, it might be a blockbuster – like Missing in Action – or it might only be discovered years later on home video. But with The Next Generation, you knew that millions of people would be watching the show and listening to your score. Believe it or not, that puts a lot of pressure on you to get things done, and done right [laughs]."

TREK VIRGIN

Nevertheless, when the call came for Chattaway to bring his talents to The Next Generation, he was excited about jumping into something new – although there was one big sticking point: the composer had never seen an episode of Star Trek, in any of its forms. The question, then, was whether or not to admit this to Paramount and the various producers of the hit series.

"I was originally asked to come in as a guest composer on an episode of The Next Generation called 'Tin Man'," he states. "It was going to be a one-off. Of course, I had heard of Star Trek, but I was not someone who knew much about it. In fact, I had never even seen one of the motion pictures! So I could not even have told you the name of a character in The Next Generation. Eventually, I decided that I'd better tell the director of music at Paramount, who had called me about the job, that I really did not know anything about the franchise. If that meant I was going to lose the job, then so be it. It would have been unfortunate, but I did not see any point in lying to people."

Luckily for Chattaway, an encyclopedic knowledge of all things Star Trek-related was not considered an essential qualification for the gig at hand. "I was basically told, 'that's okay – just do your own interpretation of what you think big, epic outer space music should sound like,'" he

Altogether, Chattaway composed 182 scores, across four Star Trek series

continues. "So the one thing I did draw on was *Star Wars*. I had seen, and enjoyed, all three of the *Star Wars* movies and I noticed how, in each film, John Williams had a separate theme tune for every different character. Of course, I figured that must be the way to do it. So there was a scene in 'Tin Man' where the Romulans attack the *Enterprise*, and I was very excited by that. I composed this great big build-up to the action – and I also gave various characters their own music in that episode. Well, I came out of the sound booth, after watching my music matched up with what was happening onscreen, and I thought it would be wildly received. I figured I had done exactly as the producers had asked."

Unfortunately for the composer, however, a score that was a blatant homage to *Star Wars* happened to be exactly what the producers of *The Next Generation* did not want. Indeed, had Chattaway asked any self-respecting *Star Trek* fan for advice, he might have saved himself a lot of time and effort.

"I remember that the producers were giving me this dumbfounded look," he smiles. "Right away I knew something was not right, so I said, 'okay, where did I mess up?' And they replied, 'Well the problem is that *Star Trek* is nothing like *Star Wars*. Our audience is much more intelligent. We don't want to tell the viewer if a character is good, bad, or indifferent – we want the fans to make up their own minds. But you have told them the whole story in what you have just conducted.' Now, in the movies that I had worked on before doing *The Next Generation*, that is exactly what the directors wanted. However, the *Star Trek* people did not like 'feeding' an audience their thoughts – they really just wanted their musicians

Picard practices Chattaway's composition in "The Inner Light"

"I REMEMBER THAT THE PRODUCERS WERE GIVING ME THIS DUMBFOUNDED LOOK."

to find the right sounds to accompany the story. So I had to take a lot of thematic stuff out and that was probably when I realized how unique the *Star Trek* universe, and its audience, are. As an aside, though, the soundtrack album for the 'Tin Man' episode finally came out and I got to put all of my original stuff back in. It was just to say to the fans 'this is how it was at one time,' so I am glad that my initial *Star Trek* experience is not lost."

Another thing that Chattaway recalls about his time on *The Next Generation* is how pressured his working environment was. "Generally when I get involved with scoring something, I get the chance to see the project in pre-production and also as it is being edited," he maintains. "But with *Star Trek* it was very different. Probably the most terrifying part about working on the series was that that we had a 65-piece orchestra to organize every week. For *The Next Generation*, we would record every Tuesday, it would be mixed on the Wednesday and usually it would be on the air by the Friday. So there really wasn't any time to fix anything. You would do all the music live with the orchestra, and no television show had really done anything that extravagant before. There was over $100,000 reserved every week just for the music. Then five or six producers would come in and they would tell you if it was what they wanted."

NEW SOUNDS

Looking back, however, Chattaway does admit that he believes he brought something new to the sounds of *The Next Generation*. "As I learned more and more about *Star Trek*, I discovered that the music on *The Next Generation*, prior to when I became involved, was very linear," he maintains. "I also don't think it was allowed to stand out so much. However, Paramount were getting letters from a lot of *Star Trek* fans who would praise the show but also mention that they wanted a more outrageous soundtrack, and who can blame them? It was an outrageous show [*laughs*]. So, for example, whenever it was time to do scenes in the holodeck, I would let the music make a little more of a statement and things would definitely pick up a bit more."

Things get explosive in the Chattaway-composed *Enterprise* episode "Zero Hour"

Composer Jay Chattaway relaxes at his Pacific coast home

Asked about his favorite piece of *Star Trek* music, Chattaway again returns to his memories of *The Next Generation*. "I really love the music that I did for 'A Fistful of Datas'," he says - referring to the installment that aired in November 1992. "The story in that features some of the crew going back in time and taking part in the Wild West. Not only did I love that episode, but I was excited about scoring it because I love Westerns. But the producers said to me that they did not want any Western music in it. Well, I thought that was a silly decision, because the actors were dressed in cowboy hats and spurs, Worf was carrying a six-shooter and dressed as an old-town Sheriff. I mean, what else could you put over that? So I said to them, 'You know what? I can't do this episode any other way. I really can't.'"

In order to stress this point further, Chattaway mentions that he went straight to his CD collection and put some suitably atmospheric tunes over the completed episode.

"I went and got some of Ennio Morricone's music from the Sergio Leone Westerns, such as *The Good, the Bad, and the Ugly*, and I began putting that over the soundtrack," he reveals. "The first time the producers saw 'A Fistful of Datas,' it had Morricone's music over it and not mine! Well, that won them over and I got to compose my very first, and last, Western [*laughs*]. I remember that we had harmonicas in that episode and all kinds of things. It was really great. The fans wrote in and praised the music – saying how much they enjoyed my homage to Morricone. However, that was one of the

other great things about doing a show like *Star Trek* – you got instant feedback. Two days after the show aired, you would get hundreds of letters telling you what worked, and what didn't, and often that stretched to the music as well."

CONTINUING MISSIONS

After *The Next Generation* finished its small screen run, in 1994, Chattaway jumped onto *Deep Space Nine*, making his debut with the third episode of the show, 'Past Prologue'. Yet, the composer is quick to admit that nothing could

Harry Groener as Tam, in Chattaway's first *Trek* episode "Tin Man"

"TWO DAYS AFTER THE SHOW AIRED, YOU WOULD GET HUNDREDS OF LETTERS TELLING YOU WHAT WORKED, AND WHAT DIDN'T."

beat the initial experience of *The Next Generation*. "I think that after *The Next Generation*, it was a bit more factory-like," he says. "I mean, maybe that is the wrong term to use. I guess what I mean is that Paramount would go from one *Star Trek* series to another: from *Deep Space Nine* to *Voyager* to *Enterprise* – and although each series was fantastic to work on, I guess you began to know what was expected from you. I think there is a lot of storytelling in the music that I composed for *Deep Space Nine*, as well as the others, and I invested a lot of time in every episode that I did. I also began to notice something quite interesting – and this might actually relate to every sci-fi movie or television show. If you analyze the music on *Star Trek* – in any of its incarnations – it generally has a negative usage. There is typically something wrong in space: and that is when you hear the really memorable scores."

Ultimately, Chattaway admits that, when *Enterprise* came to the end of its run – marking the end of his *Star Trek* experience to date – it was something that saddened him. After all, the mythology had taken up a huge part of his professional life. "The whole *Star Trek* thing lasted 18 years for me," he grins. "Although I never did become a Trekkie, I have to admit it was a wonderful thing to be a part of. Even today I miss the energy of doing a new episode of *Star Trek* – and if someone was to call me and tell me there was a new series on the way – well, I'm sure I could have my arm twisted to boldly return to the composer's chair for one more run..." ▲

Patrick Stewart as Captain Jean-Luc Picard,
in Season 1 of *Star Trek: The Next Generation*

STAR TREK
THE NEXT GENERATION

SEASON 6
September 1992-June 1993

James Doohan as Scotty, in "Relics"

For a comfortably established television program, season six remains vibrant and exciting.

We see some of the best acting of the series. Stewart bares body and soul in "Chain of Command, Part II" as he undergoes physical and psychological torture. Wendy Hughes stands out as a believable love interest for Picard, stellar cartographer Nella Darren, in "Lessons." But the season's heavy lifting belongs to Jonathan Frakes. He has to butt heads with Ronny Cox's Captain Jellico in "Chain of Command, Parts I and II," nearly go insane from hallucinations and paranoia in "Frame of Mind," and play two versions of himself – often in dialogue – in "Second Chances."

Guest stars abound, some of whose names would soon be familiar. James Cromwell ("Birthright, Parts I and II"), who plays a Yridian information broker, would later portray Zefram Cochrane in *Star Trek: First Contact*. Tim Russ, soon to be *Voyager*'s Lieutenant Tuvok, appears without Vulcan makeup in "Starship Mine" as a mercenary. There's even a brief crossover with *Deep Space Nine*, when Siddig El Fadil as Dr. Julian Bashir visits the *Enterprise* in "Birthright, Part I." Real-life astronaut Dr. Mae Jemison has a couple of lines as Lieutenant Palmer in "Second Chances," and Professor Stephen Hawking plays a holodeck version of himself in "Descent."

Brent Spiner continues to flex his comic muscles

as Data. He appears as multiple Wild West archetypes – culminating in saloon-keeper Ms. Annie – in "A Fistful of Datas." In "Schisms" Spiner recites Data's charmingly scientific poem, "Ode to Spot," though he accidentally delivers the first two lines of iambic heptameter ("*Felis catus* is your taxo-nomic nomenclature / An endothermic quadruped carnivorous by nature. . .") as a question.

Two cast changes occur this season: Miles O'Brien (Colm Meaney) and his family leave for Deep Space 9, and Spot goes from Somali to tabby as of "Birthright, Part I." This is the only season in which neither Wil Wheaton as Welsey Crusher, nor Majel Barrett as Lwaxana Troi appear, though Wesley is mentioned in "True Q" and "Lessons," and Barrett continues to be heard throughout the year as the voice of the ship's computer.

Twenty-fourth Century technology is well-represented in season six. "Realm of Fear" finally shows us what it's like to be within a transporter beam, and "Relics" delivers a Dyson Sphere, probably the largest artificial object in the galaxy. "Face of the Enemy" takes viewers inside a Romulan warbird. The exocomps from "The Quality of Life" and the holodeck Professor Moriarty in "Ship in a Bottle" continue to raise the question of the nature of artificial life forms in the *Star Trek* universe.

Careful viewers have their attention rewarded as

Time's Arrow, Part II ∧∧∧∧
Teleplay: Jeri Taylor
Story: Joe Menosky
Director: Les Landau
September 21, 1992
The *Enterprise* crew arrive in 19th-Century San Francisco, only to find a familiar face...

Realm of Fear ∧∧∧
Writer: Brannon Braga
Director: Cliff Bole
September 28, 1992
Reg Barclay must overcome his fear of transporters to prove the system is infected by an alien being.

Man of the People ∧∧
Writer: Frank Abatemarco
Director: Winrich Kolbe
October 5, 1992
An alien diplomat hides his dark side within Troi's mind.

Relics ∧∧∧∧∧
Writer: Ronald D. Moore
Director: Alexander Singer
October 12, 1992
Montgomery Scott, rescued from transporter limbo after 75 years, finds himself a man out of time..

Along with the fan thrill of seeing Scotty interacting with the *Enterprise-D*'s crew, the story tackles the serious issue of the place of this one-time "miracle worker" in a changed galaxy.

James Doohan returns, bringing his signature mix of humor and warmth to the role of the otherwise technology-obsessed engineer. Scotty's moments with La Forge sparkle, and his scene with Picard on a holodeck re-creation of the original *Enterprise*'s bridge (thanks to a combination of set replicas and the digital manipulation of footage from the 1960s) is filled with pathos.

certain story elements reverberate throughout the season. Worf experiences a crisis of faith brought about by his experiences in "Birthright, Parts I and II," but regains it in "Rightful Heir." Dr. Crusher spends a lot of time writing and directing plays, and Riker acting in them. In "A Fistful of Datas" they are rehearsing *Something for Breakfast* when "Ode to Spot" replaces some scripted lines due to a computer error. Crusher's second play, *Frame of Mind*, mirrors what's happening to Riker in that eponymous episode.

Geordi grows a beard during early episodes, but then shaves it off (actor LeVar Burton grew it for his wedding, but the producers didn't like it). At last, Troi gets a blue officer's uniform in "Chain of Command, Part I," and Worf switches to a ponytail for the first time in "Face of the Enemy."

Despite its many high points, season six features two notable bloopers. In "Relics" the *Enterprise* beams Scotty and La Forge off the *Jenolan* while its shields are up, and, in "Birthright, Part I," a production crew member can be seen in a supposedly off-camera corridor during Data's flying dream.

Finally, season six features the shortest teaser in all of *TNG*: the opening to "Chain of Command, Part I" is just 40 seconds.
Kevin Lauderdale

1992-93

Schisms ∧∧∧
Teleplay: Brannon Braga
Story: Jean Louise Matthias & Ron Wilkerson
Director: Robert Wiemer
October 19, 1992
The *Enterprise* crew are badly affected when subspace aliens abduct crewmembers in their sleep for experiments.

True Q ∧∧∧∧
Writer: René Echevarria
Director: Robert Scheerer
October 26, 1992
A young student on the *Enterprise* reveals she has powers that attract the attention of super-being Q.

Rascals ∧∧∧∧
Teleplay: Allison Hock
Story: Ward Botsford & Diana Dru Botsford and Michael Piller
Director: Adam Nimoy
November 2, 1992
It's *Star Trek Babies*, as a transporter accident turns Picard, Guinan, Ro and Keiko into children...

A Fistful of Datas ∧∧∧∧
Teleplay: Robert Hewitt Wolfe and Brannon Braga
Story: Robert Hewitt Wolfe
Director: Patrick Stewart
November 9, 1992
Trapped in a holodeck Western simulation, Troi, Worf and his son Alexander face a gang of bandits modeled after Data.

The Quality of Life ▲▲
Writer: Naren Shankar
Director: Jonathan Frakes
November 16, 1992
Robotic exocomps are declared to be sentient by Data, only to meet resistance from their creator.

Chain of Command, Part I
▲▲▲▲
Teleplay: Ronald D. Moore
Story: Frank Abatemarco
Director: Robert Scheerer
December 14, 1992
With Picard, Worf and Crusher on a mission against the Cardassians, the *Enterprise* gets a new, abrasive captain.

Chain of Command, Part II
▲▲▲▲▲
Writer: Frank Abatemarco
Director: Les Landau
December 21, 1992
Captured by Cardassian Gul Madred, Picard is tortured to reveal the secrets of Federation defenses.

Gul Madred, the at once urbane-and-savage Cardassian torturer, comes very close to breaking Picard. Gritty performances by David Warner and Patrick Stewart make this a harrowing episode.

Picard, after surviving an Orwellian psychological ordeal in which his torturer insists that there are five lights instead of the actual four, defiantly cries, "There! Are! Four! Lights!"

Ship in a Bottle ▲▲▲
Writer: René Echevarria
Director: Alexander Singer
January 25, 1993
The simulation of Professor Moriarty escapes the confines of the holodeck and demands his freedom.

Aquiel ▲▲
Teleplay: Brannon Braga & Ronald D. Moore
Story: Jeri Taylor
Director: Cliff Bole
February 1, 1993
Geordi's in love again, this time with an accused murderer!

A clunky whodunit with a heroine in whom it's hard to have any interest, a contrived twist ending (Spoiler: the *dog* did it), and when it's all over, La Forge doesn't even get the girl. Again.

Face of the Enemy ▲▲▲▲▲
Teleplay: Naren Shankar
Story: René Echevarria
Director: Gabrielle Beaumont
February 8, 1993
Troi is surgically altered to look Romulan for an undercover mission.

Even though Troi is unprepared and nothing goes according to plan, she succeeds through intelligence and guts. A rare Troi-centric story where she's not a victim.

Tapestry ▲▲▲▲▲
Writer: Ronald D. Moore
Director: Les Landau
February 15, 1993
Q shows Picard what his life would have been like had he taken a more cautious route.

This episode features some of the season's best dialogue as Q tries to convince Picard that he's God, and Picard refuses to believe that it's Q who runs the afterlife, saying, "The universe is not so badly designed."

Birthright, Part I ▲▲▲
Writer: Brannon Braga
Director: Winrich Kolbe
February 22, 1993
Could Worf's father have escaped the battle at Khitomer?

Birthright, Part II ▲▲▲
Writer: René Echevarria
Director: Dan Curry
March 1, 1993
Worf discovers a refuge where Klingons and Romulans live together in peace.

5th

Starship Mine ▲▲▲▲▲
Writer: Morgan Gendel
Director: Cliff Bole
March 29, 1993
While undergoing maintenance, the *Enterprise* is boarded by alien pirates.

Die Hard on the *Enterprise* gives Picard a chance to show that he's also a man of action. Though the episode relies on the technobabble of a baryon sweep for its premise, viewers are treated to the old-fashioned fun of outwitting enemies and throwing punches.

Lessons ▲▲▲▲
Writers: Ronald Wilkerson & Jean Louise Matthias
Director: Robert Wiemer
April 5, 1993
Picard has to deal with the ethics of starting a relationship with a new member of the *Enterprise* crew.

The Chase ▲▲▲
Teleplay: Joe Menosky
Story: Joe Menosky & Ronald D. Moore
Director: Jonathan Frakes
April 26, 1993
Attempting to solve an ancient DNA mystery, Picard finds himself in a race against a host of aliens to find the secrets of a lost civilization.

Frame of Mind ▲▲▲▲
Writer: Brannon Braga
Director: James L. Conway
May 3, 1993
Riker awakes to find himself a patient in an asylum and is told his life aboard the *Enterprise* has been an illusion.

Suspicions ▲▲▲
Writers: Joe Menosky and Naren Shankar
Director: Cliff Bole
May 10, 1993
Crusher is relieved of duty when she investigates deaths resulting from a scientific experiment.

Rightful Heir ▲▲▲▲
Teleplay: Ronald D. Moore
Story: James E. Brooks
Director: Winrich Kolbe
May 17, 1993
Worf takes part in a ceremony to summon Klingon legend Kahless, but is the being who appears the real thing?

Second Chances ▲▲▲▲▲
Teleplay: René Echevarria
Story: Michael A. Medlock
Director: LeVar Burton
May 24, 1993

First Officer Riker finds he has a double created eight years before as part of a transporter accident.

Timescape ▲▲▲▲
Writer: Brannon Braga
Director: Adam Nimoy
June 14, 1993
The *Enterprise* seems frozen in time...

Descent ▲▲▲
Teleplay: Ronald D. Moore
Story: Jeri Taylor
Director: Alexander Singer
June 21, 1993
A new strain of ruthless Borg offer Data a chance to experience human emotions.

MOST VALUABLE PLAYER

Ronald D. Moore. As the writer of two of this season's best episodes, "Relics" and "Tapestry," Moore ensures that the human condition isn't overshadowed by concerns about warp core explosions and holodeck malfunctions. Scotty's appearance, which might have been a mere stunt, becomes a completely satisfying experience, and Picard's surprising and contradictory past reminds us that our lives are merely the sum of our past choices.

STAR TREK
THE NEXT GENERATION

SEASON 7
September 1993-May 1994

Star Trek never had to deal in endings before *The Next Generation*. The original series and the animated series had both ceased, but neither had really concluded. Indeed, when *TNG* began back in 1987, that original crew was still boldly going on the big screen. When *TNG*'s turn came to bow out from television, it was already assured that they too would make the transfer to movie theaters, but this time the end of an era would be marked.

"All Good Things...", the feature-length finale for *TNG* on television, dominates the final season. Like the six years before it, season seven is a lively mix of ensemble adventures ("Gambit, Parts I and II") and focused character pieces ("Preemptive Strike", "The Pegasus"), but in the end, it's all, well... in the end.

The title is, of course, taken from the phrase spoken by Q: "All good things must come to an end," but it is also a rare nod to the viewers. Despite Q's flippant statement, the Continuum isn't out to end humanity, but to stop its very existence. In fact, there are no real endings in the story for the characters at all – only for the audience. Unlike the final stories of every *Star Trek* TV series that would follow, *TNG* ends with its crew carrying on much as ever, albeit wiser for their experiences.

It's that decision that makes "All Good Things..." the unforgettably indulgent watch that it is. By bouncing Picard around in time, it revels in icons from the past (Tasha Yar! Loquacious Data!) and explores a rich potential future (Beverly Picard! Cambridge Data!) without having to focus too hard on – or fundamentally alter – the day-to-day set-up of the show. By the end of the episode, you're in no doubt that the series is well and truly over, but know too that its legend will live on, and the adventure will always continue.

In order to justify this congratulatory finale, the rest of season seven needed its fair share of classic installments, and it doesn't disappoint on that score. The best episodes are the ones that break with tradition, and show us *TNG* in a whole new light. As the show moves beyond Gene Roddenbery's original vision, "Gambit" gives us *Star Trek*'s first space pirates, and "The Pegasus" not only presents us with a full-blown Starfleet cover-up, but one in which our very own Commander Riker is complicit! When season seven does revisit the past, it does so in exciting and unexpected ways, as when Ensign Ro returns to infiltrate the Maquis in "Preemptive Strike", or when another Bajoran, Sito Jaxa (from season five's "The First Duty"), reappears to steal the show in the format-stretching "Lower Decks."

Of course, there are low points too, mostly stemming from *TNG*'s ongoing fascination with family. Only Riker escapes a reunion this season, as Deanna finds out from her mother about the sister she never knew, Worf butts heads with his brother and his son, Picard finds out he has a 'son,' Geordi and Data unexpectedly meet their 'mothers,' and Beverly welcomes Wesley home and meets the dead body of her possessed grandmother! Even the weakest episodes have something to recommend them, though, such as the ill-conceived "Genesis," which at least allows *TNG* one more mission with Reg Barclay.

But season seven really belongs to the regular cast. Freed from the restraints of writing for an ongoing series, the *TNG* team exploited the show's definite end date to flesh out the characters' thoughts and feelings more explicitly. Most obviously, this happens with Picard and Beverly Crusher in "Attached" and thereafter, but the burgeoning romance between Worf and Troi is also allowed to be little more than just a plot point, despite paying off to great effect in "All Good Things..."

The cast take these opportunities and run with them, adding subtle new dimensions to their interplay that might have been sidelined for the sake of continuity in

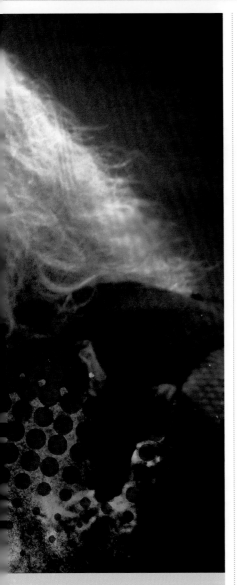

Descent, Part II ∧∧∧
Writer: René Echevarria
Director: Alexander Singer
September 20, 1993
Data's brother Lore teams up with the Borg to attack the Federation.

Liaisons ∧∧∧
Teleplay: Jeanne Carrigan Fauci & Lisa Rich
Story: Roger Eschbacher & Jaq Greenspon
Director: Cliff Bole
September 27, 1993
Picard is trapped on a planet with an alien stalker who is disguised as a beautiful woman.

Interface ∧∧∧
Writer: Joe Menosky
Director: Robert Wiemer
October 4, 1993
Going against Picard's order, Geordi sets out to find a lost ship which has his mother aboard...

Gambit, Part I ∧∧∧∧∧
Teleplay: Naren Shankar
Story: Christopher Hatton & Naren Shankar
Director: Peter Lauritson
October 11, 1993
Picard is dead: Deanna Troi and Will Riker set out to investigate among a planet's lawless underworld.

OK, so we know Picard's not really dead, but it's still great fun finding out where he is, and a great opportunity for the captain and Riker to play the bad boys.

1993-94

Gambit, Part II ∧∧∧∧
Teleplay: Ronald D. Moore
Story: Naren Shankar
Director: Alexander Singer
October 18, 1993
On an undercover mission, Picard discovers renegade Vulcans who are assembling a super weapon.

Phantasms ∧∧
Writer: Brannon Braga
Director: Patrick Stewart
October 25, 1993
Data suffers a series of disturbing visions when he engages a dreaming program.

Dark Page ∧∧
Writer: Hillary J. Bader
Director: Les Landau
November 1, 1993
Troi's mother uncovers long-suppressed personal memories when teaching a telepathic people to use their powers.

Attached ∧∧∧
Writer: Nick Sagan
Director: Jonathan Frakes
November 8, 1993
On the run from hostile aliens, Picard and Crusher are connected by a telepathic link so they can read each other's minds.

---

earlier seasons. Every main cast member also gets at least one opportunity to try something new, from Brent Spiner's multiple personalities in "Masks" to Gates McFadden's sexy Beverly in "Sub Rosa," yet it is Patrick Stewart who makes season seven his own.

In previous seasons, Picard was sometimes underused: stuck on the bridge while the ensemble cast got all the fun around him. But in a foreshadowing of the subsequent films – which set up Picard and Data as *TNG*'s Kirk and Spock – season seven puts Picard at the heart of the action wherever possible, giving Stewart plenty of opportunities to play the mentor, the diplomat, even a lover and a father. As the smuggler Galen in "Gambit," he has a cocksure swagger, and of course in "All Good Things..." he carries the entire human adventure on his shoulders. We had seen him play an old man before in "The Inner Light," but here he is pitch-perfect as three different iterations of the same man. No wonder the children on the *Enterprise* have a Captain Picard Day ("The Pegasus").

It is this performance as much as anything else that makes "All Good Things..." stand above everything else in season seven, but it is the rest of the season that justifies its wholly accurate title.
Simon Hugo

1966
1967
1968
1969
1970
1971
1972
1973
1974
1975
1976
1977
1978
1979
1980
1981
1982
1983
1984
1985
1986
1987
1988
1989
1990
1991
1992
1993
1994
1995
1996
1997
1998
1999
2000
2001
2002
2003
2004
2005
2006
2007
2008
2009
2010
2011

Force of Nature ▲▲
Writer: Naren Shankar
Director: Robert Lederman
November 15, 1993
Sibling environmental extremists who believe warp travel is damaging space invade the *Enterprise*.

Inheritance ▲▲▲
Teleplay: Dan Koeppel & René Echevarria
Story: Dan Koeppel
Director: Robert Scheerer
November 22, 1993
The woman once married to Data's creator arrives on the *Enterprise*, but the android has never heard of her.

Parallels ▲▲▲▲
Writer: Brannon Braga
Director: Robert Wiemer
November 29, 1993
Reality seems to be breaking down around Worf, as the Klingon experiences many alternate universes.

Subtle inconsistencies build to an exciting series of 'What If?' moments in this fun Worf episode that works as a kind of companion piece to "All Good Things..."

BEST MOMENT

The reveal of a desperate, ragged Riker from an alternate universe is totally unexpected and briefly puts our heroes' adventures into the context of a much bleaker multiverse.

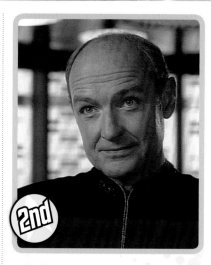

The Pegasus ▲▲▲▲▲
Writer: Ronald D. Moore
Director: LeVar Burton
January 10, 1994
Riker is ordered to recover the wreck of a ship he served on 12 years earlier during a mission that ended in tragedy.

Lost's Terry O'Quinn is great as Admiral Pressman, and the plot is one of *TNG*'s best intrigues. Probably the finest Riker episode in the whole seven-year run.

Homeward ▲▲▲
Teleplay: Naren Shankar
Story: Spike Steingasser & William N. Stape
Director: Alexander Singer
January 17, 1994
Worf has to intervene when his adopted human brother breaks the Prime Directive.

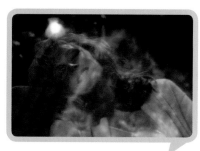

Sub Rosa ▲▲▲
Teleplay: Brannon Braga
Story: Jeri Taylor
Director: Jonathan Frakes
January 31, 1994
Attending a funeral, Crusher falls in love with a ghost.

Lower Decks ▲▲▲▲
Teleplay: René Echevarria
Story: Ronald Wilkerson & Jean Louise Matthias
Director: Gabrielle Beaumont
February 7, 1994
A day in the life of four junior *Enterprise* officers.

The ensigns we meet in this episode could easily have sustained a spin-off show all their own, which makes the ending even more memorable and unexpected.

Thine Own Self ▲▲▲▲
Teleplay: Ronald D. Moore
Story: Christopher Hatton
Director: Winrich Kolbe
February 14, 1994
Trapped on a primitive planet, Data loses his memory.

Masks ▲▲
Writer: Joe Menosky
Director: Robert Wiemer
February 21, 1994
The cultural archive of a dead civilization is downloaded into Data.

Eye of the Beholder ▲▲▲
Teleplay: René Echevarria
Story: Brannon Braga
Director: Cliff Bole
February 28, 1994
Troi and Worf investigate the suicide of an *Enterprise* crewman.

Genesis ▲▲

Writer: Brannon Braga
Director: Gates McFadden
March 21, 1994

Returning from an Away Mission, Picard and Data find the *Enterprise* crew have regressed to more primitive life forms.

Potential comedy (Spot as an iguana, the thought of Picard becoming a lemur) isn't played for laughs, leaving a Deanna Troi with gills to be unintentionally hilarious.

Worst Episode

Journey's End ▲▲▲

Teleplay: Ronald D. Moore
Story: Shawn Piller & Antonia Napoli
Director: Corey Allen
March 28, 1994

A colony of Native Americans refuse to evacuate in favor of the Cardassians, pitting Wesley against Picard.

Firstborn ▲▲▲

Teleplay: René Echevarria
Story: Mark Kalbfeld
Director: Jonathan West
April 25, 1994

Worf takes his son Alexander to experience Klingon culture, only for the pair to be caught up in a political struggle.

Bloodlines ▲▲▲

Writer: Nick Sagan
Director: Les Landau
May 2, 1994

Picard's long-lost son is kidnapped by a Ferengi who threatens to kill him.

Emergence ▲▲

Teleplay: Joe Menosky
Story: Brannon Braga
Director: Cliff Bole
May 9, 1994

A series of computer faults leads Data to conclude that the *Enterprise* has become self-aware...

Preemptive Strike ▲▲▲▲

Teleplay: René Echevarria
Story: Naren Shankar
Director: Patrick Stewart
May 16, 1994

On a mission to infiltrate the rebel Maquis, Ensign Ro Laren discovers she is sympathetic to their cause.

Best Guest Star

Michelle Forbes' return as the conflicted Ro Laren is a fitting send-off for the character that keeps you guessing to the end.

1st

All Good Things... ▲▲▲▲▲

Writers: Brannon Braga & Ronald D. Moore
Director: Winrich Kolbe
May 23, 1994

Picard is unbound in time, experiencing the past, present, and future, culminating in a confrontation with Q.

The "anti-time" plot doesn't really stand up to scrutiny, but it's impossible to resist this love-letter to seven years of adventure aboard the *Enterprise*-D.

MOST VALUED PERFORMANCE

Patrick Stewart makes the ensemble show his own in season seven, bringing more warmth and vulnerability to Picard, and flexing his muscles as Galen and the elderly Ambassador Picard.

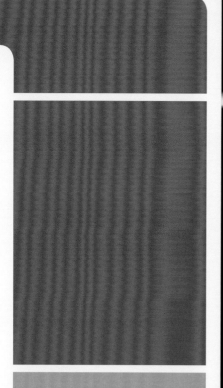

It's a story of hidden archives, technical wizardry, and passionate attention to detail. Ian Spelling speaks to Michael and Denise Okuda, among others, about the high-definition overhaul of *Star Trek: The Next Generation*.

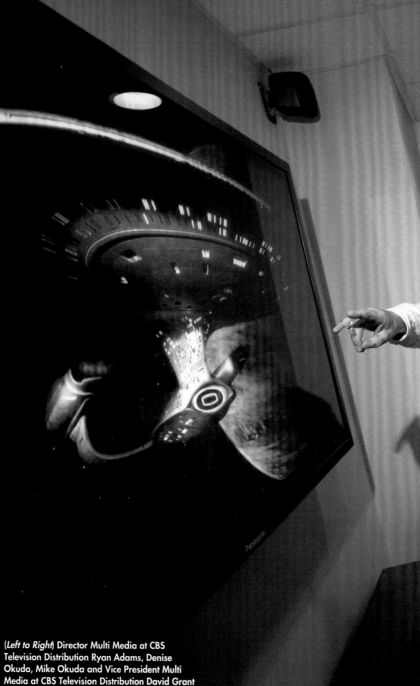

(*Left to Right*) Director Multi Media at CBS Television Distribution Ryan Adams, Denise Okuda, Mike Okuda and Vice President Multi Media at CBS Television Distribution David Grant

A VOYAGE OF REDISCOVERY

There's really no imagining *Star Trek* without Michael and Denise Okuda. Together and individually, they've lent their talents to the franchise in numerous capacities, from graphic artists to technical supervisors and consultants, from *The Next Generation*'s television and big-screen adventures, *Deep Space Nine*, *Voyager*, and *Enterprise*, not to mention assorted *Star Trek* video-games and *Star Trek Online*. And, as fans are aware, there's more. Michael Okuda also worked on *Star Trek IV*, *V*, and *VI*, while Denise co-wrote *The Star Trek Encyclopedia* with her husband, and he co-authored the *Star Trek Chronology* and *The Next Generation Technical Manual*.

The list goes on: they had a large hand in helping auctioneers Christie's stage their mega-*Star Trek* auction several years ago. More recently, they jointly worked as visual effects producers on the original *Star Trek* series Blu-ray collection.

Their latest *Trek*-centric project has them back in the Blu-ray realm, as they're serving as consultants for CBS Home Entertainment on the

> ## "WE ARE AMAZED AT THINGS WE'VE NEVER SEEN BEFORE OR NEVER NOTICED BEFORE OR ARE DISCOVERING ANEW."

remastering of all seven seasons of *The Next Generation*. Fans got their first taste of this major project earlier this year, with the four-episode sampler set "The Next Level", which included the pilot episode "Encounter at Farpoint", alongside later episodes "Sins of the Father" and "The Inner Light." The full first-season *TNG* package arrived this summer, and more packages are on the way over the next few years. *Star Trek Magazine* recently engaged the Okudas in conversation, and also spoke to other key players on the Blu-ray project, including Craig Weiss, Executive Creative Director for CBS Digital, Ryan D. Adams, Director Multi Media at CBS Television Distribution, and David S. Grant, Vice President Multi Media at CBS Television Distribution.

(*Clockwise from top*) Mike Okuda, Denise Okuda, Director Multi Media at CBS Television Distribution Ryan Adams, and visual effects colorist Deron Warner

Deron Warner touches up a scene featuring Marina Sirtis as Troi

"It's actually been quite a voyage of rediscovery," Mike Okuda says. "Twenty-five years ago, we were just immersed in this. Especially for me, it was a full-time job. It was ground-breaking and exciting and thrilling, but it's been a lot of years. So there are a lot of episodes that neither of us had seen since they first aired. To discover it again is great. We thought, 'Wow, that was fun' or, 'Look what they did in that shot' or, 'I can't believe what was done here.'"

Denise Okuda jumps in, "When you're putting something like that under a microscope, as we are, you always discover something new. We are amazed at things we've never seen before or never noticed before or are discovering anew, or, as Michael just said, that trigger memories of things that happened many years ago."

"Just to give you an example, we do the preliminary breakdown for visual effects," Mike says. "That is, we watch an episode literally shot by shot, and we write down what we think is going to need to be done to recreate the original work. It's a very painstaking, technical thing to do, and it's amazing the number of times you just get caught up in the story and think, 'Oh, wait, I have to go back.'"

So, what precisely is everyone involved doing? Are they upgrading the episodes? Modernizing them? And who's doing what?

"Everything is literally being remastered," Mike replies. "That is, CBS Digital is going back to the original film elements and re-scanning them to create a new master. The goal is to create a new master that is as much like the original as possible, just clearer, sharper, and richer. The goal is to bring out what was there to begin with."

Denise hastens to add, "It is not our intention to re-imagine *TNG*. We want to replicate exactly what you saw, just in high-definition and looking so much better."

"The original series project was very different from a technical point of view, because a lot of the film elements, the raw film, especially for the visual effects, didn't exist," Mike explains. "Also, because the original series was edited on film, cut-together film exists. So it was a matter of re-scanning the original, and when you did that, you automatically re-created the original edit. Not to trivialize what was done then, because that was a huge amount of work, most of the remastering was relatively less complicated. The only part that was more complicated was the fact that original camera elements didn't exist for the visual effects, for the ship shots, mostly. Those had to be recreated from scratch."

"WE WANT TO REPLICATE EXACTLY WHAT YOU SAW, JUST IN HIGH-DEFINITION AND LOOKING SO MUCH BETTER."

Weiss, in his capacity as Creative Director at CBS Digital, oversees the department and pretty much all the work that comes through it. "On *TNG*, I'm primarily involved in the visual effects, but I do oversee the mastering as well," he says. "On the mastering side, I just make sure that everything is working properly, and then on the visual effects side I work with the artists and make calls on our end in terms of certain approaches and techniques and work-flow, and just making sure that things get done and done correctly.

"I also oversee a bunch of stuff on a more global basis, but I have a session every week for *TNG* with the Okudas, as we review the visual effects and make notes," Weiss continues. "So I'm heavily involved on that level. I loved *TNG*, and now that I've been a part of it from this end, it makes me so much more of a fan. I've gotten to meet some of the actors, and just being able to touch the original negatives is, in an interesting way, an honor. It's something that's been put away for 25 years and that only a handful of people have ever gotten to see and touch. It's like opening a treasure and being there when it's opened."

The *TNG* footage that Weiss is referring to was in remarkable shape for its age. Paramount maintains a massive archive in an abandoned salt mine, where everything is stored in temperature- and humidity-controlled conditions. That goes a long way toward preserving *TNG* negatives.

"There was a very interesting extra feature on The Next Level that actually shows the process and how the footage is in boxes and boxes and boxes, and you have to go into those boxes, find the footage and find the right take and go from there," Denise says. "This project is so huge. It's unbelievable that CBS is doing it."

"I remember that when David Grant came back from one of his trips to the salt mine, he said it was like Indiana Jones," Mike says, laughing. "It was like the last scene of Indiana Jones, of *Raiders of the Lost Ark*."

Asked to elaborate on their role in the process, both Okudas chuckle, take a deep breath, and then accommodate the request. "The overall project involves an amazing team of archivists, led by (CBS Digital Production Coordinator) Sarah Paul," Mike says. "They're the ones who trudge through all of the reels and reels of film, scanning it and then matching it to the original episodes. On one hand, fortunately, there's an excellent template, because the original video exists. On the other hand, if there are five takes of Picard on the bridge giving an order, which take was it? In most cases, you can tell that from the camera notes, but a lot of times there were last-minute tweaks when they built the original episodes. So you have to make sure that, in fact, what is being done is what was in the notes and in the episode.

"So," Denise adds, "they have to go through, find the footage, find the right take, and if the camera

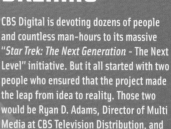

DIGITAL DREAMS

CBS Digital is devoting dozens of people and countless man-hours to its massive *"Star Trek: The Next Generation* - The Next Level" initiative. But it all started with two people who ensured that the project made the leap from idea to reality. Those two would be Ryan D. Adams, Director of Multi Media at CBS Television Distribution, and David S. Grant, Vice President of Multi Media at CBS Television Distribution.

"We had received a lot of input from the fans over the past couple of years on how much they wanted to see *TNG* in HD," Adams says. "So we are now honored to be a part of giving that to them," added Grant. "We are both so thrilled and excited to have gotten the HD remastering of *ST: TNG* off the ground and going. Since the moment we finished the original series, our goal was to get *TNG* in High Definition next. So, once we received the approval to get going on it, we were ecstatic, to say the least."

Denise and Michael Okuda check a recomposited transporter effect

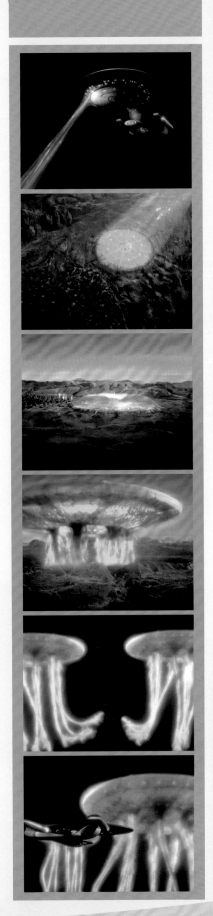

Executive Creative Director for CBS Digital Craig Weiss (standing) and lead matte painter Max Gabl re-examine an effects sequence

notes aren't specific enough, they need to look at all the takes. Then it's all edited back together to make the episode. It's huge, huge work."

"Then, for the two of us, we've been brought in as overall consultants," Mike continues. "One of our major tasks is consulting on the visual effects. That is, we see ourselves as the eyes and the ears of the original cinematographers, original directors and original visual effects

supervisors. We are trying to make it so that, even though a lot of the visual effects are recreated, when you see the finished episode, you go, 'Wow, that's what I saw 25 years ago.'"

"And, as Mike mentioned, it really starts for us in screening the episode," Denise says. "Then we do a very detailed spreadsheet, a breakdown of each visual effects shot, the in-cue and the out-cue and the dialogue. Then we submit that

Digitizing the original film reels of *Star Trek: The Next Generation* at 24 frames per second on a Spirit 2K telecine machine

Denise and Mike Okuda at
CBS Television City in Los Angeles

"And parallel to all that, CBS Digital has teams of people doing different things," Mike says. "There's a team that's restoring the film, that's looking for scratches or dirt that needs to be removed. There's a gentleman whose job is simply to make sure the color is consistent from shot to shot. David and Ryan are overseeing the conversion of the original stereo mix tracks. There are, of course, a roomful of compositors, visual effects artists whose job is to take the raw ship shots, the raw transporter elements, and put them together in a manner as close as possible to the original."

It is, the Okudas and Weiss noted, the overriding mission of everyone involved in the *TNG* remastering to render a product that resembles, as closely as possible, the original episodes that aired between 1987 and 1993. However, Weiss admits, there are exceptions to the rule. "I think, as artists, the temptation is always, 'How do I make my work better?'" Weiss

and, from there, that's where the artists go to work. Then, every week, we go into CBS. We all sit in the screening room and go through the footage. There are tweaks. There are comments. We offer those and then, when the whole thing is all done, we screen the standard-def episode next to the high-def episode and we make sure that everything is copacetic. In addition, we have input on color.

"THIS PROJECT IS SO HUGE. IT'S UNBELIEVABLE THAT CBS IS DOING IT."

says. "I don't think it's a matter of going in there and saying, 'I don't like what they did.' It's more like, 'Well, they probably didn't have the proper time or, the way the element was done, we could stabilize that or make that look a little better.' I think that's where maybe we'll do that based on just the technology and what we know they were trying to do, versus, 'Hey, let's make that a little cooler.' We don't do that. It's more about how we fix the things they probably would have wanted to have fixed as well."

While the Okudas are, as a tandem, one cog in the machine, Weiss describes their contribution as invaluable. "Mike and Denise are the *Star Trek* encyclopedia when it comes to verifying what's correct," he says. "They've been involved in consulting, pretty much weighing in on everything and verifying all the different work to make sure that it's accurate. There's really no creative license in this, in term of it's pretty much going back and being faithful to the original show. That's what everyone involved is trying to do. That's the goal."

"I'm proud that we've helped bring Gene Roddenberry's universe alive for yet another generation of viewers," Michael Okuda says. "When we started *Star Trek: The Next Generation*, the fans were understandably skeptical, but over the months and years of *The Next Generation*, people discovered, 'You know, this doesn't take away from Kirk and Spock. This adds to it.' And to have the fans accept it as another chapter in the *Star Trek* saga was very, very gratifying." ▲

OKUDAGRAMS

Michael Okuda has spent decades working in the *Star Trek* universe, and borne witness to game-changing advances in real world technologies that have echoed his visionary designs.

Okuda admits to taking tremendous pleasure in knowing that some of the computer graphics and interfaces that he helped devise 25 years ago are nudging closer and closer to reality. And, in the meantime, there are *TNG*-style apps fans can purchase to give their cell phones and other handheld devices a *TNG* look and feel. "I'm constantly amazed that real-life computers are not only resembling, but in some cases overtaking what we did back in the days of *Star Trek: The Next Generation*," he says. "I remember that we did a whole sequence where Data was doing a keyword search. I did like four or five different computer-screen animations. This was for the episode '11001001.' This is something that you do with two clicks of a mouse, using Google. The iPad app is a lot of fun, but there's no greater honor than there being a fair number of people at computer companies who say, 'We were inspired by *Star Trek*'s computers.' To have had a bit of a hand in that is just amazing."

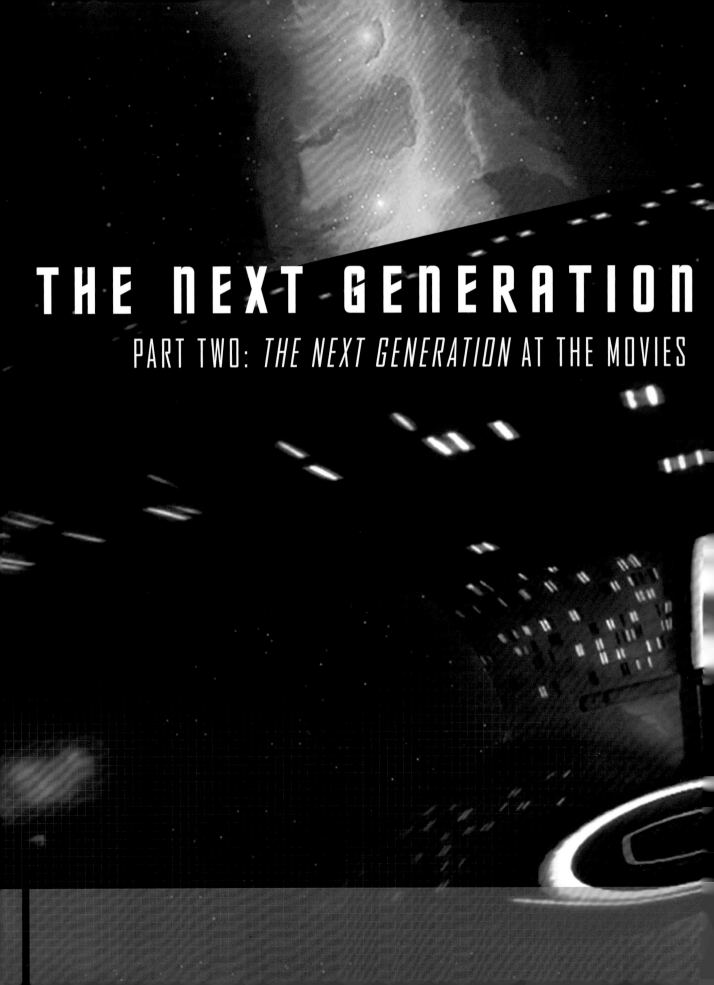

THE NEXT GENERATION

PART TWO: *THE NEXT GENERATION* AT THE MOVIES

When *The Next Generation*'s TV run ended with the sublime series finale, "All Good Things..." the cast and crew were already preparing for their transition to the big screen. Four very different movies followed, which would see the destruction of the *Enterprise*-D, an all-action encounter with the Borg, the discovery of the fountain of youth, and the "death" of a much-loved character...

THE DECLINE AND FALL

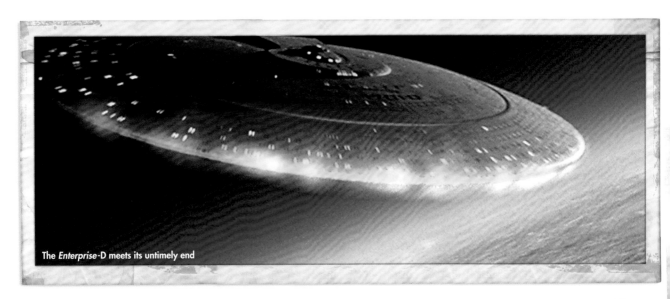

The *Enterprise*-D meets its untimely end

T he memory cheats. It's difficult to imagine now, when a *Star Trek* film can garner nigh-universal critical praise, but *Star Trek* was, for a few brief months in 1994 – dare we say it? – cool. Sixteen years ago, it truly seemed that *Star Trek* would conquer the world. *Star Trek: The Next Generation* had just finished its final season with an Emmy nomination for Best Drama. *Star Trek: Deep Space Nine* was about to enter its third season, Paramount would soon launch a new television network to be anchored by *Star Trek: Voyager*. Patrick Stewart and William Shatner appeared together on the cover of *Time*. *Star Trek* was clearly more popular, more influential that it had ever been. There were summits still to climb, and it was hoped the film *Star Trek Generations*, bringing together two generations for a single adventure, would lead the way.

Ask a *Star Trek* fan about *Generations*, and the responses may be about the story – "It's the crossover film," "Data gets his emotion chip," "The *Enterprise* crashes," "Kirk dies" – but, more than likely, it will be

a subjective judgment on the film: "It's not very good." The fan consensus is remarkably uniform; no fan would call the film the best of the 11, and it would be a rare fan that would rank it even in the top half.

With a feeling that the original series cast was spent as a box office draw executives at Paramount decided to retire *TNG* on television and relaunch it as a film series to create a run of low-budget, high-profit films utilizing the proven – and cheaper – *TNG* stars. Producer Rick Berman, who had been a part of *TNG* since its birth, was handed the reins of the film series, and he made the early decision that the first *TNG* film should incorporate the cast of the original series as much as possible, to pass the torch from one generation to the next.

Berman put two scripts into development. The first, by former *TNG* producer Maurice Hurley, was not precisely a crossover film – Picard calls upon a simulation of Kirk on the Holodeck for advice when the Federation is threatened. The second, by then-current *TNG* writers Ronald D. Moore and Brannon Braga, was more

conventional, utilizing both crews. Their initial idea, to have Kirk and his crew battle Picard and his because of the potential teaser image of two *Enterprises* locked in battle, was irresistible, but it was also unworkable; they could not construct a story that made both crews appear heroic. They came up with another idea in its place – a mystery that spanned the 23rd and 24th Centuries, bringing the two captains, Kirk and Picard, together for the climax. This second story would evolve into *Generations*.

Fan mythologies have accreted to *Generations* over the past 15 years – the studio had a "laundry list" of story elements; Kirk had to die; the *Enterprise*-D had to be destroyed, though none of these beliefs are true. There was no requirement to kill Kirk from on high; Hurley's script presumed that Kirk was dead, and while Moore and Braga's script included a death scene for Kirk, as Berman believed that a death scene would interest Shatner in the film. Similarly, the *Enterprise*'s demise was planned for the end of the sixth season of *TNG*, except the effects could not be done effectively on a television budget.

STAR TREK
THE MOTION PICTURE

STAR TREK II
THE WRATH
OF KHAN

STAR TREK III
THE SEARCH FOR
SPOCK

STAR TREK
IV
THE VOYAGE HOME

STAR TREK
THE FINAL FRONTIER

STAR TREK
VI

STAR TREK
GENERATIONS

STAR TREK
FIRST CONTACT

STAR TREK
INSURRECTION

STAR TREK
NEMESIS

STAR TREK

"In the end, time is going to hunt you down, and make the kill."

Malcolm McDowell as Soran
Star Trek Generations

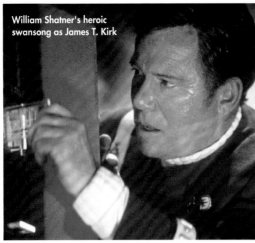

William Shatner's heroic swansong as James T. Kirk

Captain Harriman (Alan Ruck)

The film's prologue was to be set aboard the successor to the ship seen in the previous movies, the *Enterprise*-B, during her maiden voyage, and Moore and Braga wrote dialogue for the entire original *Star Trek* crew as they were on hand to witness the occasion. These scenes became crowded and unwieldy, with too little for the actors to do. The original cast was ultimately pared from seven to three – Kirk, Spock, and McCoy – and would be altered further to Kirk, Scotty, and Chekov when Leonard Nimoy and DeForest Kelley passed on appearing.

In spite of Nimoy's decision not to appear in the film, Berman approached him to direct. Nimoy saw places where the script could be improved. Berman, however, felt there was no time for revisions and wanted the script shot as written. Without changes,

> ## "The visual style brought to *Generations* lends an air of finality to *The Next Generation* in a way that its TV finale did not."

Nimoy passed on helming the film, and Berman turned to British television director David Carson, an experienced *Star Trek* hand with *TNG*'s two-crew story "Yesterday's Enterprise" and *DS9*'s pilot to his credit.

On its own merits, *Generations* is an adequate, if deeply flawed film. Moore and Braga never find a balance between plot and character, spending their time on Picard's emotional crisis and Data's discovery of human emotions, neither of which drive the story nor bear any relevance to Tolian Soran's alliance with renegade Klingons and his decision to kill millions in pursuit of his goal. *Generations*' plot beggars logic, introducing blind alleys that go nowhere – why is there no follow-up to a Romulan attack on a Federation research outpost, and why does Picard choose the film's least decisive moment to defeat Soran? Worse, the film lacks a sense of the stakes involved. While Malcolm McDowell's Soran conveys menace, he never comes across as evil or insane, only misguided, and the destruction of Veridian IV is presented as abstract, a

faceless consequence of Soran's pursuit of an aim that the audience never quite understands.

Even the film's performances are mixed. Shatner brings some intensity to the film's early sequences, but his later scenes have a languid feel, matched by Stewart's own apathetic performance. Stewart, by his own admission, was extremely tired following nine months of filming *TNG*'s final season, and he comes across on-screen as disengaged. The rest of the *TNG* cast fares better, and McDowell has genuine presence on screen.

Carson and cinematographer John Alonzo created a visually impressive film. The sets and costumes of *TNG*, in daily use for seven years, were worn-down and unsuited to film. With no money in the budget to upgrade sets that would be destroyed anyway, Alonzo bathed the sets in darkness and ambient lighting. After new costumes were created, the decision was made to use the ones designed for *DS9* instead. Working within these limitations, Carson and Alonzo shot a visually somber film. The darkness of the *Enterprise* bridge, the haunting illumination of Picard's and Guinan's cabins, once so bright on television, now convey an air of gloom and pessimism.

Generations is emblematic of its time, just as much as *Star Trek VI* was, but unlike its predecessor, *Generations* is a fundamentally pessimistic film. Just

two weeks before the film opened the Republicans took both houses of Congress, and Clinton argued that as President he was still relevant. Though not intended as such, the film represents a passing of one ideology to the next, from liberalism as embodied by Kirk and the original series to conservativism as embodied by Picard and the 24th Century. The film lacks in hope; the visual style brought to the film lends an air of finality to *TNG* in a way that its TV finale "All Good Things..." did not.

Star Trek reached the summit in 1994. There were no higher peaks ahead. Only in retrospect can we see that *Star Trek: Generations* represented the franchise reaching its zenith, not a new and higher plateau from which new heights could be scaled.

Or so it seemed...

Allyn Gibson

Kirk (William Shatner) clings on for dear life, during the climax of *Generations*

Riker (Jonathan Frakes) rescues Soran (McDowell) from the wreckage of the Amargosa Observatory

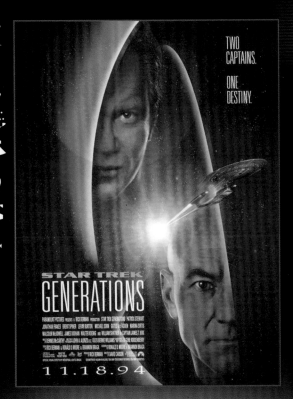

TWO CAPTAINS.

ONE DESTINY.

STAR TREK
GENERATIONS

11.18.94

CRITICS' VERDICT:

GENERATIONS

Generations was the movie that killed Kirk. But that was mostly a problem for *Star Trek* fans, not for film critics, who tended to be more interested in craft than the demise of a beloved pop-culture icon with Rita Kempley calling it "a flawed but funky adventure" in her review for *The Washington Post*.

"The problem is that while *Star Trek Generations* is undeniably a major motion picture," notes ReelViews's James Berardinelli, "too often it seems like little more than an overbudgeted, double-length episode of the *Next Generation* television series."

"*Star Trek Generations* has enough verve, imagination and familiarity to satisfy three decades' worth of Trekkers raised on several incarnations of the television skein," wrote Leonard Klady for *Variety*. "While the abundance of narrative thread tends to slow matters to less than warp speed, that's offset by a lot of character detail."

"*Generations* is predictably flabby and impenetrable in places," according to Janet Maslin of *The New York Times*, "but it has enough pomp, spectacle and high-tech small talk to keep the franchise afloat. And in an age when much fancier futuristic effects can be found elsewhere, even its tackiness is a comfort."

DATA LOG

The Torch of Adventure is About to be Passed

"I take it the odds are against us, and the situation is grim?"
James T. Kirk

FEATURING:

Kirk

Scotty

Chekov

Picard

Riker

Data

La Forge

Crusher

Troi

Worf

Guinan

GUEST STARRING:

Soran
(Malcolm McDowell)

Captain John Harriman
(Alan Ruck)

Demora Sulu
(Jacqueline Kim)

Lursa
(Barbara March)

B'Etor
(Gwynyth Walsh)

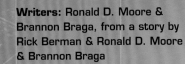

Writers: Ronald D. Moore & Brannon Braga, from a story by Rick Berman & Ronald D. Moore & Brannon Braga

Director: David Carson

Released: USA: November 17, 1994
UK: February 2, 1995
Australia: March 30, 1995

First weekend: $75,671,262
Worldwide gross: $120,000,000

STAR TREK FIRST CONTACT

ASSIMILATING
A GENERAL AUDIENCE

The *Enterprise*-E takes on a Borg cube

1996 was a banner year for *Star Trek*. The franchise celebrated the 30th anniversary of the original series' televised debut, while the show's second spin-off, *Star Trek: Deep Space Nine*, aired its 100th episode, and its third, *Star Trek: Voyager*, began its third year as the number one show on the UPN Network schedule. Marvel launched the Paramount Comics imprint, dedicated primarily to publishing comics based on *Star Trek* in all its incarnations, and Pocket Books published over 30 *Trek* titles, including a line of *Trek* books for young readers, and the very first crossover event connecting all four crews in an overarching story.

Star Trek was quite arguably at its peak of popularity – and the creators of *Star Trek: First Contact*, released that November, knew it. After all, you don't toss out a shameless joke like, "…you're all astronauts on some kind of star trek," unless you're damned sure of your audience's affection, utterly

confident that they'll be giggling more than groaning, and stay right with you all the way to the credits. Up until summer 2009, *First Contact* held the record for the biggest opening weekend box office take of any *Trek* film, evidently managing to attract an audience beyond the ranks of fandom. All the same, *First Contact* is very much a film for the fans – and it's not the least bit ashamed to admit it.

More so than probably any other film in the series, *First Contact* draws on established canon – not terribly surprising, given that it was scripted by two of *TNG*'s most prolific veteran scriptwriters, Ronald D. Moore and Brannon Braga, and directed by another long-time alumnus, Jonathan Frakes. The opening scene is a nightmare flashback to Jean-Luc Picard's assimilation by the Borg in "The Best of Both Worlds," which then segues into the current Borg threat, and Starfleet's concern over how Picard's history with the Borg will affect his performance in battle. Then we cut to the battle in progress, and onto the bridge of the *Defiant*, under the command of Lieutenant Commander

Worf. It is never explained to those audience members who may have never seen an episode of *DS9* why Worf is aboard this other ship, or why Riker later kids him about remembering how to do the job he did for almost seven years on the TV show, but that's beside the point, because now the real story starts.

The Borg cube is quickly destroyed once Picard joins in, and with the requisite big space battle out of the way, the film then switches to that other venerable *Star Trek* story trope: time travel. A small Borg sphere, followed by the *Enterprise*, goes back to the mid-21st Century, where they encounter Zefram Cochrane. Cochrane, we learned in the original series episode "Metamorphosis," was the discoverer of space warp, and one of the most influential figures in human history. As our heroes now try to ensure Cochrane keeps his appointment with destiny, while they are also at the same time engaged in a battle with a Borg boarding party for control of the *Enterprise*, we also revisit Picard's Dixon Hill holodeck program, are reminded of Data's "fully functional" tryst with Tasha

"I am such an idiot. It's so simple. The Borg hurt you, and now you're going to hurt them back."

Alfre Woodard as Lily Sloane

The Borg Sphere emerges
(*Star Trek: First Contact*)

Alice Krige as the Borg Queen

Yar back in season one, and meet another copy of *Voyager*'s Emergency Medical Hologram, who appears here primarily to crack a Bones McCoy "I'm a doctor, not a..." joke.

And yet, even with all these gifts for the continuity mavens in the audience, *First Contact* is still easily accessible to the uninitiated. The story of Picard's assimilation is neatly summarized by the opening dream sequence and the scenes leading up to the battle. And for those new-to-*Trek* viewers who, like Lily, hear the name "Borg" and are put in mind of the Swedes, Frakes does a fantastic job of building the fear of these creatures: we don't actually get a good look at a Borg until a third of the

"Up until this past summer, *First Contact* held the record for the biggest opening weekend box office take of any *Trek* film."

way into the film. Like the best classic monster movies, the audience is encouraged to use their own imaginations as strange shadows move through dimly-lit Jefferies tubes, and as the camera zooms in on a horrified engineer's face, before cut away from her in mid-scream.

Likewise, you don't need to have seen Cochrane's first on-screen appearance to understand his role here. In fact, it would probably be to the viewer's benefit to not even have any knowledge of Glenn Corbett's guest-starring role 30 years earlier, and to be blissfully unaware of the contradictions the casting of James Cromwell seemingly created. All the better to simply enjoy his performance: Cromwell had previously appeared twice on *TNG* before his Best Actor Oscar nomination for the film *Babe*, and he's clearly having a great time back among this group, playing this eccentric, cynical, broken genius, swilling bad liquor and dancing with loose-limbed abandon to classic Roy Orbison. All more the pity that Cochrane ended up being used primarily for comic relief, and is reduced almost to a puppet that Riker and La Forge use to ensure their history books remain literally accurate, if not quite in any deeper sense.

And then, there is the Borg Queen, who flips everything we thought we knew about the Borg on its head. Whereas the Borg of *TNG* were a faceless mass without even the concept of individuality, the Queen is an individual being who actually controls this unrelenting force, and "bring[s] order to chaos." Whereas the old Borg were simply mindless conquerors, the Queen offers a reason – a quest for perfection – for their relentlessness. And rather than lumbering, deformed, largely asexual cybernetic zombies, we have a lithe, graceful and disturbingly sensual Borg who not only tries to seduce Data, but, it turns out, had also tried to seduce Picard/Locutus years earlier. The Queen spends surprisingly little time on screen, but the impression she makes in that short time is indelible.

Of course, a big part of this impression was her entrance, as a disembodied head and upper torso hanging from umbilical cords, flown across the engineering section and lowered into its awaiting body. All the more impressive, in this day when computer generated effects are common even in contemporary films and television

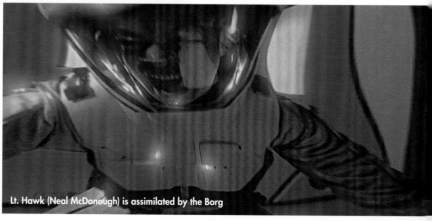
James Cromwell as Zefram Cochrane

programs, to realize this remarkable effect was achieved with old-school optical effects, by putting Alice Krige into a physical harness with an artificial neck and shoulders attached beneath her chin. *First Contact* was in fact a major transitional production: it was the first *Trek* film to make extensive use of digital effects – primarily during the battle with the Borg, and the evacuation of the *Enterprise* – and the last to use actual physical models for the *Enterprise* and the majority of the other ships. And while there are a few spots in the film where the limitations and shortcomings of both practical special effects and early CGI technology stand out, the film still looks great: the *Enterprise*-E movie sets are a marked improvement over the darkened television sets used for *Generations*, and the new and improved Borg make-up is subtle yet highly effective.

But perhaps what really makes this movie, and makes it so easily relatable and timeless, is that, as formidable as the Borg are, our protagonists' real struggles are within themselves. Picard is forced to face his obsession and to overcome it, Data is subjected to temptations of the flesh (both figuratively and literally), and Cochrane finds himself confronted by a destiny that he neither wants nor of which he believes himself capable. In the end, all three manage to overcome their self-doubts... and the confidence the filmmakers displayed coming into this film is proven to have been absolutely justified.
William Leisner

Lt. Hawk (Neal McDonough) is assimilated by the Borg

RESISTANCE IS FUTILE

STAR TREK
FIRST CONTACT

11.22.96

CRITICS' VERDICT:
FIRST CONTACT

The Next Generation cast's first solo outing in movie theatres was largely well received by mainstream critics:

"Here, for a change, is an action movie that takes its subject but not itself seriously," said Richard Corliss in *Time*. "The movie glides along with purpose and style."

George Powell of the *San Francisco Examiner* wrote, "Even those unfamiliar with the entire *Star Trek* phenomenon…will find this a clever action movie, with a well-written screenplay and tight direction of a fine cast….The *Next Generation* cast clearly demonstrate they are more than adequate heirs to what has preceded them."

Susan Stark's review in *Detroit News* was more measured: "The first stretch and the home stretch are so filled with visual interest and, more importantly, with the patented *Star Trek* philosophical and humorous tidbits that fans will gladly suffer the dull Borg patch for the pleasure of the rest."

"The script by Brannon Braga and Ronald D. Moore provides [Patrick Stewart and Alfre Woodard] with the kind of meaty, energetic dialogue that keeps Trekkies coming back for more," declared Margaret A. McGurk for the *Cincinnati Enquirer*.

And *USA Today* noted, "While *First Contact* espouses the usual lofty *Trek* ideals, it never forgets to factor in the fun."

DATA LOG

Resistance is Futile.

"You people, you're all astronauts, on some kind of star trek?"
Zefram Cochrane

FEATURING:

Picard

Riker

Data

La Forge

Crusher

Troi

Worf

Barclay

GUEST STARRING:

Borg Queen
(Alice Krige)

Zefram
Cochrane
(James Cromwell)

Lily Sloane
(Alfre Woodard)

Lt Hawk
(Neal
McDonough)

The Doctor
(Robert Picardo)

Lt Daniels
(Michael Horton)

Writers: Brannon Braga & Ronald D. Moore, based on a story by Rick Berman, Brannon Braga & Ronald D. Moore

Director: Jonathan Frakes

Released: USA: November 18, 1996
UK: December 13, 1996
Australia: November 28, 1996

Opening weekend: $30,716,131
Worldwide gross: $150,000,000

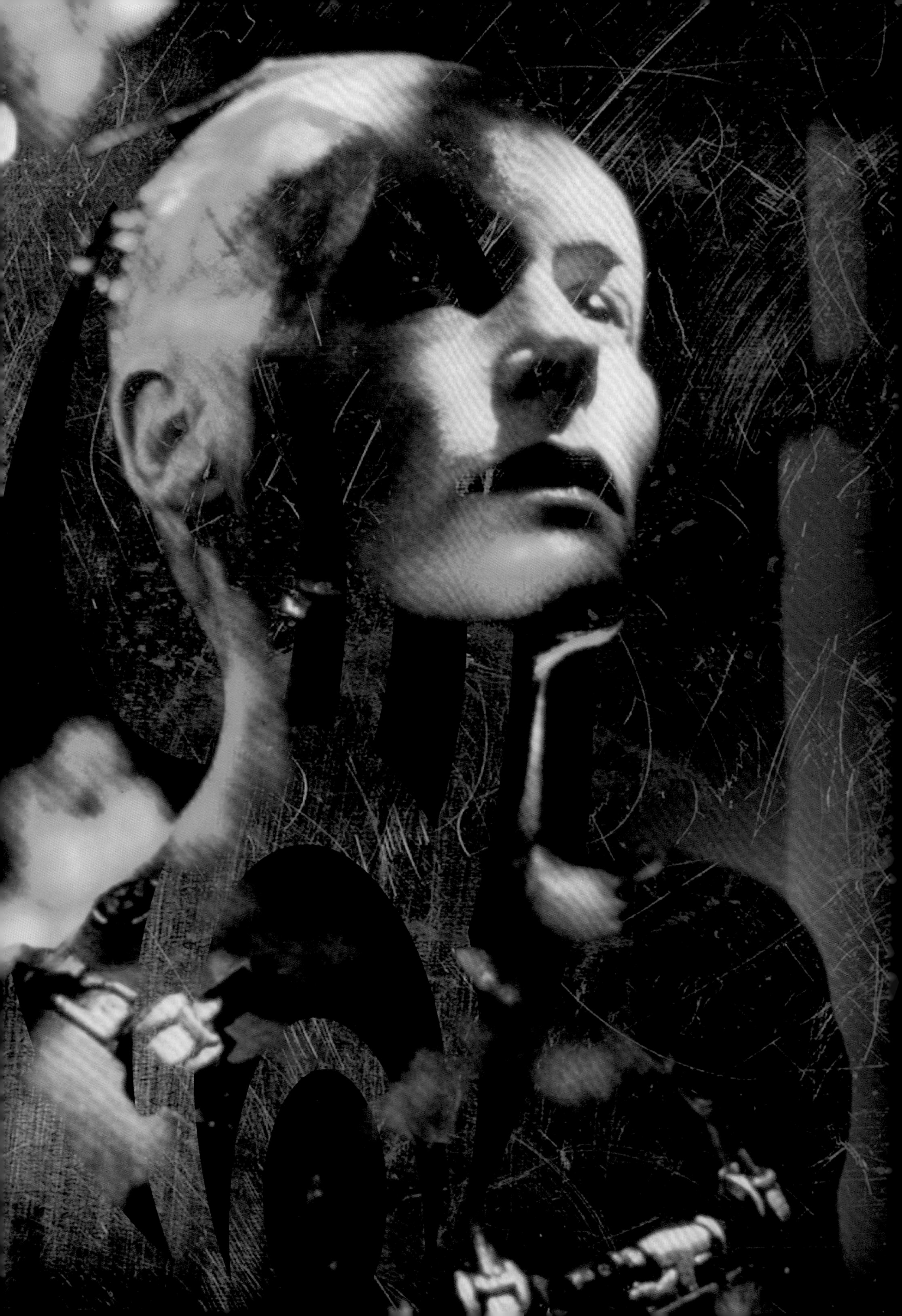

The Borg Queen (Alice Krige) sizes up a potential companion in Locutus (Patrick Stewart) in *Star Trek: First Contact*

THE ONE WHO IS MANY

As the actress most associated with the ruthless Borg Queen, Alice Krige knows better than most how it feels to be assimilated into the Borg collective – and stitched into *that* costume.
Words: Bryan Cairns

The various incarnations of the *U.S.S. Enterprise* have encountered plenty of scary, savage, and cunning adversaries during their exploration of space, although perhaps none as creepy or relentless as the Borg. After being flung across the universe into an uncharted region by the omnipotent Q in "Q Who", Captain Jean-Luc Picard (Patrick Stewart) and his crew barely survived their initial run-in

> "I KNEW NOTHING ABOUT *STAR TREK* WHATSOEVER. I HAD GROWN UP IN A COUNTRY THAT DIDN'T HAVE TELEVISION."

with the lethal species. Since then, the zombie-like Borg have sporadically popped up to terrorize the Federation, but it wasn't until the movie *Star Trek: First Contact* that the seductive Borg Queen, portrayed by actress Alice Krige, was introduced. As it turns out, back then, Krige had no idea what she was getting herself into.

"I knew nothing about *Star Trek* whatsoever," says Krige. "I had grown up in a country that

Starfleet fight a losing battle, in *Star Trek: First Contact*

didn't have television. Television arrived in South Africa the year after I left to go to England. I read books, so I didn't really have any idea of the implications of *Star Trek*. I never even got a script. I got three scenes. I said to my agent, 'This is no good. I need the whole script. How can I come to grips with her if I haven't got the whole story in my head?' And my agent said, 'You don't understand. No one sees the script. People only get scenes.' I went to a friend's house who had written some episodes for *Star Trek*, and he gave me the Borg episodes.

"The character didn't really get a hold of me until I went in and did the audition," continues Krige. "Actually standing there doing it for Rick Berman and the casting director Junie Lowry-Johnson, I suddenly felt the power of the character. By the time I walked out of the audition, which I thought I had done really poorly, I wanted the role terribly. It was before we had mobile phones, so I ran off the lot, found the first pay phone, called my agent and said, 'I've just done a terrible audition, but I badly

"THE BORG QUEEN FELT SHE WAS DOING EVERYONE A BIG FAVOR"

want to play this part. Will you call them right away and tell them I would really value the opportunity of having another go. I promise to do better next time.' We didn't hear from them for three weeks. And then, lo and behold, they asked me to come in."

Not much is known about the Borg. Apparently thousands of years old and not overly big talkers, their prime objective has always remained relatively the same: to achieve perfection by taking over other races, and adding them to their collective consciousness through a painful ordeal known as assimilation.

"The Borg Queen felt she was doing everyone a big favor," Krige remarks. "There's no way I can perceive anyone I play as a villain. They may

have aspects of their personality that are problematic for other people, but I can't have bad feelings about anyone I play. Certainly the Borg Queen thought she was offering a kind of salvation to any being she assimilated."

A captured Picard experienced assimilation firsthand, in the season three finale "The Best of Both Worlds", when he was surgically altered and transformed into Locutus of Borg. Fortunately, the process proved reversible. Given Picard's history with the Borg, Krige naturally assumed the Queen was once again focusing her attention on him. Upon arriving on the *First Contact* set, Krige discovered that wasn't the case at all.

"What happened was everyone went to film in the Angeles National Forest, except for Brent [Spiner]," recalls Krige. "Brent and I met on the lot and it was incredibly instructive. He opened my eyes. I thought the Borg Queen was still interested in Picard, and Brent said 'No, no, no. She's been there and done that. The one that she's really interested in is Data.' And, of course, he was right. Picard was really no match for her. The Queen was messing around with Data and she didn't think for a minute he would mess around with her, and he did. He was not quite her match, but almost."

A STITCH IN TIME

Character motivations were not the only elements Krige had to wrestle with. It was the Queen's pale and cybernetically enhanced exterior, combined with a smooth, authoritative voice, that gave her a commanding presence. Scott Wheeler created the Borg Queen's face and head, while Todd Masters built the suit. Krige herself took an active role in developing the costume and giving suggestions, noting: "as we put it all together, I was very instrumental in defining what she ultimately became." However, on the first day of shooting, the costume became excruciating.

"I started filming on the Friday," says Krige. "We had done tests where I was put in the costume, but then I got out of it. On the Friday, I left home at 2am and joined Scott in my little trailer. To start with, it was very complex to do and got easier and easier. By the time I was doing the installation in Vegas, it was a breeze because we had done it so often. Scott was happier with it in the end than he was in the beginning. So I got to Paramount around 3am and I think we wrapped at 1am the next day."

"We started at 3am, I had cups of coffee and more coffee and then juice and then a cup of tea and some water," continues Krige. "Then around noon, they stitched me into the costume. At

The Borg Queen was given a more flexible, feminine costume than the stiff, rubber outfits reserved for the regular Borg

Alice Krige as the Borg Queen makes her unforgettable entrance, in *Star Trek: First Contact*

about 5pm, I was desperate to pee. I knew I couldn't hold out any longer. I went to the first assistant and said, 'I have to go to the bathroom.' It took 45 minutes to get me out of the costume, but what happened is they couldn't get me back in. My hands and feet had swollen because of how tight it was around my wrists and ankles. The costume had done something Todd had not expected it to do. The rubber had set harder than he thought it would. The edge really chafed. By the time they finally took the costume off me, they knew they couldn't do this on a daily basis."

Masters had to roll with the punches and tweak the outfit. Miraculously, he delivered what was requested.

VOICE ACTIVATED

Beyond *First Contact* and *Voyager*, Krige has gone on to encounter the Borg in different media, voicing the Borg Queen in video game *Star Trek: Armada II*, and filming scenes for the Borg4D interactive adventure at the *Star Trek: The Experience* in Las Vegas.

Portraying the Borg Queen as a solely vocal performance, in particular, was a different experience for the actress.

"I wasn't especially thinking about either my voice or the absence of her physical presence," says Krige. "I just went back into that imaginative space. I actually forgot all about the video game and have never seen it. But I found the installation in Vegas quite difficult. I wasn't interacting with anyone. It was just me on a blue box for several days, talking, and I was filmed in isolation, which is simply not enjoyable, because what is interesting is the exchange between you and other characters. It was much more challenging."

"They told Todd he had to make another suit that weekend," states Krige. "So Todd gathered up the hard rubber suit at 1am, drove across L.A. to his workshop and worked all weekend. As I remember, on Monday at noon, they delivered a soft suit. Well, it was like being wrapped up in a marshmallow. It was fantastic and I was pain-free for the remaining 13 days of the shoot. I have to say, all my poor Borg suffered the way I suffered on the first day for the rest of the shoot. They just couldn't remake every suit."

Nonetheless, the Borg Queen certainly knows how to make an impressive entrance. With Data strapped down and a prisoner, the Queen's severed head, upper torso and spine were lowered-down to connect with the rest of her body.

"I had never done this degree of blue screen work," explains Krige. "I had done some on a film called *Habitat,* in Montreal. Now, it's constant. You work with it all the time. The technology and the whole process of doing it interested me greatly, because it was done with the most controlled camera head. I was in the picture, then out of the picture and they explained it would be put together in the computer.

"I had to re-voice the whole role because there were cranes," adds Krige. "It was all comparatively noisy for a film set. The sound crew wants absolute silence when you are filming, and they didn't have it. Two things happened when I went to do the re-voicing. I did the first lot of

ADR (Automatic Dialogue Replacement) and we didn't finish it in one session, so I had to come back at a later date. When we got to the end, it didn't quite fit. There was a little jump. The head came down in one place and the spine was in another. There was a little jump as the head fitted into the body. But I didn't say anything. I thought, 'They said this was going to be the most memorable entrance of all time, but they aren't there. I went back a second time and there was still a little jump. I thought, 'Hold your peace and wait to see what happens.' That was one thing. The other thing was the second time I went back, as I walked into the recording studio, I thought it sounded really good. I was listening to my own voice. They were playing back what I had already recorded. And they said, 'Well, Alice, we have to tell you. We enhanced what you did.' It was a good reality check."

Inevitably, Picard, Data, and the *Enterprise* get the better of the Borg Queen, and she seemingly died. Of course, in sci-fi, death is rarely an insurmountable condition, and the Borg Queen subsequently reappeared in the *Voyager* episodes "Dark Frontier" and "Unimatrix Zero". While a busy Krige was unavailable to guest star in those episodes (instead actress Susanna Thompson filled the bodysuit), Krige later reprised the part she'd created in the *Voyager* series finale, "Endgame".

"Yes, I was doing something," confirms Krige. "When they asked me to do the finale, I believe it was because Susanna was doing something else. I was very happy to go back and join everyone. I didn't watch Susanna's episodes, but I asked to read the scripts. I don't like to see myself anyway, and I thought to actually see someone else's performance would throw me off course. It was already going to be fairly different because it was the Borg Queen with two females, as opposed to the Borg Queen with two males. It was not out of any disrespect to Susanna. I just felt it wouldn't help the process. And it was very intense. We filmed my work on *Voyager* on two very, very long days, because I had to fly to England to start another project. We did two 20-hour days."

The episode featured an epic confrontation between the Borg Queen and Janeway. Krige was excited to return to the *Star Trek* universe, but unexpectedly became panic stricken the night before, as she prepared for her scenes. Suddenly, there was a new dynamic that Krige had never explored before.

"I was thinking, 'Oh goodness. That kind of sexual tension that existed between Data and the Borg Queen, and indeed Picard and the Borg Queen, I am now doing it with two women!'" explains Krige. "I called one of the producers and said, 'Now what?' And the producer, with good insight, said, 'Don't worry. Just think of the Borg Queen as omni-sexual.' Well, it just became very interesting. The thing

The introduction of the Borg Queen added an extra dimension to an already-complex foe

"DON'T WORRY. JUST THINK OF THE BORG QUEEN AS OMNI-SEXUAL."

about the Borg Queen, Data, and Picard is it's all about power. There really was no reason why she wouldn't use the same energy on Seven of Nine, to manipulate her. With Janeway, it was two fairly formidable opponents coming up against each other."

FANTASY ROLES

On top of her *Star Trek* appearances, Krige has racked up plenty of genre credits. Among them are *Sleepwalkers*, *Dinotopia*, *Children of Dune*, *Ghost Story*, *The 4400*, *The Sorcerer's Apprentice*, *Silent Hill*, *Reign of Fire*, and *Spooks*, to name a few.

"The only one I found difficult was *Silent Hill*," offers Krige. "Because my character, Christabella, wasn't so fantastical; she was so close to a current reality, a religious fanatic who kills people in the name of religion. The script became more extreme and violent. It became exceedingly difficult to channel that energy." Krige had more fun in *Reign of Fire*, although her character was short-lived, "I was dead before the dragon attack. But that fantastical element is wonderful, because you can enter a space that is larger than life. It's fun to let your imagination go and draw very broad strokes." She'll no doubt enjoy her upcoming role in superhero sequel *Thor: The Dark World*, then.

The Borg Queen (Krige) toys with Data's emotion chip, in *Star Trek: First Contact*

"I thought the Borg Queen was still interested in Picard, and Brent said, 'No, no, no. She's been there and done that.'"
Alice Krige on the Borg Queen's taste in men

But it's her new movie, *StringCaesar*, that is Krige's current passion, a film in which she stars and also produced. It's an unconventional exploration of the early life of Roman Emperor Julius Caesar, told in the contemporary setting of three prisons. Krige believes people who love *Star Trek* will be equally engaged by *Jail Caesar*.

"It looks at what takes him from the age of 14 to 33, that period that makes him become this man considered one of the greatest statesmen of all time, and yet if he was alive today, he would probably be charged with war crimes," explains Krige. "He was savagely cruel, if he deemed it necessary. It's a look at history as a series of parallel universes that keep this idea of the string theory of multiple universes on a spindle of time, constantly repeating. It's a very interesting and complex piece."

Krige couldn't be more thrilled to have been involved with a franchise that has such loyal and vocal fans. "I didn't really do a convention until about three years after [*Star Trek: First Contact*] was released," concludes the actress. "It was at that point I understood the dimension of what I had become a part of. It's actually an abiding joy to me, because there are Trekkies all over. They are everywhere." ▲

THE QUEEN IS DEAD. LONG LIVE THE QUEEN.

"I am the beginning; the end; the one who is many. I am the Borg"
The Borg Queen, *Star Trek: First Contact*

Created to "bring order to chaos", the Queen appears to be some kind of hub for the hive-mind of the Borg Collective. But what happens to the Collective if they lose their Queen? Considering how many times we've watched her die, they must simply install a new one!

We first saw the Borg Queen face her mortal end at the climax of *Star Trek: First Contact*. Data released a cloud of warp core plasma coolant, which obliterated all that remained of her pre-assimilated organic body. Picard made doubly sure the job was done, by snapping her cybernetic spinal cord. Surely there's no coming back from that?

Unfortunately for the crew of *Voyager*, there was, and they were to encounter, and defeat, the dreaded Queen on more than one occasion. In the episode "Dark Frontier", we find the Borg Queen trying to re-assimilate Seven of Nine. Things end badly for the Queen, as *Voyager*'s away team make a daring escape aboard the *Delta Flyer*, through a transwarp conduit in which the Borg Queen's vessel is apparently destroyed.

In the two-part *Voyager* tale "Unimatrix Zero", the Borg Queen once again butts heads with Janeway's brave crew, as they attempt to protect a virtual haven for renegade Borg from the Queen's ruthless attempts to destroy it. The Queen appears to perish aboard her own exploding Borg Cube, when she orders it to self-destruct.

The Borg Queen meets her match in *Voyager*'s "Endgame"

She faces yet another final end in the *Voyager* series finale, "Endgame". This time, a future Admiral Janeway infects the Borg Queen with a neurolytic pathogen, and she goes to pieces – literally – as her drone Borg body falls apart!
By Christopher Cooper

163

STAR TREK INSURRECTION

HEART OF LIGHTNESS

Picard (Patrick Stewart) fights to protect the Ba'ku, in *Star Trek: Insurrection*

tar Trek: Insurrection starts with a bang. As the inhabitants of the idyllic Ba'ku world go about their daily routines, turmoil suddenly shatters the tranquility. Shopkeepers inexplicably are knocked to the ground by an unseen force. Then the head of a man appears, apparently floating in air. But it's not just any head. Stripping off an invisibility suit he's been wearing, Starfleet's Lieutenant Commander Data struggles against other invisibles who are attempting to apprehend him. To the dismay of his pursuers, Data fires a well-placed phaser blast at the cliff overhead. Is he out of his positronic mind? Then the dust clears, revealing the previously cloaked observation post where Starfleet and Son'a scientists secretly have been observing the Ba'ku. A million questions are about to be raised, and the audience is as eager to hear the answers as the bewildered Ba'ku people.

It's a great opening sequence, filled with intricate stunt work and clever visual effects. But the momentum quickly dissipates as the scene cuts to more familiar territory – the *Enterprise*-E, where Captain Picard and his crew are hosting a diplomatic gathering. The atmosphere

is as pleasant and reassuring as a family reunion, or as a peaceful Ba'ku village. The only element missing is... action.

Aye, there's the rub. *Star Trek: Insurrection* suffered the misfortune of following a very successful older sibling. With the Borg pressing hard upon Picard and company, *Star Trek: First Contact* was, as old-time critics used to say, an "actioner," and it popped in all the right places. Despite the promise of Data's exciting entrance, *Insurrection* set much of the action aside in exchange for a thought-provoking, but subdued, mystery. Rings around the Ba'ku planet emit "metaphasic radiation" that rejuvenates life. The young-appearing villagers, it turns out, are hundreds of years old – and they even have the ability to slow down time. And that appears to be the message for viewers: Slow down; enjoy the view; take time to play and to observe the hummingbirds. Movie-goers hoping for an exhilarating sequel to the Borg onslaught of *First Contact* felt let down.

The irony here is that the screenplay to *Insurrection* was written by veteran *Star Trek* producer Michael Piller, who knocked viewers' collective socks off with his script

to the quintessential Borg episode "The Best of Both Worlds" for *Star Trek: The Next Generation*. However, faced with the assignment to write the third movie featuring the *TNG* characters, Piller opted not to try to top the Borg. Blockbuster though it was, Piller found *First Contact* to be "a bit dark." The next film, he decided, should make people feel good.

To reach that goal, Piller fell back on his greatest strength as a writer – characterization. And in fact, *Insurrection* is the most character-driven script of the *TNG* movies, with noteworthy scenes that better define the personalities of nearly all the regulars. This isn't surprising. Piller was a much-loved figure in the *Star Trek* community, largely credited with helping *TNG* fulfill its potential. Flux in the writers' room during *TNG*'s first two seasons contributed to on-screen characters that remained ill-defined. Invited aboard during Season Three, Piller arrived fully aware of his lack of science fiction expertise. But he made up for it by helping the scriptwriters transform the men and women of the *Enterprise* into flesh and blood beings, including Data, the show's one "artificial" crewmember.

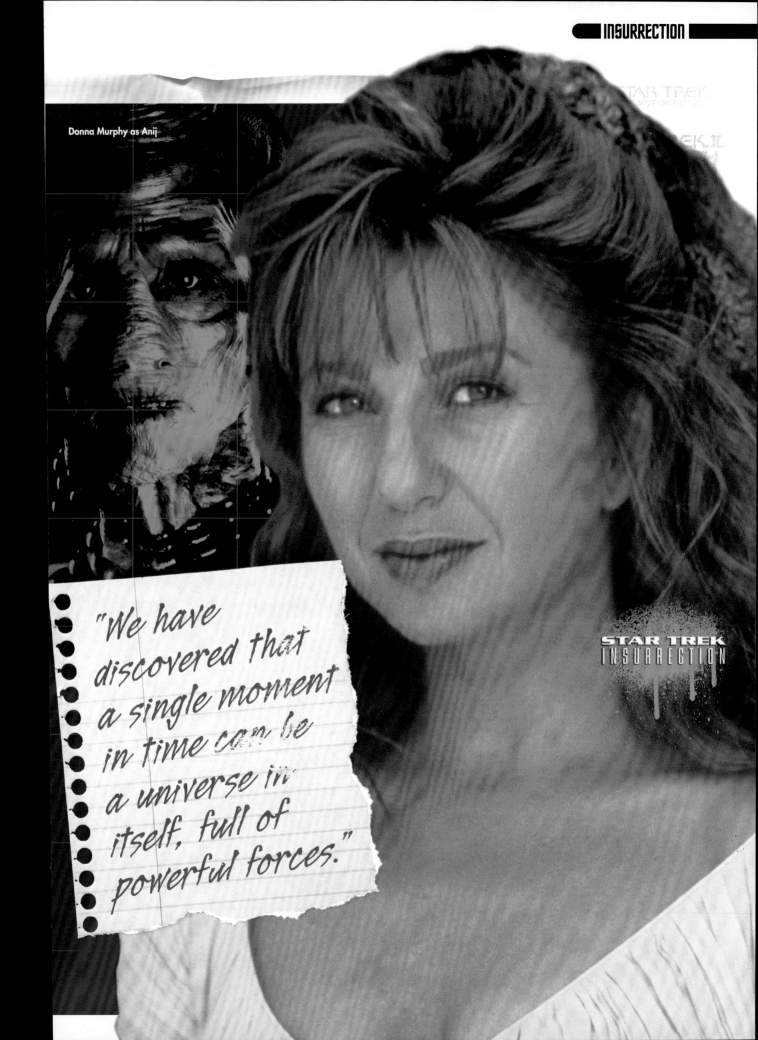

Donna Murphy as Anij

"We have discovered that a single moment in time can be a universe in itself, full of powerful forces."

STAR TREK
INSURRECTION

Piller approached the new feature in much the same way, constructing a story from the inside out, rather than from the outside in. Prompted by executive producer Rick Berman's suggestion to use a classic piece of literature as a foundation, Piller delved into Joseph Conrad's classic novella, *Heart of Darkness*. That established a framework in which Captain Picard was to pursue an old friend into the "wilderness" of space, much like Conrad's protagonist Marlow pursued Kurtz. When the story didn't quite gel, Berman provided another suggestion: substitute Data for Picard's anonymous old friend. Piller recognized at once the increased stake that Picard and the audience would have in such a story. He later came up with a crucial final element off the top of his head – literally – while applying a bit of hair color restorer Rogaine to his middle-aged hairline. As he glumly reflected on the impact of time's passage, he realized that Picard's pursuit of Data should take him to a *Star Trek* version of the Fountain of Youth.

"*Insurrection* stands as a testament to the *Next Generation* characters, while offering newcomers a solid introduction to them."

F. Murray Abraham as the villainous Ru'afo, leader of the Son'a

The Son'a attack the Ba'ku village (*Star Trek: Insurrection*)

Tongue in cheek, Piller began referring to his new screenplay as "Heart of Lightness."

Lightness, however, doesn't mean lack of conflict, and the script would hurl Picard to the brink of a personal crisis. After Data's addled behavior draws the *Enterprise* to the Ba'ku world, it doesn't take long for Picard to figure out that Starfleet and the Son'a are interfering with the populace in a major way. The dilemma he faces could destroy his career: Should he support a Federation policy that ignores its long-revered Prime Directive, or take a unilateral stand and support the innocent?

Is there any question which course of action he will choose? And is there a member of the audience who would disagree with him?

Reviews of *Insurrection* were not unkind, although they were predictably comparative to the film's predecessor. *Variety*, for example, noted that the film was "a distinct comedown after the smashingly exciting *Star Trek: First Contact*," adding that *Insurrection* struck

"a deft balance of heroics and quirky humor," even as it sniped that the movie "played less like a stand-alone sci-fi adventure than an expanded episode of *Star Trek: The Next Generation*."

Given *Star Trek*'s notoriously loyal audience, *Insurrection* might have done fine at the box office had it debuted at a different time of year. But Paramount chose to open *Insurrection* in mid-December, a period when competition between the studios is notoriously cutthroat. And it was that business decision, as much as anything else, that reduced *Insurrection*'s fortunes at the box office.

Initially it seemed that the studio had made the right decision. It opened as the week's top-ranked film, grossing twice as much as *A Bug's Life*, the film in second position. But *Insurrection*'s momentum did not sustain. Box office was down by 50 per cent the second week – the

week prior to Christmas – while *A Bug's Life*, entering its fifth week in theaters, was actually up 28 per cent. Worse yet, the other studios brought out their big guns for the holidays: *The Prince of Egypt*, *You've Got Mail*, *Patch Adams* and *Stepmom*.

Each of these competitors fell into easily categorized holiday genres, whether comedy, romance or cartoon. But *Insurrection* was neither fish nor fowl. In the end, the film's reputation as well as its profits were fair-to-middling: about $120 million worldwide. Not a disaster by any means, but the film never received the respect it was due. Its primary failure, apparently, was that it didn't live up to "expectations."

On the other hand, *Insurrection* struck a chord with an unexpected segment of the audience; current events followers saw Picard's crew leading the beleaguered Ba'ku through the mountains as a metaphor for a United Nations peacekeeping force and the heated activities leading up to Kosovo Albanian's movement for independence. It wasn't an unrealistic assumption, although the film's producers didn't claim to intentionally having crafted the correlation.

Nevertheless, movie-goers who brought nothing with them but a love of *Star Trek* found they could enjoy *Insurrection* as a kind of "expanded episode." *Insurrection* stands as a testament to the *TNG* characters, while offering newcomers a solid introduction to them. So don't be afraid to do what the Ba'ku do – learn to live in the moment, and relax with the hummingbirds.

Paula M. Block and Terry J. Erdmann

CRITICS' VERDICT:
INSURRECTION

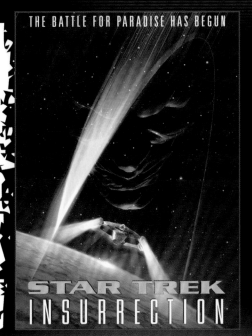

THE BATTLE FOR PARADISE HAS BEGUN

STAR TREK
INSURRECTION

Insurrection is another of those *Star Trek* movies that seemed to receive both rhapsodies and raspberries – sometimes within the same write-up. "Outsiders will find this schtick-laden, mildly exciting adventure yarn an inoffensive triviality," wrote Andrew O'Hehir for Salon.com, "while fans will savor one more encounter with Picard, Riker, Data, Worf and the gang, replete with all the well-worn character tics and platitudinous parables about the contemporary world they expect."

"The artistry is intense," said Peter Stack of the *San Francisco Chronicle*, "though it could have used a little more warp speed at times."

Praise often came in the form of left-handed compliments, as it did from Stephen Holden of *The New York Times*: "An appealing millennial throwback to the hippie dream that is part and parcel of *Star Trek*'s utopian ethos."

Other critics lambasted the film: "More of the same old, same old," lamented *Globe and Mail*'s Liam Lacey; "Inert and unconvincing," wrote Roger Ebert for the *Chicago Sun-Times*; and "A muddled, gimpy mess, filled with the worst sort of *Trek* clichés and ill-timed humorous outbursts," judged Marc Savlov of the *Austin Chronicle*.

DATA LOG

Eternity Awaits Beyond The Final Frontier

"We are betraying the principles upon which the Federation was founded. It's an attack upon its very soul."
Jean-Luc Picard

FEATURING:

Picard | Riker | Data | La Forge | Crusher | Troi | Worf

GUEST STARRING:

Ru'afo (F. Murray Abraham) | Vice Admiral Dougherty (Anthony Zerbe) | Anij (Donna Murphy) | Gallatin (Gregg Henry) | Lt Daniels (Michael Horton)

Writers: Michael Piller, based on a story by Rick Berman & Michael Piller

Director: Jonathan Frakes

Released: USA: December 11, 1998
UK: December 15, 1998
Australia: December 31, 1998

First weekend: $22,052,836
Worldwide gross: $117,800,000

STAR TREK NEMESIS

THE CLONE WARS

A Reman strikeforce boards the *Enterprise*-E
(*Star Trek Nemesis*)

The tagline for *Star Trek: Nemesis* made it clear that this was to be the farewell voyage for Picard and crew, and this freed the writers to shake things up. The screenplay therefore wrapped up some story arcs that had been spread across seven years of *Star Trek: The Next Generation* and the three previous films featuring the series' stars. For example, Commander William Riker finally accepts promotion to captain and also finally marries Deanna Troi, ending his "always a bridesmaid, never a bride" syndrome on multiple levels. Although these long-awaited character developments are nice, neither the wedding nor the new ship, the *Titan*, appear in *Nemesis*, failing to deliver an emotional pay-off for fans – contrast this with *Star Trek VI: The Undiscovered Country*, which featured Captain Sulu's *Excelsior* as an integral part of the plot.

These are not the only interesting developments to take place off-screen. Continuity-loving fans do a double-take at the cameo of Dr. Beverly Crusher's son, Wesley, at the wedding reception (in *TNG* he had ascended to a higher plane of existence) and the reappearance of Lieutenant Commander Worf in uniform

(on *Star Trek: Deep Space Nine* he became Federation ambassador to the Klingon homeworld). Because of this lax handling of series continuity, *Nemesis* often works differently for fans than it does for casual moviegoers. While fans are distracted by the confused back-story during the reception, newcomers simply enjoy the friendly banter. Parsing out such details would inspire the *A Time To...* miniseries of novels, which ironed out the various continuity wrinkles between *Star Trek: Insurrection* and the beginning of *Nemesis*.

Wrinkles aside, the focus of *Nemesis* is action. The reception is a quiet interlude between an attention-grabbing scene in the Romulan senate and a *Road Warrior*-like chase on a remote desert planet where the crew discovers a lost android "brother" of Data. That Data's other brother, encountered during *TNG*, was a sociopath who allied with the Borg and was responsible for the deaths of hundreds of people goes unmentioned by everyone – a serious lapse in believability for the long-term fan as the "B-4" android is reactivated without hesitation. There's no explanation for this amnesia other than the need to

move the story along, but viewers unfamiliar with the TV series did not notice this plothole.

With all the pieces now in place, the crew of the *Enterprise*-E is drawn into an increasingly catastrophic confrontation with Shinzon, the human leader of a Reman slave rebellion against the Romulans. The writing team seized on a hot-button topic of the day for Shinzon's origins – Shinzon is a clone of Picard, created then discarded and imprisoned by the Romulans. *Nemesis* was released in December 2002; cloned sheep such as Dolly had been making headlines since the late 1990s, and Pope John Paul II declared human cloning immoral in 2000. The summer before the film, the U.S. House of Representatives had passed the Human Cloning Prohibition Act of 2001 (it did not pass the Senate).

Although entire armies of clones were unleashed that summer of 2002 in *Star Wars Episode II: Attack of the Clones*, the writers could have avoided Shinzon becoming an also-ran character if they had gotten a handle on his relationship with Picard. Does Shinzon consider Picard his archenemy, or a long-lost father? Does Shinzon want Picard dead, or does he need Picard

Brent Spiner as Data

"'Never saw the sun shining so bright. Never saw things going so right.'"

STAR TREK
THE MOTION PICTURE

STAR TREK II
THE WRATH OF KHAN

STAR TREK III
THE SEARCH FOR SPOCK

STAR TREK
IV
THE VOYAGE HOME

STAR TREK
THE FINAL FRONTIER

STAR TREK
VI
THE UNDISCOVERED COUNTRY

STAR TREK
GENERATIONS

STAR TREK
FIRST CONTACT

STAR TREK
NEMESIS

STAR TREK

alive for transfusions to treat his clone-related health issues? Actor Tom Hardy gives it a run and is effectively creepy, especially in his first meeting with Picard and crew, but his motivation lurches around, driven by what the screenplay needs to get to the next scene. In the end Hardy is not able to synthesize these disparate elements into a cohesive character, and the whole clone subplot seems much ado about nothing. It's simply inexplicable why Shinzon's need for revenge seems more focused on Picard and Earth instead of the Romulans who did him wrong. Shinzon is more like a Bond villain than Picard's Khan, complete with the requisite super-weapon with which to threaten destruction and domination.

Nevertheless, the clash between Picard and Shinzon provides a workable set-up for continuing action, including a Reman invasion of the *Enterprise* and escalating space battles. Although these set-pieces are a bit by the numbers, they build to an I-did-not-see-that-coming scene which nicely echoes the crash of the *Enterprise*-D in *Star Trek Generations*. The special effects are exciting – if a bit static compared to the hyperkinetic *Star Wars* movies – and there's the best use

> ## "Shinzon is more like a Bond villain than Picard's Khan, complete with the requisite super-weapon with which to threaten destruction and domination."

The *Enterprise*-E's newset shuttlecraft, *Argo*, comes fully equiped with an all-terrain buggy

Picard (Patrick Stewart) confronts Shinzon (Tom Hardy)

A Klingon *Bird-of-Prey* bears down on the *Enterprise*-E (*Star Trek Nemesis*)

Picard makes a toast at the Rikers' wedding

of the vacuum of space since the on-the-hull fight with the Borg in *Star Trek: First Contact*.

The "final journey" becomes literal for Data, as the dire situation forces a heroic sacrifice to save his captain. While not inherently a series ending development – *TNG* weathered the death of security officer Lt. Tasha Yar, which led to Worf's promotion to that position – a follow-up film would have necessarily taken a new course. Tagline aside, had *Nemesis* been a huge success, it's easy to imagine a sequel introducing new officers to the *Enterprise*-E to replace Riker, Troi, and Data, with Riker's *Titan* ready to assist Picard. Indeed, this is what the novels have done, albeit with *Titan* getting its own book series.

At the end of the day, however, *Nemesis* did not resonate within the *Trek* fanbase or reach a wider audience. Adjusted for inflation, the worldwide box office gross of *Nemesis* was $80,270,545 (not much above its budget), while J. J. Abrams' *Star Trek (2009)* made $79,204,289 in its first weekend. It's not an entirely fair comparison, given that Abrams had twice the budget, but its obvious that the new *Star Trek* pulled in an audience far beyond that of *Nemesis*.

It may be tempting to blame the lackluster performance on director Stuart Baird and screenwriter Logan for being new to the franchise, but director Nicholas Meyer and producer Harve Bennett were also newbies when tapped for *Star Trek II: The Wrath of Khan*,

and they made a fan favorite that grossed an impressive eight times its meager budget. Perhaps the continuing television spin-offs reached a saturation point that weakened the box-office draw of the films. Maybe seven years of *TNG* episodes and four films were more than the characters could sustain. And certainly there were weaknesses in the screenplay obvious to fans and general moviegoers alike; there was no convincing reason, other than that it would have ended the story before it began, for the Romulans not to simply kill young Shinzon when they no longer wanted him. Probably all of these factors and more contributed to the disappointing box-office performance of *Nemesis*.

Regardless of the exact causes, it was clear after *Nemesis* that the franchise was due for some sort of reinvention and reinvigoration. The final television series to date, *Star Trek: Enterprise*, which was on the air when *Nemesis* was released, left the air in 2005 after only four seasons, also unable to bring in the necessary viewers – the three previous spin-offs had each run for seven years. After almost 20 years of continuous series – *TNG* had debuted in 1987 – and concurrent films, there was no filmed *Star Trek* in production.

Scott Pearson

CRITICS' VERDICT:
NEMESIS

Nemesis received mostly tepid reviews, and seemed widely regarded as an unfortunate note upon which to conclude the cinematic exploits of the *Next Generation* crew, as observed by Shannon J. Harvey of Australian *Sunday Times*: "If this is *The Next Generation*'s final voyage, then it goes somewhat gently into that good night rather than raging against the dying of the light."

"Doesn't feel like an appropriate send-off," echoed Marc Mohan for the *Oregonian*.

Richard Roeper of *Ebert & Roeper* liked the film, which "...stands alone as an engaging intergalactic thriller with a lot of spirit – and some rousing action scenes."

"It doesn't deliver anything new to the series, and even fans might find parts distinctly slow," concluded *Empire* magazine, "but it finally hits most of the right buttons."

Jim Laden of Sacramento *News & Review* was less enthusiastic: "John Logan's script hasn't enough invention or suspense even for an hour-long episode of the series, Stuart Baird's direction is leaden, and the look of the film is murky and dismal."

On ReelViews, James Berardinelli called *Nemesis* "watchable, and, at times, enjoyable. But it doesn't feel like *Star Trek*, despite the presence of so many familiar faces. There's no real sense of character for any of the protagonists."

DATA LOG

A Generation's Final Journey Begins

"Are you ready to plunge the entire Quadrant into war to satisfy your own personal demons?"
Jean Luc Picard

FEATURING:

Picard | Riker | Data | La Forge | Crusher | Troi | Worf | Wesley

GUEST STARRING:

Guinan

Shinzon (Tom Hardy) | Viceroy (Ron Perlman) | Commander Donatra (Dina Meyer) | Admiral Janeway (Kate Mulgrew) | B-4 (Brent Spiner)

Writers: John Logan, based on a story by John Logan & Rick Berman & Brent Spiner

Director: Stuart Baird

Released: USA: December 9, 2002
UK: January 3, 2003
Australia: January 17, 2003

First weekend: $18,513,305
Worldwide gross: $67,312,826

"It was really, really good fun to play the villain. You have so much freedom when you play villains. There are so many avenues you can explore."

THE YOUNG

PRETEN

Tom Hardy enbraces the role of *Star Trek Nemesis* villain, Shinzon

"**Y**ou'd be surprised at how many Trekkies came out of the woodwork," marvels Tom Hardy. "I have some very close friends who I didn't know were *Star Trek* fans, and I've got some friends who I knew were fans. It was very interesting. A good friend of my wife's is a massive, massive fan and we had some chats. Another director I've worked with is a fan as well. So it's opened up some doors in different social surroundings, that's for sure."

Hardy practically went to university on *Star Trek* after being selected for the role in *Star Trek Nemesis*. After chatting to friends and family, watching old *Star Trek: The Next Generation* episodes and a few of the *Star Trek* features, the young Brit winged his way to Los Angeles and Paramount Pictures, where he played Shinzon, the Reman clone of Captain Jean-Luc Picard (Patrick Stewart). So vehemently did the Praetor Shinzon despise the captain of the *U.S.S.*

Enterprise NCC-1701-E, and so distracted was he by his attraction to Deanna Troi (Marina Sirtis), that he squandered his window of opportunity to destroy Earth and bring the Federation to its knees.

"It was really, really good fun to play the villain," Hardy says. "You have so much freedom when you play villains. There are so many avenues you can explore. Khan [Ricardo Montalban] and the Borg Queen [Alice Krige] were my favourite *Star Trek* villains out of all of them, but I didn't really put too much stress on myself about things like that. I didn't try to defeat somebody else's performance. That's nonsense. You just go in and do your best. I was already absolutely terrified anyway, throughout the whole thing. Trying to compare myself to another character, or trying to impose myself upon that which had had life previously, would only have been putting more pressure on myself."

And though Shinzon was a nasty creature and no doubt the villain of the piece, Hardy stops short

of calling the bald character evil. Pure malevolence, he argues, is something entirely apart from villainy. "A baby is not born evil, I don't believe, personally," says the 26-year-old actor. "I think that you attain baggage through circumstances, through various issues with the world. Shinzon is very much the orphan, the lonely child who was abused. Unless you get right to the centre or the essence of a character, there's no point.

"Also, when it comes to villains, why is this person a monster? Why is someone suddenly so vile and distasteful? Because of what he's been through. That makes for understanding a character. Three-dimensional bad guys are much more interesting than one-dimensional bad guys."

Though the finished film didn't perform to expectations upon its release in December 2002, Hardy liked it. And he's quick to point to several particular scenes that he rather enjoyed.

"I liked the scene when I first come down the stairs," Hardy recalls. "I'm in the Reman observation lounge and I walk down a lot of stairs, a *lot* of stairs. I thought, 'I should have on a nice, long dress, a pair of high heels and have a very loud, sexy voice.' I felt very small right then and I suddenly realised how vast that set was. That was something. That gobsmacked me a bit. I thought, 'Well, we are here now and this is big.'

"Another scene I remember in particular is when I fight Picard. They were blowing up my ship and I had to live-fight Patrick while wearing a pair of contact lenses that I couldn't see through. The whole ship was made of this gridiron metal and I had to run up these stairs after Patrick and fight him. And I couldn't see anything. That was another one of those 'Oh my God' moments. I was kind of hoping that everyone was insured. And all these explosions were going off, which I loved, though they were destroying the sets. And those sets, they were unbelievable. They put so much time and effort into creating these elaborate sets."

Hardy was busy before *Nemesis* and he's been very busy since its completion. His films pre-*Nemesis*, among them *The Reckoning*, *Simon: An English Legionnaire* and *Dot the I*, are all still in the process of seeking distributors, although you may be familiar with him from *Black Hawk Down* and TV's *Band of Brothers*. Right after *Nemesis*, Hardy filmed *LD-50*. "It's a horror movie," he explains. "I get to run around and beat up poltergeists. It's about a group of anti-vivisectionists who go to liberate the animals from this factory or warehouse, somewhere

As the new praetor, Shinzon had the Reman and Romulan Star Empire at his beck and call, but it was his desire for revenge against his 'brother', Jean-Luc Picard, which would eventually bring about his downfall. Young actor Tom Hardy recalls what it was like playing the dark side of Picard for Jennifer Jackson...

Shinzon (Tom Hardy) and Picard (Patrick Stewart) in Star Trek Nemesis

"I think that you attain baggage through circumstances, through various issues with the world. Shinzon is very much the orphan, the lonely child who was abused."

in the countryside, and end up coming undone. Things get a bit horrible. I'm the reluctant hero in that, the ordinary person asked to do extraordinary things. Really, he just wants to get himself out of there and everybody else with him. Katharine Towne is in it with me. She's the female lead. Melanie Brown [Melanie B or Scary Spice] from the Spice Girls is in it, too."

Upon finishing *LD-50*, Hardy began work on *Get a Grip*, a music-oriented feature of his own making. "*Get a Grip* isn't a movie like *8 Mile* at all. It's actually quite the opposite. It's a mock documentary about a white rapper. Have you seen a movie called *Man Bites Dog*? It's a bit like that. We follow this one guy. It's a sort of black and white MTV documentary about a white rapper in London. It's all very unglamorous, and it's just about the days leading up to his big gig. I play the rapper, but the whole thing is freestyle. We used non-actors and I directed it with my DJ.

"It's kind of a community piece. People that I know – DJs, music industry people, dancers – are all helping me. We're keeping it in-house and trying to form a group of people, a production company. As our careers grow and develop and the team gets bigger, we can hopefully pick each other up so that, eventually, there will be a time when we can walk into a joint and stand there 40-strong. It's the same type of vibe as what Ewan McGregor and Jude Law have with Natural Nylon. We're slowly, slowly putting things together, because there's no longevity in just being an actor."

Even with all of his post-*Nemesis* endeavours, Hardy, in certain circles, will now and forever be associated with *Star Trek*. Over time, Shinzon just might be recalled in the same breath as the Borg Queen and Khan. Asked if he's ready to be invited to conventions, stopped on the street by Trekkers and asked for autographs until the end of his days, Hardy laughs. "No," he says, mock-seriously. "Thanks. That's the last question. No, absolutely, I'm looking forward to it all. Even though it's all very new to me, this whole [fame] thing, it's all right. It's an important part of the job and I'm looking forward to it."

Likewise, Hardy is looking forward to the next phase of his career. And he's hopeful that his performance in *Nemesis* will lead to increasingly bigger, better and more challenging opportunities. "Obviously, I'd love to work more," says the actor, who, in the spring and summer of 2003, acted in back-to-back Robert Delamere plays, *In Arabia, We'd All Be Kings* and *The Modernists*, both of which were staged in London.

"I'd like *Nemesis* to be a calling card, to show people that I can do the work. I think any performance is a testament to where you are in your training as an actor. So you're never entirely pleased, never entirely comfortable with a performance. You could always do better, couldn't you? But at the same time you've got to turn it off and say, 'Hang on a minute. This is where I'm at. This is what I could do. I've done my best.' That's all you can do. At the end of the day you're never going to be entirely happy, but you've got to cut it off somewhere or you'll go mad. So, I'm pretty satisfied with the film and my work in it."

And so far as the future is concerned, Hardy is optimistic. "I don't think there's any need to relocate [to America from England, where he lives with his wife]. I think what I would do is go wherever the work demanded me to go. It's very much like being in the military. You just have to go. You have to be on call, and you go whenever anyone needs help. In an ideal world you wouldn't have to choose. You could just relax and sit on the beach or whatever is your ideal utopia. It was always mine to go through school, be with my wife and to act, and to do it all well.

"If I'm lucky, everything fits into place. If not, if the heavens do fall as they're fated to, at least I had a go at something and I did one movie, once, at Paramount Pictures and had a crack at Picard. That's something to hang your gloves on." ■

Picard's nemesis – his clone, Shinzon (Tom Hardy)

He's behind you!

A GENERATION'S FINAL JOURNEY BEGINS

STAR TREK
NEMESIS

DECEMBER 13

One of several theatrical
posters designed to promote
the final *Next Generation*
movie, *Star Trek Nemesis*

OTHER GREAT TIE-IN COMPANIONS FROM TITAN

ON SALE NOW!

Star Trek: The Movies
ISBN 9781785855924

Fifty Years of Star Trek
ISBN 9781785855931

Buffy - Welcome to the Hellmouth
ISBN 9781782763642

Buffy - Fear, Itself
ISBN 9781782763659

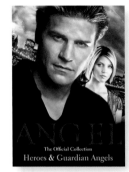

Angel - Heroes & Guardian Angels
ISBN 9781782763680

Star Wars - The Official Collection Volume 1
ISBN 9781785851162

Star Wars - The Official Collection Volume 2
ISBN 9781785851179

Star Wars - The Official Collection Volume 3
ISBN 9781785851896

Star Wars - The Official Collection Volume 4
ISBN 9781785851902

Star Wars - The Official Collection Volume 5
ISBN 9781785851919

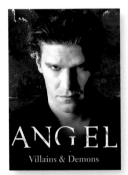

Angel - Villains & Demons
ISBN 9781782763697

The X-Files - The Bureau and The Syndicate
ISBN 9781782763710

The X-Files - Monsters and Villains
ISBN 9781782763727

The X-Files - The Truth, Secrets & Lies
ISBN 9781782763734

Once Upon a Time - Behind the Magic
ISBN 9781782760290

TITANCOMICS

For more information visit www.titan-comics.com

STAR TREK MAGAZINE SUBSCRIPTIONS: TITANMAGAZINES.COM/TREK